# Empirical Finance

**Empirical Finance: Theory and Application** offers a modern, data-driven introduction to the field of finance, tailored for undergraduate students and practitioners seeking to bridge theory with real-world evidence. In an era defined by abundant data and computational power, this book emphasizes hands-on learning by integrating financial theory, empirical analysis, and practical implementation using Python and R. Each chapter balances intuitive explanations with mathematical rigor, ensuring that readers not only understand key concepts but also learn how to test them with actual data.

Structured in two parts, the book begins with a thorough review of essential quantitative tools—optimization, probability, and statistics—providing the foundation needed for empirical work. The second part applies these tools to core topics in finance, including asset pricing, portfolio choice, market efficiency, event studies, and volatility modeling. Real-world examples and case studies—such as testing the Efficient Markets Hypothesis, analyzing stock splits, and evaluating the equity premium—bring the material to life and illustrate how empirical methods can validate or challenge economic intuition.

A distinctive feature of this text is its emphasis on reproducibility and application. Code snippets, exercises, and datasets enable readers to replicate results and develop their own analyses. Topics like time-series properties of returns, portfolio management and behavioral finance are treated with both theoretical and empirical depth, preparing students for quantitative internships, graduate studies, or roles in the financial industry.

Ideal for courses in Empirical Finance, Financial Econometrics, or Quantitative Finance, this book stands out for its clear exposition, relevance to contemporary practice, and commitment to evidence-based reasoning. It empowers a new generation of finance students to think critically, work with data, and understand markets not as a set of abstract rules, but as a dynamic interplay of economics, data, and technology.

**Key Features:**

- Seamlessly integrates hands-on coding in both Python and R with financial theory, enabling readers to replicate results and conduct their own empirical analysis.
- Strikes a unique balance between financial intuition, mathematical clarity, and real-world application, avoiding the common extremes of abstract theory or mere data manipulation.
- Structured in two distinct parts—first building essential quantitative tools (optimization, probability, statistics) before applying them to core finance topics—ensuring a solid foundation for empirical work.
- Uses contemporary, relevant examples throughout, such as testing market anomalies, analyzing cryptocurrency returns, and conducting event studies on recent scandals.
- Emphasizes a data-centric approach to validate or challenge economic reasoning, teaching students to treat finance as a dynamic, evidence-based discipline.

**CHAPMAN & HALL/CRC Series on Statistics in Business and Economics**

**Recently Published Titles**

**Empirical Research in Accounting**
Tools and Methods
*Ian D. Gow and Tongqing Ding*

**Risk and Predictive Analytics with R**
*Ozgur M. Araz and David L. Olson*

**Empirical Finance: Theory and Application**
*Oliver Linton, Shaoran Li, and Shuyi Ge*

For more information about this series, please visit: https://www.routledge.com/Chapman-and-HallCRC-Series-on-Statistics-in-Business-and-Economics/book-series/CHSBE

# Empirical Finance

## Theory and Application

Oliver Linton, Shaoran Li, and Shuyi Ge

CRC Press
Taylor & Francis Group
Boca Raton London New York

CRC Press is an imprint of the
Taylor & Francis Group, an **informa** business
A CHAPMAN & HALL BOOK

Designed Cover Image: Shutterstock

First edition published 2026
by CRC Press
2385 NW Executive Center Drive, Suite 320, Boca Raton, FL 33431

and by CRC Press
4 Park Square, Milton Park, Abingdon, Oxon, OX14 4RN

*CRC Press is an imprint of Taylor & Francis Group, LLC*



ISBN: 978-1-032-89470-6 (hbk)
ISBN: 978-1-032-89494-2 (pbk)
ISBN: 978-1-003-54312-1 (ebk)

DOI: 10.1201/9781003543121

Typeset in CMR10
by KnowledgeWorks Global Ltd.

Publisher's Note: This book has been prepared from camera-ready copy provided by the author.
Access the Support Material: www.routledge.com/9781032894706

# Contents

# *Preface*

Over the past two decades, the financial industry has undergone a remarkable transformation, driven by the explosive growth of data availability, computational resources, and algorithmic decision-making. In this environment, understanding **empirical finance**—the use of data to test and apply financial theories—has become not just desirable but essential.

This book, *Empirical Finance: Theory and Application*, is written to meet the growing demand for a **data-centric and conceptually rigorous** introduction to finance for undergraduate students. Our aim is to strike a balance between **financial intuition**, **mathematical clarity**, and **practical implementation**.

We believe that finance should not be taught as a collection of formulas to memorize, but rather as a **living discipline**, where economic reasoning is validated—or challenged—by data.

This book is suited for:

- Undergraduate students in finance, economics, and data science
- Students preparing for quantitative internships or graduate programs
- Instructors seeking a modern, application-oriented text for empirical finance

The book is designed for **hands-on learning**, with each chapter blending:

- **Theory**: Fundamental concepts in asset pricing, portfolio theory, and volatility
- **Application**: empirical examples with real world data
- **Computation**: Codes in Python and R for replicating results

Each chapter ends with:

- *Key Takeaways*
- *Conceptual and Empirical Exercises*

This book may be used as a:

- Primary textbook for **Empirical Finance**, **Financial Econometrics**, or **Quantitative Finance** courses

- Supplementary reference for students in finance, accounting, or macroeconomics
- Self-study guide for students and practitioners seeking to bridge theory and data

To benefit fully from this book, readers should have familiarity with:

- Introductory finance (e.g., diversification)
- Basic statistics (e.g., linear regression, hypothesis testing)
- Programming fundamentals (preferably in Python or R)

We intentionally balance mathematical rigor with economic intuition. Where derivations are included, we emphasize their empirical implications rather than purely theoretical elegance.

We are grateful to the many students who piloted early drafts of this text and offered insightful feedback. We also thank colleagues, teaching assistants, and reviewers for their constructive comments and continuous encouragement.

We hope that this book inspires young readers to explore finance not merely as a set of rules, but as a dynamic discipline that blends economics, data, and technology in shaping our understanding of markets.

*The Authors*
September 2025

# List of Figures

# *List of Tables*

# Part I

# Tools

# 1

# Optimization

## Outline

Economics is fundamentally the art of allocating scarce resources to achieve the best attainable outcomes. This chapter introduces the principles of optimization, treating both unconstrained and constrained problems.

After reading this chapter, you will be able to:

- Understand the role of optimization in economics and its importance for efficient resource allocation.
- Identify conditions for the existence of a minimum or maximum in unconstrained optimization problems.
- Apply differential calculus to locate optimal points, interpreting first- and second-order conditions.
- Utilize methods such as grid search and Newton's method to find extrema of functions.
- Recognize the complexities inherent in multivariate optimization and its applications.
- Analyze constrained optimization problems that involve equality or inequality restrictions.
- Solve constrained problems with substitution methods and grasp the essentials of the Lagrange-multiplier approach.

Economics is all about doing the best we can with the limited resources we have. This can be formulated in the mathematical terms of optimization (maximization or minimization). For example

- (Production) What is the best combination of inputs, given their unit costs, to produce a certain output? What is the best quantity of output to produce given the consumer demand?
- (Consumption) What is the best combination of purchases given their prices to maximize my satisfaction (utility) subject to my budget constraint?

DOI: 10.1201/9781003543121-1

- (Portfolio) What is the best combination of investments to maximize my expected return given a certain level of risk?

We consider several different optimization problems and sketch the analysis of these problems.

## 1.1 Unconstrained Optimization

Suppose that $x$ is a choice variable and $f(x)$ is the payoff to that choice. We wish to choose $x$ to maximize or minimize the payoff $f(x)$. First note that maximizing $f$ is the same as minimizing $-f$. There are several questions about this problem:

1. Does there exist an optimizing value of $x$?
2. Is it unique?
3. How do we find the optimizing value(s)?

**Example 1** *Suppose that $f(x) = x^2$ and we are to choose $x \in \mathbb{R}$ to minimize $f(x)$. The function $f$ is graphed below on the range $[-5,5]$.*

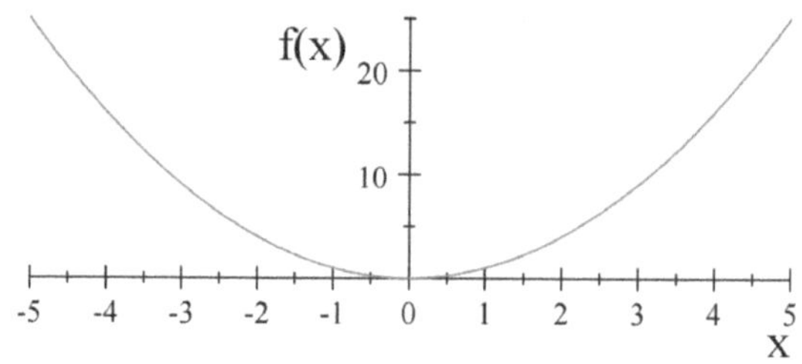


*Clearly, there is a unique minimizing value at $x = 0$.*

**Example 2** *Suppose that $f(x) = \sin(x)$ and we are to choose $x \in \mathbb{R}$ to minimize $f(x)$.*

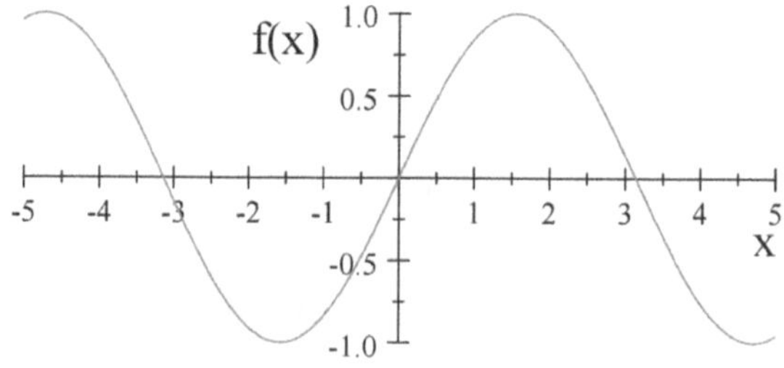

*In this case, there are a countable number of minimizing values at $x = 2j\pi - \pi/2$ for $j = 0, \pm 1, \ldots$*

**Example 3** *Suppose that $f(x) = -1/x$ and we are to choose $x \in \mathbb{R}$ to minimize $f(x)$.*

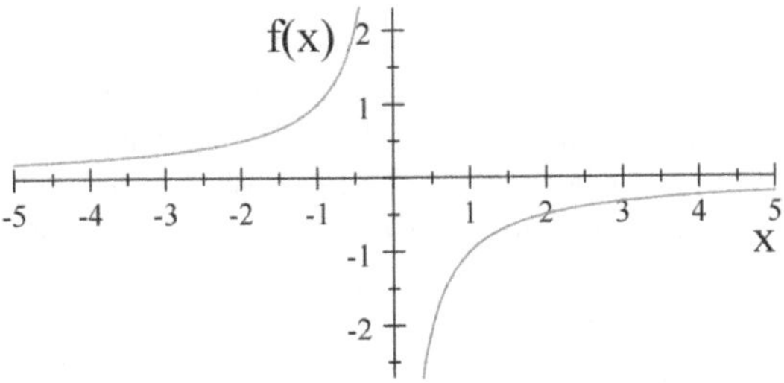


*In this case, $x = 0$ seems to be both a minimizing and a maximizing value depending on how you approach $x = 0$, i.e., $f(0)$ is not well (properly) defined.*

### 1.1.1 Existence of a Minimum

In this section, we give the most well-known theoretical result that guarantees, under some conditions, the existence of a minimum of a function. A compact interval is a set of real numbers of the form

$$\{x : a \leq x \leq b\} = [a, b] \tag{1.1}$$

with $a > -\infty$ and $b < \infty$. That is, the set is bounded and closed (includes its endpoints). For such a set, any sequence of points with elements $x_n \in [a, b]$ has a limit that is contained in $[a, b]$. An open interval $(a, b) = \{x : a < x < b\}$ or half-open intervals $(a, b] = \{x : a < x \leq b\}$ and $[a, b) = \{x : a \leq x < b\}$ are not called compact because there are sequences of points inside these sets that "escape" from the set. For example, the sequence $\{1/n, n = 1, 2, \ldots\}$ lies inside the open interval $(0, 1)$, but its limit point 0 does not, although its limit 0 does lie in $[0, 1]$.

A continuous function $f$ satisfies

$$\lim_{x \to x_0} f(x) = f(x_0), \tag{1.2}$$

meaning that however $x$ approaches $x_0$ (from above or below), $f(x)$ approaches $f(x_0)$. For example, the function $f(x) = x^2$ is continuous everywhere because for any $x_0$,

$$f(x) = x^2 = (x_0 + x - x_0)^2 = x_0^2 + (x - x_0)^2 + 2x_0(x - x_0)$$

and for $x$ close to $x_0$, $x^2$ is close to $x_0^2$. The "step" function (sometimes called the **Heaviside** function)

$$f(x) = \begin{cases} 1 & \text{if } x < 1 \\ 0 & \text{if } x \geq 1, \end{cases}$$

however, is discontinuous at $x_0 = 1$, since as $x \to 1$ from above $f(x) \to 0$, but as $x \to 1$ from below $f(x) \to 1$. The function $f(x) = 1/x$ is said to be discontinuous at the point $x_0 = 0$ because $f(0)$ is not well defined, i.e., it is either plus or minus infinity, depending on whether one approaches from above or below. On the other hand, the limit of this function at infinity does exist, i.e., $\lim_{x\to\infty} 1/x = 0$. The function $\sin(x)$ is continuous everywhere, but the limit at infinity does not exist, i.e., $\lim_{x\to\infty} \sin(x)$ does not exist because the function oscillates indefinitely and has no limit.

We have the famous Weierstrass theorem for continuous functions.

**Theorem 1** *Any function continuous over a compact interval has a minimum and a maximum on that interval.*

For example, the sin function is continuous, and so over any interval such as $[0, \pi]$, it achieves both a maximum and a minimum. The reciprocal function is continuous over any interval $[a, b]$ that does not include the origin and so achieves a maximum and a minimum there. This is nice to know, but is not very useful. How do we actually find the maximum and minimum, where it is located, and what is the value achieved?

### 1.1.2 Necessary Conditions for a Minimum

Calculus is the main tool that we use. The main idea it exploits is that the top of a hill is flat, and so to find the maximum, we look for the flat points. This line of argument can be extended to the multivariate case and to the case with equality constraints and inequality constraints, but we shall start with the simplest one-dimensional case without constraints.

A function $f$ is said to be differentiable at $x$, if the following limit exists

$$\lim_{\epsilon\to 0} \frac{f(x+\epsilon) - f(x)}{\epsilon}, \tag{1.3}$$

and the derivative is called $f'(x)$. This can be rewritten as saying that for small values of $\epsilon$, we have "approximately"

$$f(x+\epsilon) \simeq f(x) + \epsilon f'(x). \tag{1.4}$$

This means that the function $f$ is approximately linear close to $x$. A quadratic function is differentiable everywhere, and the sine function is differentiable everywhere. Suppose that a function $f$ is twice differentiable, meaning that the function $f'$ itself is differentiable. In this case, for small values of $\epsilon$, we have approximately

$$f(x+\epsilon) \simeq f(x) + \epsilon f'(x) + \frac{1}{2}\epsilon^2 f''(x).$$

This means that the function is approximately quadratic close to $x$. The second derivative itself is denoted $f''$ when it exists. In particular, for a quadratic function $f(x) = a + bx + cx^2$ with constants $a, b, c$, we have $f'(x) = b + 2cx$ and $f''(x) = 2c$.

**Theorem 2** *For differentiable functions defined over* $\mathbb{R}$*, a necessary condition for* $x_0$ *to be a minimum is that*

$$\overbrace{f'(x_0) = 0}^{\textit{first order condition}} \quad , \qquad \overbrace{f''(x_0) > 0}^{\textit{second order condition}} \quad . \tag{1.5}$$

**Example 4** *If* $f(x) = x^2$*, then*

$$f'(x) = 2x, \quad f''(x) = 2.$$

*This satisfies the conditions for a minimum at* $x = 0$ *but for a maximum nowhere.*

**Example 5** *If* $f(x) = \sin(x)$*, then*

$$f'(x) = \cos(x), \quad f''(x) = -\sin(x).$$

*This satisfies the conditions for minimum at* $x = 2j\pi - \pi/2$ *for* $j = 0, \pm 1, \ldots$. *All of these minimum values have the same value of* $f(x) = -1$.

**Example 6** *If* $f(x) = 1/x$*, then*

$$f'(x) = \frac{-1}{x^2}, \quad f''(x) = \frac{2}{x^3}, \quad x \neq 0.$$

*No* $x$ *satisfies the first-order condition. On any interval* $[a, b]$ *not containing* 0*, there is a minimum and a maximum, but it is always at the endpoint of the interval and not findable by the calculus method.*

We next discuss some exceptions. The function

$$f(x) = |x|$$

is continuous everywhere but is not differentiable at the point $x = 0$ (the slope to the right is $+1$, while the slope to the left is $-1$), which is where the unique minimum is!

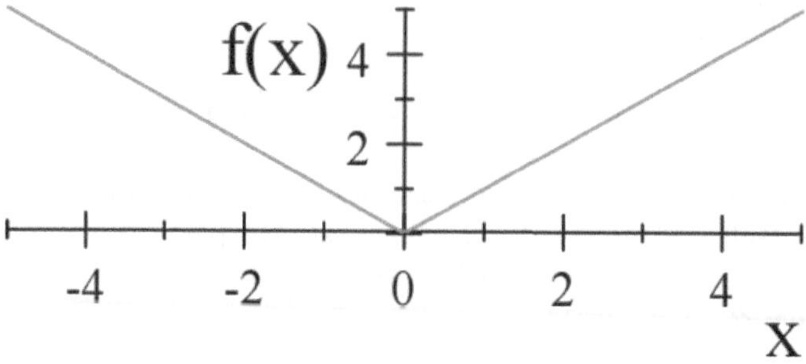


This example shows that calculus has limitations and sometimes other tools may be necessary. The absolute value is a **convex function** (like the quadratic), and there are some special arguments available for such functions. A second exception arises if the function is defined over a compact interval like $[a, b]$ with either $a > -\infty$ or $b < \infty$. In this case, the result needs to be modified to account for the possibility that the minimum occurs at either endpoint $a$ or $b$. For example, suppose that $f(x) = x^2$ is defined on $[1, 2]$. Then the minimum occurs at $x = 1$, but the condition $f'(1) = 0$ is not satisfied. In that case, the first condition is helpful only for **interior** minima.

In the differentiable case, the first-order condition can often be solved to find the maximum or minimum.

**Example 7** *Suppose that*

$$f(x) = ax^2 + bx + c.$$

*Then*

$$f'(x) = 2ax + b \Longrightarrow x_0 = \frac{-b}{2a}$$

*solves the first-order condition. Furthermore,*

$$f''(x) = 2a,$$

*so if $a > 0$, then $x_0 = -b/2a$ is a minimum, while if $a < 0$, then $x_0 = -b/2a$ is a maximum. If $a = 0$, then no max or min.*

**Example 8** *Suppose that*

$$f(x) = ax^3 + bx^2 + cx + d.$$

*Then*

$$f'(x) = 3ax^2 + 2bx + c \Longrightarrow x_0 : 3ax_0^2 + 2bx_0 + c = 0$$

*solves the first-order condition. Two solutions, one solution, or no solutions. Furthermore,*

$$f''(x) = 6ax + 2b.$$

Consider the special case $f(x) = x^3 - x : f'(x) = 3x^2 - 1 = 0$ at $x = \pm 1/\sqrt{3}$, $f''(x) = 6x$, which is positive at $x = 1/\sqrt{3}$ and negative at $x = -1/\sqrt{3}$.

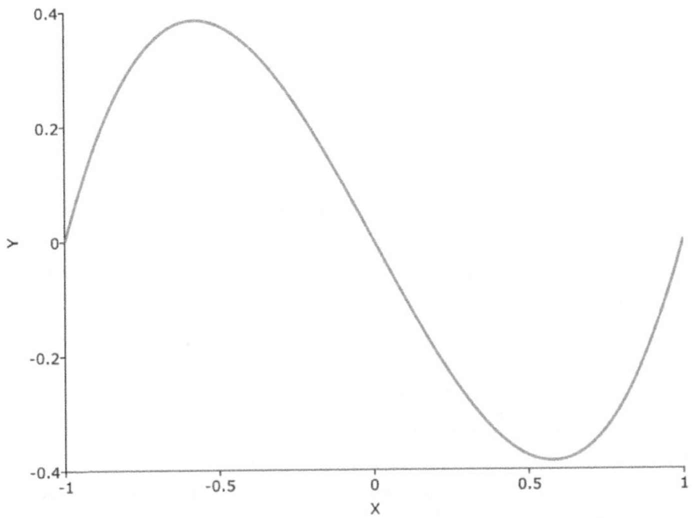


**Example 9** $f(x) = x^3$. *In this case,* $f'(x) = 3x^2 = 0$ *at* $x = 0$, $f''(x) = 6x = 0$ *at* $x = 0$, *the value* $x = 0$ *is neither a minimum nor a maximum; it is called a "turning point" or a "saddle point".*

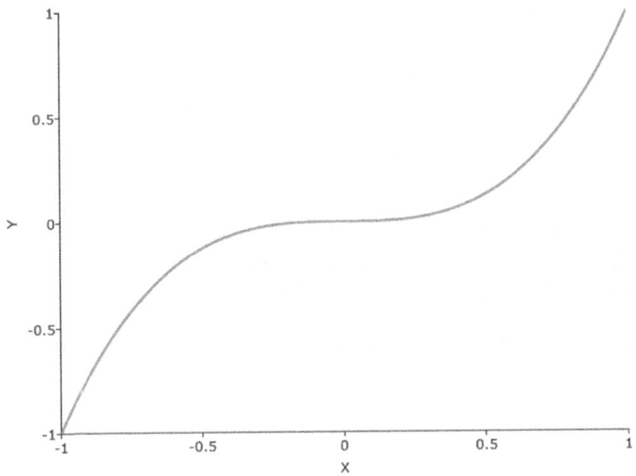

### 1.1.3 How Do We Find the Minimum of a General Function?

How do we find the minimum in general situations? There are two approaches.

- **Grid search**
  - Let $\{x_1, \ldots, x_n\}$ be a grid of points arranged in decreasing order so that $x_1 > x_2 > \cdots > x_n$. Calculate $f(x_1), \ldots, f(x_n)$
  - Find $x_{\max} \in \{x_1, \ldots, x_n\}$ such that

$$f(x_{\max}) \geq f(x_i), \text{ for all } x_i \in \{x_1, \ldots, x_n\}.$$

  - Maybe refine the grid in a second step. If $x_{\max} = x_i$, then construct a new grid on the interval $[x_{i-1}, x_{i+1}]$ and search over the refined grid.

This method works well in the one-dimensional case where the domain is compact. However, it does not work so well in the multivariate case and unbounded domain case. The reason is that when the space is high-dimensional, grid points end up being far apart. In the unit interval $[0, 1]$, the grid with $n$ points equally spaced is separated by $1/n$; if you place $n$ equally spaced points in the unit square $[0, 1]^2$, say $\{(i, j)/\sqrt{n}, i, j = 1, \ldots, \sqrt{n}\}$ you see the points are now separated by $1/\sqrt{n}$, in the general case, the spacing is of order $1/n^{1/d}$. This is sometimes called the **curse of dimensionality**.

An alternative approach to finding maximums and minimums is to use an iterative calculus-based method, for example, Newton's method. This is a method for finding the zeros of a function (such as zeros of the derivative of a function, which can be part of the defining property of a maximum or minimum) and works iteratively, namely, you start with an initial value and then improve your guess repeatedly.

- Let $x_1$ be some guess, and define the recursion $n = 2, 3, \ldots$

$$x_{n+1} = x_n - \frac{f'(x_n)}{f''(x_n)}.$$

Under some conditions one can show that $x_n \to x_0$, a zero of $f'(x)$, as $n \to \infty$. If the function $f$ has a unique maximum or minimum, then the Newton iteration will converge to that value.

**Example 10** $f(x) = x^2$. *Suppose that* $x_1 = 3$

$$x_2 = 3 - \frac{6}{2} = 0.$$

*That is, the correct value is achieved after one round.*

**Example 11** *$f(x) = x^4$, $f'(x) = 4x^3$ and $f''(x) = 12x^2$, $x_0 = 0$ is the unique global minimum. Suppose that $x_1 = 1$*

$$x_2 = 1 - \frac{4}{12} = \frac{2}{3}$$

$$x_3 = \frac{2}{3} - \frac{4\left(\frac{2}{3}\right)^3}{12\left(\frac{2}{3}\right)^2} = \frac{4}{9}$$

$$x_4 = \frac{4}{9} - \frac{4\left(\frac{4}{9}\right)^3}{12\left(\frac{4}{9}\right)^2} = \frac{8}{27}.$$

*In this case, the algorithm takes some time to approach the correct value, but you can see that at each stage it is getting closer.*

In general, derivative functions may have many flat points, some that correspond to local maxima or local minima of the original function. The calculus method only finds the local minimum and local maximum. For example, suppose that $f(x) = x\sin(2\pi x)$, in which case $f'(x) = \sin(2\pi x) + 2\pi x\cos(2\pi x)$. This function is plotted below. It has many local minima over the range $[-5, 5]$; there are two global minima over this range at close to $\pm 5$.

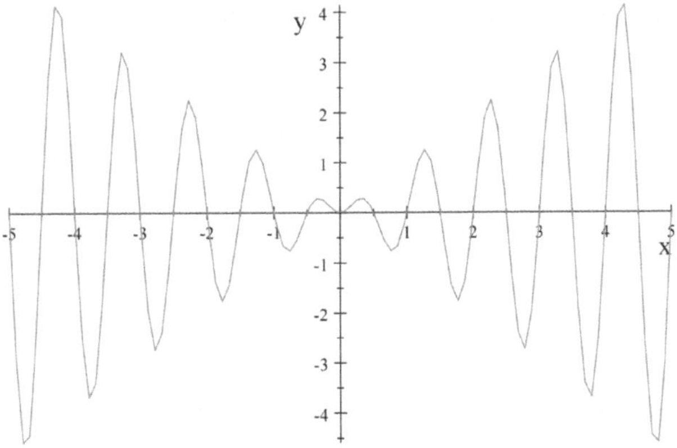


If we apply the Newton algorithm to this function, it will converge to the closest local minimum to the starting point $x_1$. For example, if we set $x_1 = 0$, then the algorithm will stop there. We may address this problem by the following more general algorithm:

1. Choosing distinct starting values $x_1^1, \ldots, x_1^K$
2. For each starting value run the Newton recursion to obtain $x_0^1, \ldots, x_0^K$
3. Compare $f(x_0^1), \ldots, f(x_0^K)$ and take the largest

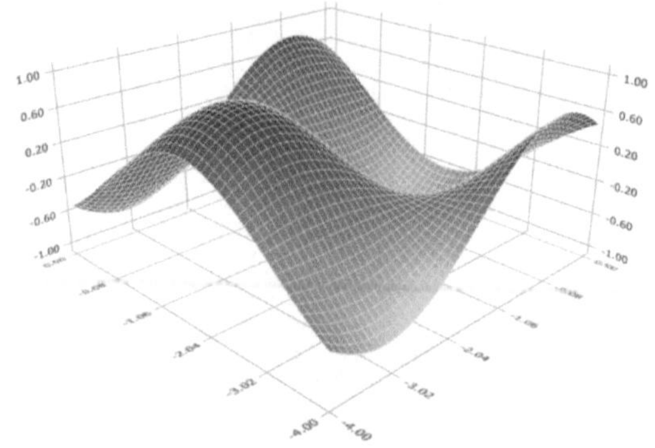


**FIGURE 1.1**
Surface plot of bivariate function

### 1.1.4 Multivariate Optimization

In practice, we often have to find the maximum or minimum of a function $f$ or several variables, e.g., $f(x_1, \ldots, x_n)$, say. Below we show a two-dimensional example, its surface plot (in Figure 1.1) and contour plot (in Figure 1.2). To find the maximum or minimum here requires the use of multivariable calculus. The so-called partial derivative of the function $f$ with respect to its separate components is defined as

$$\frac{\partial f}{\partial x_i}(x_1, x_2, \ldots, x_n) = \lim_{\epsilon \to 0} \frac{f(x_1, \ldots, x_{i-1}, x_i + \epsilon, x_{i+1}, \ldots, x_n) - f(x_1, x_2, \ldots, x_n)}{\epsilon}, \tag{1.6}$$

when this limit exists. We may define a multivariate version of the Newton algorithm to find the maximum or minimum of this function. We do not pursue this in detail here.

## 1.2 Constrained Optimization

In many cases, there are constraints on the values of the choice variable. For example, an individual's budget constraint says that you can't spend more than you earn. We seek to maximize an output $f(x)$ subject to the constraint that $x \leq a$. Suppose that $f(x) = x^2$ and we want to minimize $f$ for all $x \leq -1$ (an inequality constraint). In this case, the value 0 is not allowed, and so we cannot use calculus to find the solution. However, in this case it is straightforward to see that $x_0 = -1$ is the minimizing value. We next consider the case where there are two control variables $x, y$.

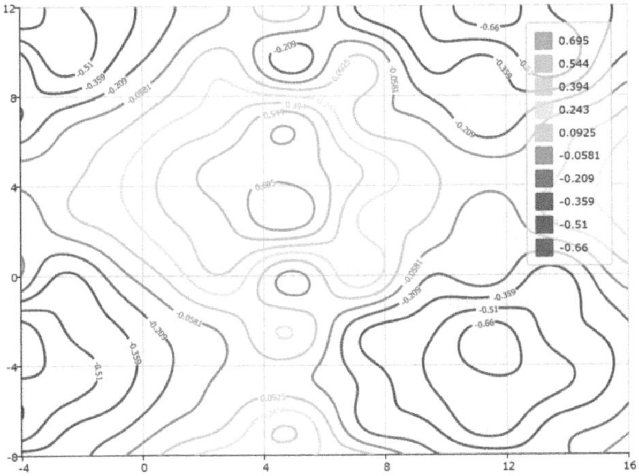


**FIGURE 1.2**
Contour plot showing lines of equal height

Suppose we have to minimize a function

$$f(x, y) = ax^2 + by^2$$

by choosing $x, y$ where $a, b > 0$. Without any restriction clearly $x = y = 0$ minimizes $f$. Now suppose that the choice of $x, y$ is limited in the sense that it should satisfy the equality restriction that $x+y = 1$. The constraint $x+y = 1$ changes the problem dramatically. Certainly, $x = y = 0$ does not satisfy the restriction, so we have to find values of $x, y$ that do satisfy the restriction and minimize the objective function.

A useful tool here is **substitution**. We substitute for $y$ using budget constraint, that is, we must have $y = 1 - x$. Then we have to minimize the function

$$f(x) = ax^2 + b(1-x)^2$$

with respect to the scalar value $x$ without any restriction. We have

$$f'(x) = 2ax - 2b(1-x) \Longrightarrow x_0 = \frac{b}{a+b}, y_0 = \frac{a}{a+b}$$

$$f''(x) = 2a + 2b > 0.$$

If $a = b = 1$, then $x_0 = y_0 = 1/2$. The minimizing value of $f$ satisfies

$$f(x_0, y_0) = a\left(\frac{b}{a+b}\right)^2 + b\left(\frac{a}{a+b}\right)^2 = \frac{ab}{a+b} > 0.$$

If $a = b = 1$, then $x_0 = y_0 = 1/2$ and $f(x_0, y_0) = 1/2$.

If we change the constraint to $x + y = \frac{1}{2}$, what is the solution and the minimizing value of $f$?

**Example 12** *Suppose that we wish to find the rectangle whose area is largest for a given perimeter. For example, you are a farmer who wants to enclose the largest piece of land with a given length of fence. If the rectangle has sides $x$ and $y$ it has an area $xy$ and perimeter $2(x+y)$. Therefore, the farmer wishes to maximize*

$$A = xy$$

*subject to the restriction that $2(x+y) = P$ for some perimeter $P$.*

To solve this problem, we first substitute the constraint, i.e., let $y = \frac{1}{2}P - x$, and then we have to maximize

$$A = x\left(\frac{1}{2}P - x\right)$$

with respect to $x > 0$. The first order condition is

$$\frac{1}{2}P = 2x \Longrightarrow x = \frac{P}{4},\ y = x,\ A = \frac{P^2}{16},$$

that is, the square is the most efficient use of his fencing among all rectangles. Actually, the circle is even more efficient, since the circle with perimeter $P$ has radius $r = P/2\pi$ and area $P^2/4\pi$. However, a farmer is not going to do that.

Finally, we can state the general case where we have to minimize the value

$$f(x_1, \ldots, x_n)$$

by choosing $x_1, \ldots, x_n$ subject to some restrictions that the choice variables must satisfy, for example:

$$r_1(x_1, \ldots, x_n) \geq 0, \ldots, r_p(x_1, \ldots, x_n) \geq 0.$$

Everything is a special case of this. If the number of equality restrictions $p = n - 1$, then we can substitute out all but one variable and turn this into an unconstrained univariate problem. To solve this general problem, we need to use Lagrange multipliers and matrix algebra, which is beyond the scope of this course.

## 1.3 Key Points

1. Many economic choices can be represented as optimization problems with respect to the choices available.
2. Unconstrained optimization can often be solved by finding first order conditions and then solving them for the optimal choice and then checking that the second order conditions are satisfied appropriately. Constrained optimization can often be turned into an unconstrained optimization problem by substitution.

## 1.4 Exercises

1. Suppose that your company produces cars in quantity $y$ with inputs tires $x$ and steering wheels $z$, and that

$$y = \frac{x}{4} \times \frac{z}{2}$$

where the total available inputs $x, z$ satisfy $x, z \geq 0$ and

$$x + z \leq 10.$$

Find the optimal choice of $x, z$ i.e., the input choice that maximizes the output $y$? Clearly, we should take

$$x + z = 10$$

why? In that case, we have to maximize

$$x\,(10 - x)$$

why? The first order condition is

$$10 - 2x = 0 \Longrightarrow x = 5, z = 5, y = \frac{25}{8}$$

is second-order condition satisfied?

2. Suppose that we want to minimize the function

$$f(x, y, z) = ax^2 + by^2 + cz^2,$$

where $a, b, c > 0$, with respect to $x, y, z$ subject to the two constraints that $x + y + z = 1$ and $x + 2y + 3z = 3$. By substituting out $y, z$ write the function $f$ solely in terms of $x$ and find its minimum.

3. Suppose that your company produces cars in quantity $y$ with inputs tires $x$ and steering wheels $z$, and that

$$y = \min\left\{\frac{x}{4}, z\right\}$$

(the minimum value of $x/4$ and $z$), where the total available inputs $x, z$ satisfy $x, z \geq 0$ and

$$x + z \leq 28.$$

Find the optimal choice of $x, z$ i.e., the input choice that maximizes the output $y$ when

(a) $x, z$ are integers and

(b) when $x, z$ can be real numbers (so you may produce a fractional number of cars).

In neither case is it possible to use calculus. First, use the constraint to write $z = 28 - x$. Blue line is $28 - x$ and red line is $x/4$

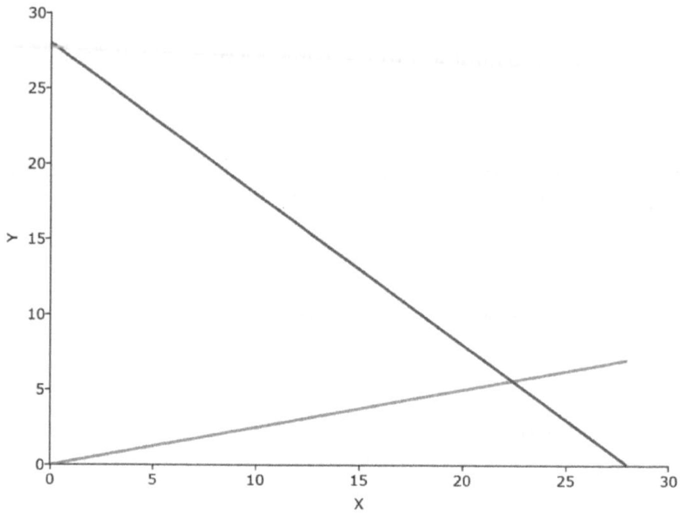


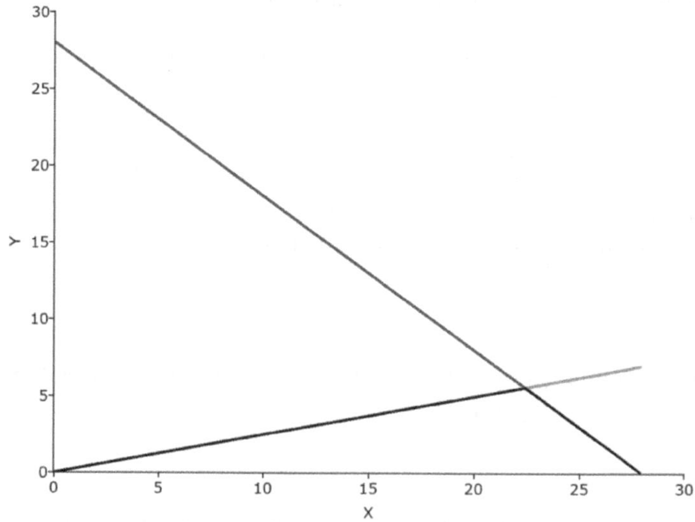

# 2

# *Probability*

## Outline

Probability theory offers a rigorous language for quantifying uncertainty and guiding decisions when information is incomplete. This chapter begins by defining an experiment and its sample space, reviews essential set-theoretic notation, and builds the structure of a probability model. It then presents the fundamental rules and theorems of probability, investigates conditional probability, independence, and Bayes's theorem, and distinguishes between discrete and continuous random variables. Throughout the chapter, real-world examples—from games of chance to horse-race wagering—demonstrate the practical power of probabilistic thinking.

After reading this chapter, you will be able to:

- Understand the concept of probability and its role in measuring uncertainty.
- Interpret and manipulate common set-theoretic symbols and operations.
- Define and analyze probability models, including sample spaces, events, and probability measures.
- Apply fundamental probability rules and theorems, such as De Morgan's laws and the law of total probability.
- Calculate conditional probabilities and understand the concept of independence.
- Utilize Bayes' theorem in various contexts, including medical statistics and legal reasoning.
- Distinguish between discrete and continuous random variables, along with their probability mass and density functions.
- Calculate the expectation and variance of random variables.
- Analyze games of chance and calculate expected values and risks.
- Understand betting strategies in horse racing, and calculate implied probabilities.

DOI: 10.1201/9781003543121-2

Probability theory is a set of useful tools for understanding uncertainty. The basis of probability is the so-called **Experiment**. An experiment is a (repeatable) procedure that has an outcome that is not known ahead of time. The classic examples that arise from gambling include rolling six-sided dice, roulette wheels, and so on. We will later use probability theory to understand the stock market and many other phenomena that don't exactly fit into this framework.

$$A^c = \{x \in S,\ x \notin A\}$$

$$A = B \text{ if } A \subseteq B \text{ and } A \supseteq B,\ A \cup B = \{x : x \in A \text{ or } x \in B\}.$$

We use $\phi$ to denote the empty set, that is, the set with no elements, which is kind of hard to imagine but is important as a construct in mathematics. We use $\mathcal{P}(S)$ to denote the set of all subsets of $S$ (called the **power set** of $S$). For a finite set this is easy to specify and to imagine. For $S = \mathbb{R}$, the power set is very complicated and large, and the concept is not manageable.

Union, intersection, and complement are mathematical operations on sets that obey certain rules, which we list below:

| | | |
|---|---|---|
| (1) | $A \cup B = B \cup A$,<br>$A \cap B = B \cap A$ | Commutativity |
| (2) | $A \cup (B \cup C) = (A \cup B) \cup C$;<br>$A \cap (B \cap C) = (A \cap B) \cap C$ | Associativity |
| (3) | $A \cap (B \cup C) = (A \cap B) \cup (A \cap C)$;<br>$A \cup (B \cap C) = (A \cup B) \cap (A \cup C)$ | Distributive |
| (4) | $(A \cup B)^c = A^c \cap B^c$;<br>$(A \cap B)^c = A^c \cup B^c$ | DeMorgan's |

Rules 1-3 are like the operations + and × in arithmetic according to their properties, for the most part. However, these rules can be extended to an infinite number of sets, specifically to **countably** many sets. A set $S$ is countable if the set is equivalent to the set of natural numbers, specifically, if there exists a **one-to-one** function $f$ from $S$ to the natural numbers $\mathbb{N} = \{0, 1, 2, \ldots\}$. In this case, we define the corresponding unions and intersections as follows:

$$\begin{aligned} A &= \cup_{i=0}^{\infty} A_i = \{x : \text{ There exists } i \in \mathbb{N} \text{ such that } x \in A_i\} \\ A &= \cap_{i=0}^{\infty} A_i = \{x : \text{ For all } i \in \mathbb{N},\ x \in A_i\}. \end{aligned}$$

Notice that these unions and intersections are always defined, whereas infinite sums of numbers may or may not be well defined. For example, what is the correct value of $+1 - 1 + 1 - 1 + \cdots$

The **Venn Diagram** is a classical way of presenting set theoretic ideas and results, see Figure 2.1, which shows three sets $A, B, C$ in a general configuration.

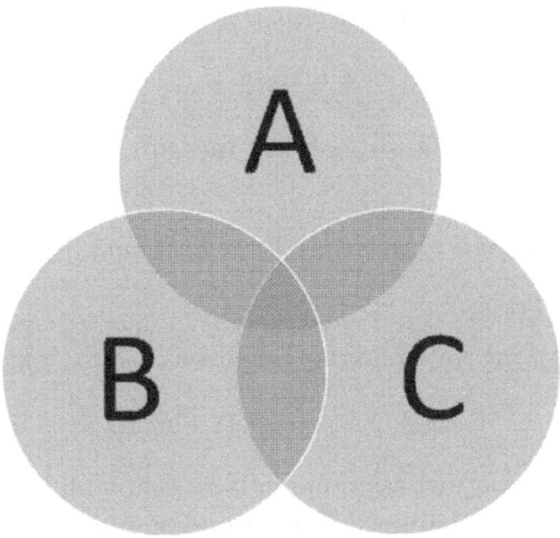


**FIGURE 2.1**
Venn diagram showing three general events A, B, C

The probability model consists of three ingredients:

1. A sample space $S$, the set of possible outcomes of the experiment
2. A collection $\mathcal{A}$ of events (called the sigma algebra), which are subsets of $S$, and are said to occur as the outcome of an experiment.
3. A probability measure $P$ that assigns a real number between zero and one to events (the "probability of the event occurring as the outcome of the experiment"), i.e., for each $A \in \mathcal{A}$, we can define $P(A) \in [0, 1]$.

The sample space $S$ can contain: a finite number of elements, e.g., $\{H, T\}$, an infinite but countable number of elements, e.g., $\mathbb{N} = \{1, 2, \ldots\}$, or an uncountable number of elements, e.g., $\mathbb{R}$ the set of real numbers.

An event $A$ is any subset of $S$ including the empty set $\phi$ and $S$ itself. Other special events are the singleton events $A = \{x\}$, for $x \in S$, which we will consider below. Essentially, events are questions about which we can answer yes (it occurred) or no (it did not occur). The collection of events $\mathcal{A}$ has to obey certain properties, namely, it should be closed under union and complement, that is, if $A, B \in \mathcal{A}$, then $A^c, A \cup B \in \mathcal{A}$.

**Example 13** *Suppose that the sample space is $S = \{0, 1, 2, \ldots\}$ and that $\mathcal{A}$ is all possible subsets of $S$. Then, possible events include*

$$A = \{2\}, \;\; A = \overbrace{\{2, 4, 6, \ldots\}}^{\textit{even numbers}}, \;\; A = \overbrace{\{2, 3, 5, 7, \ldots\}}^{\textit{prime numbers}}$$

**Example 14** *Suppose that the sample space is the unit circle, i.e.,* $S = [0, 2\pi] = \{x : 0 \leq x \leq 2\pi\}$. *Then possible events include*

$$A = \{\pi\},\ A = [0, 1],\ A = (\pi/2, \pi) = \{x : \pi/2 < x < \pi\}.$$

We will require that the probability measure satisfies the axioms given next.

**Definition 1** *A probability measure* $P$ *is a mapping from* $\mathcal{A} \to [0, 1]$ *such that:*
*(1)* $P(S) = 1$;
*(2) If* $A, B$ *are disjoint (or mutually exclusive) events, i.e.,* $A \cap B = \phi$, *then*

$$P(A \cup B) = P(A) + P(B).$$

The first assumption just says that $S$ is basically all the possible outcomes and that set itself always happens. The second assumption is quite reasonable, it says that the measure of weight of the combined set is equal to the combined weights of the two separate bodies. In fact, this last property should hold for a countable set of pairwise disjoint events, that is, for events $\{A_i\}_{i=1}^{\infty}$ with $A_i \cap A_j = \phi$ we must have

$$P\left(\cup_{i=0}^{\infty} A_i\right) = \sum_{i=1}^{\infty} P\left(A_i\right). \tag{2.1}$$

The meaning of $P(A)$ is the probability that event $A$ occurred so that the meaning of $P(A \cup B)$ is the probability that either event $A$ or event $B$ occurred, while the meaning of $P(A \cap B)$ is the probability that both event $A$ and $B$ occurred.

When $S$ is a finite set with $n$ elements, we may just take, without loss of generality, $\mathcal{A}$ to be the power set of $S$, and it suffices to pay attention just to the so-called singleton sets $\{x\}$. We often suppose that for any $x \in S$

$$P(\{x\}) = \frac{1}{n}. \tag{2.2}$$

From the second property of $P$, it then follows that for any compound event $A = \{x_1, x_2, \ldots, x_m\}$ containing $m$ distinct elements of $S$ we have

$$P(A) = \frac{m}{n}.$$

Many problems fall into this case in which calculating the probability amounts to finding $m$ or counting the elements of $A$. But this is not necessarily the case; we may have a probability measure $P$ that assigns different probability to different singletons. For example, suppose we have a biased coin with a 55% chance of landing on heads and a 45% chance of landing on tails, then we take

$$P(\{H\}) = 0.55, \quad P(\{T\}) = 0.45.$$

In fact, when $S$ is an infinite set, we cannot have equal positive probability for singletons, because the sum of the probabilities has to equal one, which implies that these singleton probabilities must approach zero.

**Example 15** ***Poisson distribution***. *Suppose that the outcomes are any non-negative integers, i.e., $S = \{0, 1, 2, \ldots\}$, a countable but infinite set. Then specify*

$$P(\{x\}) = e^{-\lambda}\frac{\lambda^x}{x!}, \quad P(\{0\}) = e^{-\lambda}, \; P(\{1\}) = e^{-\lambda}\lambda, \ldots$$

*This distribution is applied in many contexts in finance. One common application is in modeling the time between events, such as the time between trades or the arrival of information. Using the rules of probability, we can calculate the probability of compound events, even complicated ones with infinitely many elements. For example, if $\lambda = 1$,*

$$\begin{aligned} P(\{prime\ numbers\}) &= \sum_{i=1}^{\infty} P(\{prime\ number_i\}) \\ &= e^{-1} \sum_{x:prime} \frac{1}{x!} \simeq 0.24839162. \end{aligned}$$

*The numerical answer is obtained by computing the sum for a large number of prime numbers, which gives an approximation to the truth.*

We next identify some key properties of probabilities that are consequences of the axioms we specified above.

**Theorem 3** PROPERTIES OF ***P***
*1. $P(\phi) = 0$*
*2. $P(A) \leq 1$*
*3. $P(A^c) = 1 - P(A)$*
*4. $P(A) = P(A \cap B) + P(A \cap B^c)$ (Law of Total Probability)*
*5. If $A \subset B \Rightarrow P(A) \leq P(B)$*
*6. $P(A \cap B) = P(A) + P(B) - P(A \cup B)$*
*7. $P(A \cup B) \leq P(A) + P(B)$ for any sets $A, B, \ldots$*

The proofs of these properties involve manipulating sets to obtain disjoint sets and then apply the axioms. For example, $A$ and $A^c$ are mutually exclusive and exhaustive so that

$$1 = P(S) = P(A \cup A^c) = P(A) + P(A^c),$$

which establishes property 3. For property 6, see Figure 2.2.

We next come to an important example that we will use in a number of contexts.

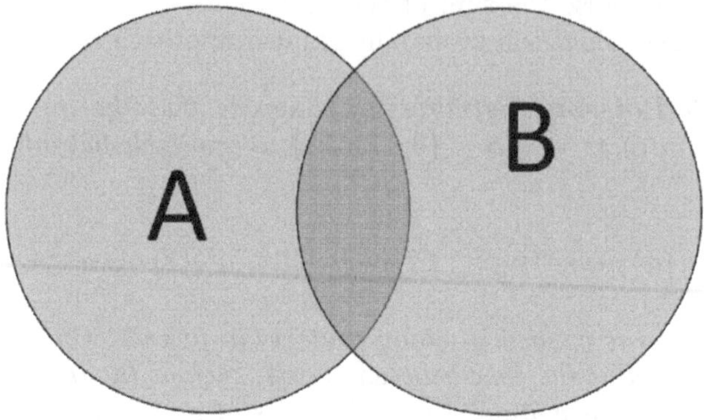


**FIGURE 2.2**
Demonstration of Property 6

**Example 16** *Birthday Problem. Suppose that there are n people in a room, what is the probability that at least two of them will have the same birthday?*

For many people, intuition says that this should be roughly (n-1)/365, which turns out to be wrong and badly wrong except when $n = 2$. There are many different approaches to solving this problem, we choose a bottom-up approach by specifying the details like sample space and event, and probability measure in turn. Suppose that $n = 2$, Alice and Bob, and forget about February 29th. The sample space can be represented as $S = \{(i, j), \quad i = 1, \ldots, 365, \ j = 1, \ldots, 365\}$, and in table format this looks like

| $A/B$ | 1 | 2 | 3 | $\cdots$ | 365 |
|---|---|---|---|---|---|
| 1 | | | | | |
| 2 | | | | | |
| 3 | | | $\ddots$ | | |
| $\vdots$ | | | | $\ddots$ | |
| 365 | | | | | |

, $365 \times 365$ elements

The typical element of the sample space is $(i, j)$, which corresponds to Alice having her birthday on day $i$, while Bob having his birthday on day $j$.

**Axiom 1** *We assume that each singleton $\{(i, j)\}$ has equal probability, i.e.,*

$$P(\{(i, j)\}) = 1/365^2. \tag{2.3}$$

That is, the probability that Alice has her birthday on day $i$ and Bob having his birthday on day $j$ is $1/365^2$. Obviously, Alice and Bob are unrelated people not identical twins, for example, otherwise this would be a bad assumption, see below.

The event that Alice and Bob have the same birthday can be represented as

$$E = \{(i, i), \quad i = 1, \ldots, 365\} \subset S,$$

which corresponds to the diagonal elements of the matrix

| $A/B$ | 1 | 2 | 3 | $\cdots$ | 365 |
|---|---|---|---|---|---|
| 1 | $A = B$ | | | | |
| 2 | | $A = B$ | | | |
| 3 | | | $\ddots$ | | |
| $\vdots$ | | | | $\ddots$ | |
| 365 | | | | | $A = B$ |

, $365 \times 365$ elements

By counting the elements of $E$, we obtain that

$$P(E) = \frac{365}{365^2} = \frac{1}{365}.$$

Now suppose that $n = 3$, Alice, Bob and Charlie. In this case, the sample space can be denoted

$$S = \{(i, j, k), \quad i, j, k = 1, \ldots, 365\},$$

which contains $365 \times 365 \times 365$ elements.

**Axiom 2** *We assume that each singleton* $\{(i, j, k)\}$ *has equal probability, i.e.,*

$$P(\{(i, j, k)\}) = \frac{1}{365^3}.$$

The event that two or more people have the same birthday can be satisfied in a number of different ways: Alice has the same birthday as Bob, or Alice has the same birthday as Charlie, or Bob has the same birthday as Charlie, or all three have the same birthday. That is, this event is the union of the following sets:

$$AB = \{(i, i, j), \quad i, j = 1, \ldots, 365\}, \; AC = \{(i, j, i), \quad i, j = 1, \ldots, 365\}$$

$$BC = \{(j, i, i), \quad i, j = 1, \ldots, 365\}, \; ABC = \{(i, i, i), \quad i = 1, \ldots, 365\},$$

but if we just add up all the elements of these sets, there is a double count because, for example, the event that *Alice* $=$ *Bob* includes also the possibility that *Alice* $=$ *Bob* $=$ *Charlie*. Therefore, we need to subtract off the intersections of these sets, which need to be enumerated. This is left as an exercise.

It is easier to calculate the probability that they all have different birthdays. Define the event where they all have different birthdays to be

$$E = \{(i, j, k), \quad i = 1, \ldots, 365, \; j \neq i, k \neq i, k \neq j\}.$$

This set has a total of $365 \times 364 \times 363$ elements. Therefore,

$$P(E) = \frac{365 \times 364 \times 363}{365^3}.$$

The probability that at least two of them have the same birthday is equal to 1 minus the probability that they all have different birthdays using the properties of sets. Therefore, we obtain

$$P\,(\text{at least two have same birthday}) = 1 - \frac{365 \times 364 \times 363}{365^3} = 0.0082.$$

In the general case the sample space $S$ has $365^n$ elements. The event $E$ that all $n$ individuals have different birthdays has $365 \times 364 \times \cdots \times (365 - (n-1))$ elements. Therefore,

$$\begin{aligned} &P\big(\text{at least two out of } n \text{ have same birthday}\big) \\ &\quad = 1 - \frac{365 \times 364 \times \cdots \times (365 - (n-1))}{365^n} \\ &\quad = 1 - \frac{365!}{(365-n)! \cdot 365^n}. \end{aligned}$$

For $n = 23$, this probability is just over 1/2. In Figure 2.3 we show how this probability increases with $n$.

In reality, the probability of a given day being a birthday is not equal across days within the year. In Figure 2.4, we show the empirical probability of births on each of 365 days in the calendar year for the US and the UK, averaged over the previous 20 years. Clearly, in both countries December 25th and January 1st are very low points for birthdays, and in the USA July 4th is another low point. In both countries, the late summer and early fall period is the most common for birthdays, the maximum is achieved in the UK on 26th September. The effect of non-equal probability (each day has probability $p_i$) on the coincident probability (the probability that at least two out of $n$ have the same birthday) can be calculated numerically; the deviation from the equal probability case depends on the variance of $p_i$ and is small in this case.

## 2.1 Continuous Versus Discrete Random Variables

A random variable $X$ is just a cardinalization (making into a numerical value) of the sample space (e.g., $\{H, T\} \mapsto \{0, 1\}$).

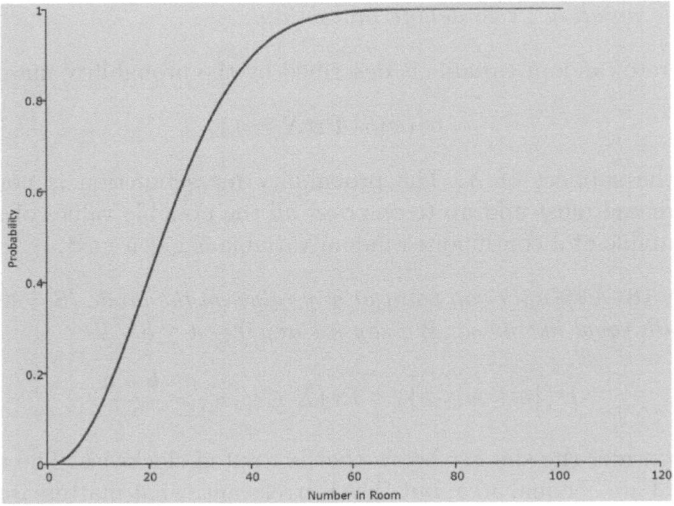


**FIGURE 2.3**
Probability of coincident birthday in a sample of size n

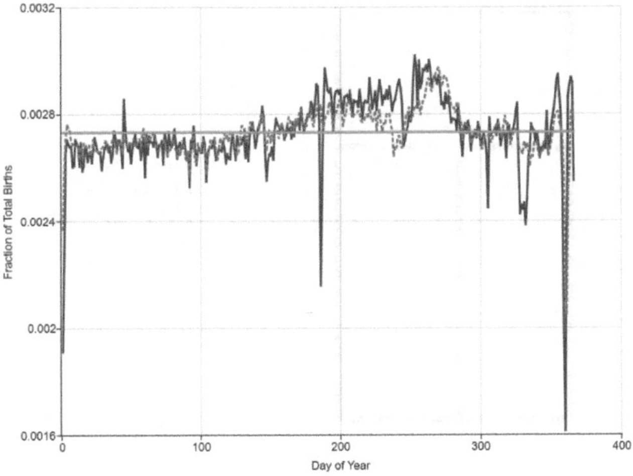


**FIGURE 2.4**
US and UK birthday fractions by day of the year, average of last 20 years

**Example 17** *The die with six sides* $\{1, 2, 3, 4, 5, 6\}$ *and equal probability of each side occurring.*

$$P(\{i\}) = \Pr(X = i) = \begin{cases} \frac{1}{6}, & i \in \{1, 2, 3, 4, 5, 6\} \\ 0 & \textit{any other } i. \end{cases}$$

*We use the notation* Pr *to denote probability.*

A discrete random variable is described by the probability mass function

$$f_X(x) = \Pr(X = x)$$

for $x$ in the support of $X$. The probability mass function is non-negative everywhere and must add up to one over all the possible values of $x$.

An example of a continuous random variable is given next.

**Example 18** *A spinner can point at any value on the circle ($S = [0, 2\pi]$) and does so with equal likelihood. We say for any $0 \leq a \leq b \leq 2\pi$*

$$P(\{a \leq x \leq b\}) = \Pr(X \in [a, b]) = \frac{b-a}{2\pi}.$$

Now consider the spinner below that is rotated clockwise. The three rectangles 1,2,3 are of equal area, but that is irrelevant; what matters is the angles they occupy. If the spinner ends up pointing in 1, this is equivalent to the event $A = [0, \pi]$ (if we set the origin to west) and so has probability 1/2.

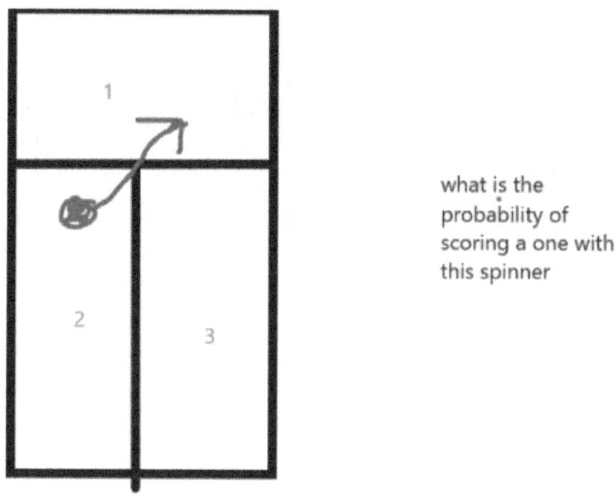


A defining property of a continuous random variable is that for any given $x$

$$P(\{x\}) = \Pr(X = x) = 0.$$

If this were not the case, we would end up with a contradiction, as we have already discussed. Further to that, the following calculation obviously makes no sense:

$$1 = P([0, 2\pi]) = P\left(\cup_{x\in[0,2\pi]}\{x\}\right) = \sum_{x\in[0,2\pi]} P(\{x\}) = 0.$$

The issue here is that $[0, 2\pi]$ is an **uncountable set** and the laws of probability were only defined for countable sets. Specifying probabilities of singleton events is not much use in this case, and instead we must specify probabilities of intervals (formally called **Borel sets**) and work from there.

In particular we may define $\Pr(X \in [a, b])$ for numbers $a, b$. The cumulative distribution function (c.d.f.) is defined as

$$F_X(x) = \Pr(X \leq x),$$

i.e., the case where $b = x$ and $a = -\infty$. A continuous random variable is described by the **probability density function** $f_X(x)$, where

$$\Pr(X \in [a, b]) = \int_a^b f_X(x)dx$$

for $x$ in the support of $X$. In fact, $f_X(x) = F_X'(x)$. The density function $f_X$ is non-negative and integrates to one over its domain $S$, i.e.,

$$\Pr(X \in S) = \int_S f_X(x)dx = 1.$$

We next define the mean and variance of a general random variable.

**Definition 2** *We say that the expectation of a random variable exists if* $\sum_x |x| f_X(x) < \infty$ *or* $\int_{-\infty}^{\infty} |x| f_X(x)dx < \infty$ *in the discrete and continuous cases, respectively. When the expectation exists, we define it as either*

$$E(X) = \sum_x x f_X(x), \quad E(X) = \int_{-\infty}^{\infty} x f_X(x)dx$$

*in the discrete and continuous case, respectively.*

This is a measure of the "central tendency" of the random variable $X$. A key property of expectation is that for any random variables $X, Y$ and any constants $\alpha, \beta$

$$E(\alpha X + \beta Y) = \alpha E(X) + \beta E(Y).$$

This is called "linearity". In practice, accountants and spreadsheets love the feature that averages of averages are averages, which is a manifestation of this property.

**Definition 3** *We say that the variance of a random variable exists if* $\sum_x x^2 f_X(x) < \infty$ *or* $\int_{-\infty}^{\infty} x^2 f_X(x)dx < \infty$ *in the discrete and continuous cases, respectively. When the variance exists, we define it as equivalently*

$$\text{var}(X) = E\left[(X - E(X))^2\right] = E(X^2) - E^2(X). \tag{2.4}$$

*The standard deviation is defined as* $\text{stdev}(X) = \sqrt{\text{var}(X)}$.

A key property of variance is that for any random variable $X$ and constants $a, b$, we have

$$\text{var}(a + bX) = b^2 \times \text{var}(X), \quad \text{stdev}(a + bX) = |b| \times \text{stdev}(X). \tag{2.5}$$

For example, the random variable $2X$ has a variance four times the variance of $X$. For any random variable $X$ (for which the moments exist), we may define a standardized random variable

$$\boxed{Z = \frac{X - E(X)}{\text{stdev}(X)}},$$

which by construction has $E(Z) = 0$ and $\text{var}(Z) = 1$. We will make a lot of use of standardized random variables in statistics.

We next give some examples of continuous random variables, their distributions and their means and variances.

**Example 19** *Uniform Distribution $X \sim U[0, a]$ (e.g., $a = 2\pi$) i.e.,*

$$f_X(x) = \begin{cases} \frac{1}{a} & \text{if } 0 \le x \le a \\ 0 & \text{else.} \end{cases}$$

*This has*

$$E(X) = \int_0^a x f_X(x) dx = \frac{1}{a} \int_0^a x dx = \frac{1}{a} \left[ \frac{x^2}{2} \right]_0^a = \frac{a}{2}$$

$$\text{var}(X) = \frac{1}{a} \int_0^a x^2 f_X(x) dx - E^2(X) = \frac{a^2}{3} - \left( \frac{a}{2} \right)^2 = \frac{a^2}{12}.$$

**Example 20** ***Normal or Gaussian distribution.*** *Suppose that*

$$f_X(x) = \frac{1}{\sqrt{2\pi\sigma^2}} \exp\left( -\frac{1}{2} \left( \frac{x - \mu}{\sigma} \right)^2 \right), \tag{2.6}$$

*we say that $X \sim N(\mu, \sigma^2)$. This has*

$$E(X) = \int_{-\infty}^{\infty} x f_X(x) dx = \mu, \quad \text{var}(X) = \sigma^2.$$

*For the special case $\mu = 0$ and $\sigma^2 = 1$ we have the standard normal density*

$$\phi(x) = \frac{1}{\sqrt{2\pi}} \exp\left( -\frac{1}{2} x^2 \right). \tag{2.7}$$

*This is the density of the standardized random variable $Z = (X - E(X))/\text{stdev}(X)$ that has mean zero and variance one. Figure 2.5 shows the shape of this density.*

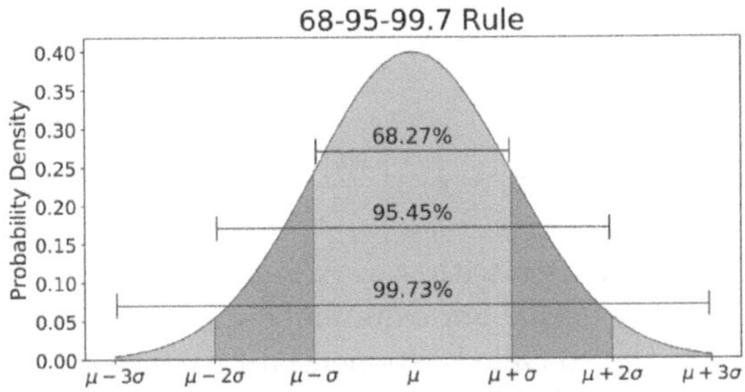


**FIGURE 2.5**
Normal or Gaussian density

**Example 21** *Human height (and weight and IQ) is approximately normally distributed. The average male height is $\mu$ with a variance of height across the population is $\sigma^2$. In practice $\mu, \sigma^2$ vary across different populations, such as male/female etc., and across cohorts. For males $\mu = 70''$ (178cm) and $\sigma = 4''$; Robert Wadlow measured 107" (272cm) on June 27th 1940, the tallest of all time. John Brower Minnoch weighed 635kg compared to $\mu = 75kg$ and $\sigma = 15kg$ (out of the estimated 107 billion people who ever lived)*

Suppose that IQ is normally distributed across the population; typically, it is thought that $\mu = 100$ and $\sigma = 15$. How many geniuses are there in the world? Suppose genius is defined as someone whose intelligence is more than six standard deviations above the mean, i.e., an IQ of 190. There are around $n = 8{,}000{,}000{,}000$ people in the world, so using the normal distribution we expect there to be

$$8{,}000{,}000{,}000 \times \Pr(X > \mu + 6\sigma) \simeq 8$$

people to be geniuses according to this definition. What about very smart people with intelligence more than three standard deviations above the mean (IQ of 145)? In this case, we have

$$8{,}000{,}000{,}000 \times \Pr(X > \mu + 3\sigma) \simeq 10{,}799{,}184,$$

which is a lot more common. Divide the answer by 80 say, then this says that there are around 134,990 people your age in the world who are that smart.

What we have just learned is that the tails of the normal distribution are thin, that is, the probability of extreme events is low and declines very quickly as you go further and further into the extremity. For example, we have

$$\frac{\Pr(X > \mu + 3\sigma)}{\Pr(X > \mu + 6\sigma)} = \frac{\Pr(X < \mu - 3\sigma)}{\Pr(X < \mu - 6\sigma)} = 1{,}368{,}250,$$

so that when you go from 3 to 6 standard deviations the **exceedance** probability shrinks by a factor of over a million. For a standard normal random variable, we have for any $x > 0$

$$\Pr(X > x) \leq \frac{\exp(-x^2/2)}{1+x}. \tag{2.8}$$

The right-hand side decreases with $x$ very rapidly. It says that large events are relatively unlikely to occur. For example, for $x = 10$ the right hand side is $1.91 \times 10^{-24}$. This is the so-called exponential tail property. This property is felt to be unrealistic for use in high-frequency financial markets where large (in both positive and negative senses) events occur quite frequently. The so-called **Pareto law** (also known in some applications as **Gibrat's law** or **Zipf's law**) is an alternative modeling assumption widely used for that purpose. It is an empirical question whether Gaussianity is a good model for, say, IQ or human height. In practice, standardized testing companies transform the scores on their tests exactly so that they conform to a normal distribution, so we will never know. Income and wealth distributions are far from normally distributed and are better described by a Pareto law.

## 2.2 Conditional Probability and Independence

In many applications, we have events $A$ and $B$ , and we want to explain or predict $A$ by $B$. We are not just interested in **marginal** probabilities, but also in **conditional** probability, that is, we want to incorporate some information into our predictions about whether event $A$ is likely to occur.

**Example 22** *Suppose you are a college admissions officer and you have to choose between applicants based on their High School grades (and perhaps other information). Let*

$$A = \{\textit{got g.p.a. 4.0 in college}\} \quad ; \quad B = \{\textit{got g.p.a. 4.0 in High School}\}.$$

*You observe on file the value of* $B$. *Of interest is* $P(A|B)$; *the extent to which this is larger (or smaller) than* $P(A)$ *is a measure of the value of the information in* $B$ *for this purpose.*

**Example 23** *Suppose you are deciding whether to invest in the stock market at the end of the day. Let*

$$A = \{\textit{stocks up Tomorrow}\} \qquad ; \qquad B = \{\textit{stocks up Today}\}.$$

*You observe* $B$ *before you make your investment decision. Of interest is* $P(A|B)$; *the extent to which this is larger (or smaller) than* $P(A)$ *is a measure of the value of this information.*

In both cases, we might expect the event $B$ to give relevant and useful information about event $A$. Sometimes the information has value, and sometimes it does not. Knowing the answer to one question, may or may not help you in answering another question. Knowing whether the dog found the chocolate or not is relevant for determining whether there is any chocolate for you or not.

**Definition 4** *The probability of an event $A$ given an event $B$, denoted $P(A|B)$, is given by*

$$P(A|B) = \frac{P(A \cap B)}{P(B)},$$

*when $P(B) > 0$.*

Note that $P(\cdot|B)$ is itself a probability measure meaning that

$$P(A_1 \cup A_2|B) = P(A_1|B) + P(A_2|B)$$

for any disjoint sets $A_1, A_2$. Show that $0 \leq P(A_1 \cup A_2|B) \leq 1$. We next discuss some properties of conditional probability. If $A$ and $B$ are mutually exclusive events, i.e., $A \cap B = \varnothing$, then $P(A|B) = 0$; if $A$ and $B$ can never happen simultaneously, then knowing that $B$ has occurred means that $A$ has not occurred. If $A \subseteq B$, then $P(A|B) = P(A)/P(B) \geq P(A)$, with strict inequality unless $P(B) = 1$; if $A$ is a special case of $B$, then knowing that $B$ has occurred improves the likelihood that $A$ has occurred. If $B \subseteq A$, then $P(A|B) = 1$; if $B$ is a special case of $A$, then knowing that $B$ has occurred implies that $A$ has occurred.

**Example 24** *"Mr. Jones has two children. The older child is a girl. What is the probability that both children are girls?" "Mr. Smith has two children. At least one of them is a boy. What is the probability that both children are boys?"*

The sample space is

$$S = \{(Boy, Boy), (Boy, Girl), (Girl, Boy), (Girl, Girl)\},$$

where the first component of each pair signifies the sex of the first child, and the second component indicates the sex of the second child. Let us assume that each pair is equally likely, which is close to sensible assumption.

Using the definition of conditional probability, we can derive the result

$$\begin{aligned} P(\text{Younger is Girl} \mid \text{Older is Girl}) &= \frac{P(\text{Older is Girl and Younger is Girl})}{P(\text{Older is Girl})} \\ &= \frac{1/4}{1/2} = \frac{1}{2} = P(\text{Younger is Girl}). \end{aligned}$$

As for Mr. Smith, we know that he does not have $\{girl, girl\}$, but all three other outcomes are possible, and equally likely. Since $\{boy, boy\}$ is only one of three possible outcomes, the probability that Mr. Smith has two boys is 1/3.

We next consider the **Monty Hall problem**. There was a famous American TV game show with a host called Monty Hall. The game was as follows. The contestant is shown three doors, he is told that behind one door is a brand new car, and behind the other two doors are goats. The contestant must choose one door, and he will get to keep what is behind the door he chooses. The game proceeds as follows:

1. The contestant makes a choice of a door.
2. Then Monty Hall opens one of the remaining doors to reveal a goat.
3. Then Monty Hall asks if the contestant wants to change his choice.
4. Finally, all the remaining doors are opened to reveal which door had the car and whether the contestant has won or not.

The question is, should the contestant stick or switch when they are asked? A lot of people view this as an exercise in probability theory and intuitively say there is no reason to switch, the car cannot be moved, so my chances of success cannot be improved by switching. The key thing here is the fact that this Monty Hall has an objective and knows where the car sits (it is really a two-person game). His objective is to make good TV! Of course, he is not going to open a door with a car behind it because that would cut the excitement short. He specifically opens a door with a goat in it and this has valuable information. In particular, if your first choice is correct, then MH chooses one of the other doors at random (both doors contain a goat). On the other hand, if your first choice is incorrect, then MH chooses the single remaining door that contains a goat. Sticking gives a probability of 1/3 of success. However, switching gives a probability of 2/3 of success, since in the event that your first choice was incorrect (which happens with probability 2/3), your switching gives you a 100% chance of winning. Let $B$ be the event that your first choice is correct, and let $A$ be the event that your switched choice is correct. Then $P(B) = 1/3$ and so $P(B^c) = 2/3$. Then $P(A|B) = 0$, whereas $P(A|B^c) = 1$. By the law of total probability

$$P(A) = P(A \cap B) + P(A \cap B^c) = P(A|B)P(B) + P(A|B^c)P(B^c).$$

In this case

$$P(A) = P(A|B)P(B) + P(A|B^c)P(B^c) = \frac{2}{3}.$$

We next consider the concept of **independence**. This corresponds to the case where the conditioning information has no value, as is reflected in the definition below.

**Definition 5** INDEPENDENCE. *Suppose $P(A), P(B) > 0$, then $A$ and $B$ are independent events if*
*(1) $P(A \cap B) = P(A) \cdot P(B)$ [symmetric in $A$ and $B$]*

*(2) $P(A|B) = P(A)$ [easier to interpret]*
*(3) $P(B|A) = P(B)$ [easier to interpret]*

**Example 25** *In the six-sided die example take $A = \{2,4,6\}$, $B = \{1,2,3,4\}$. Then $A, B$ are independent since*

$$P(A \cap B) = \frac{1}{3} = P(A) \times P(B)$$

$$P(A|B) = \frac{1/3}{2/3} = \frac{1}{2} = P(A), \ P(B|A) = \frac{1/3}{1/2} = \frac{2}{3} = P(B).$$

Independence is a **symmetric relationship**, so that $A$ is independent of $B$ is the same thing as $B$ is independent of $A$. Furthermore, if $A$ is independent of $B$, then $A$ is independent of $B^c$, $A^c$ is independent of $B$, and $A^c$ is independent of $B^c$ (If you know $B$, then you know $B^c$). These can easily be verified in the above example. On the other hand, Independence is not a **transitive relationship**, i.e., $A$ independent of $B$ and $B$ independent of $C$ does not imply that $A$ is independent of $C$.

**Example 26** *In the six-sided die example, take*

$$A = \{2,4,6\}, \ B = \{1,2,3,4\}, \ C = \{1,3,5\}.$$

$$P(A \cap B) = \frac{1}{3} = P(A) \times P(B)$$

$$P(B \cap C) = \frac{1}{3} = P(B) \times P(C)$$

$$P(A \cap C) = 0 \neq P(A) \times P(C)$$

Independence is an important property that is often assumed in applications. For example, in games of chance such as roulette or craps, consecutive plays are assumed to be independent. For example, it is often assumed that stock returns are independent from day to day; For example, it is usually assumed that different households' spending decisions are independent of each other. In fact, independence is widely used in statistics as the basis of **sampling** from a population.

**Example 27** *Birthday problem continued. Another way of approaching this problem is to specify the probability of Alice having birthday on day $i$ ($P(A_i)$) as being $1/365$ and assuming that the events $A_i$ and $B_i$ are independent for all $i$, i.e., $P(A_i \cap B_i) = P(A_i) \times P(B_i) = 1/365^2$. Then the probability that Alice and Bob have the same birthday is*

$$P\left(\cup_{i=1}^{365} A_i \cap B_i\right) = \sum_{i=1}^{365} P(A_i \cap B_i) = \sum_{i=1}^{365} P(A_i)\, P(B_i) = \frac{1}{365}.$$

The Independence property guarantees, for example, that for independent random variables $X, Y$ and constants $a, b$

$$\mathrm{var}(aX + bY) = a^2\mathrm{var}(X) + b^2\mathrm{var}(Y). \tag{2.9}$$

In particular, this says that for independent and identically distributed random variables $X_i$ with common variance $\sigma^2$, we have

$$\mathrm{var}(X_1 + \ldots + X_n) = \mathrm{var}(X_1) + \ldots + \mathrm{var}(X_n) = n\sigma^2.$$

This property is important in both statistics and finance. In finance, it says essentially that risks are additive, i.e., can be added together. Independence can also be assumed inappropriately.

**Example 28** *The* ***Sally Clark/Roy Meadow*** *case. Expert Meadow testified that the probability of two cot deaths occurring in the same family was 1 in 73,000,000, a figure which he erroneously obtained by squaring the observed ratio of live-births to cot deaths in affluent non-smoking families (approximately 1 in 8,500). See Phil Dawid expert witness statement in the retrial.*

## 2.3 Bayes Rule

We next give the famous **Bayes Rule**. Often, we have prior information about a marginal probability and about a conditional probability. However, we are most interested in the reverse direction of conditional probability. In some application fields, this is called signal extraction or extracting the signal from the noise.

**Theorem 4** *(Bayes Rule). For two sets $A$ and $B$ with $P(A) \neq 0$*

$$P(B|A) = \frac{P(A|B) \cdot P(B)}{P(A)} = \frac{P(A|B) \cdot P(B)}{P(A|B) \cdot P(B) + P(A|B^c) \cdot P(B^c)}. \tag{2.10}$$

**Proof 1** *The first equality follows from the definition of conditional probability,*

$$P(A \cap B) = P(A|B) \cdot P(B) = P(B|A) \cdot P(A).$$

*The second equality follows from the law of total probability*

$$P(A) = P(A \cap B) + P(A \cap B^c) = P(A|B)P(B) + P(A|B^c)P(B^c).$$

We may also write this formula in different ways for interpretations. First,

$$\frac{P(B|A)}{P(B)} = \frac{P(A|B)}{P(A)}.$$

This says that the ratios of the conditional probability to the marginal probability are the same whether $A$ or $B$ is chosen as the conditioning variable. Second,

$$\frac{P(B|A)}{P(A|B)} = \frac{P(B)}{P(A)}.$$

This says that the ratios of the conditional probabilities are the same as the ratios of the marginal probabilities.

In Bayesian Statistics, the probability $P(B)$ is frequently called the **prior** probability, and $P(A|B)$ is called the **likelihood**, while $P(B|A)$ is called the **posterior**. There are many applications of Bayes theorem in medical statistics and law.

**Example 29** *Suppose that a person takes a covid-19 lateral flow test and receives bad news: a "positive" test. However, since not every positive result is correct, what is the probability that she actually has covid-19? Suppose that: the fraction of people who have covid-19 is 0.014, the fraction who do not have covid-19 is 1 − 0.014 = 0.986, the probability that a person who has covid-19 will get a positive result on a lateral flow test is 0.75, and the probability that a person who does not have covid-19 will get a false positive is 0.1.*

Let

$$A = \{\text{person tests positive}\}, \; B = \{\text{person has covid}\}$$

We have $P(B) = 0.014$, $P(A|B) = 0.75$, $P(A|B^c) = 0.1$. Therefore,

$$\begin{aligned} P(B \mid A) &= \frac{P(A \mid B)P(B)}{P(A \mid B)P(B) + P(A \mid B^c)P(B^c)} \\ &= \frac{0.75 \times 0.014}{0.75 \times 0.014 + 0.1 \times 0.986} \\ &= \boxed{0.096} \end{aligned}$$

This seems like quite a low probability. It happens because the tested population has a low incidence of disease. Suppose there are 1000 people, roughly 14 of them will have COVID-19. Of the 986 who do not have COVID-19 approximately 99 will test positive, while of the 14 with COVID-19, maybe 11 will test positive. The positive tested set will contain 99 without and 11 with so numerically, the withouts dominate the withs. One can improve the false positive rate by only screening a population with a higher incidence. In fact, the statistics of COVID-19 tests is more complicated, since the results depend on when, relative to infection, a patient is tested.

The **Prosecutor's fallacy** is a fallacy of statistical reasoning involving a test for an occurrence, such as a DNA match. Such matches often feature in criminal trials. A positive result in the test may paradoxically be more likely to be an erroneous result than an actual occurrence, even if the test itself is very accurate. The fallacy is named because it is typically used by a prosecutor to exaggerate the probability of a criminal defendant's guilt. Suppose that $E$ is evidence and $I$ is the event that the suspect is innocent. Then we have

$$P(I|E) = \frac{P(E|I) \times P(I)}{P(E)}.$$

Therefore, even if $P(E|I)$ is small, $P(I|E)$ could be large if $P(E)$ is equally small. In the Sally Clark case, suppose the evidence was two dead babies. According to expert Meadows, $P(E|I)$ is $1/73000000 = (1/8500)^2$ (he assumed independence). But $P(E)$ is also very low by the same reasoning, i.e., double homicide of babies by their mother is very uncommon.

In an influential paper, Ioannidis (2005) used Bayes theorem to argue that most published empirical research is false! His argument is as follows. The probability that a research claim is true may depend on study power and bias, the number of other studies on the same question, and, importantly, **the ratio of true to no relationships** among the relationships probed in each scientific field. In this framework, a research finding is less likely to be true when the studies conducted in a field are smaller; when effect sizes are smaller; when there is a greater number and lesser preselection of tested relationships, where there is greater flexibility in designs, definitions, outcomes, and analytical modes; when there is greater financial and other interest and prejudice; and when more teams are involved in a scientific field in chase of statistical significance. Simulations show that for most study designs and settings, it is more likely for a research claim to be false than true. Moreover, for many current scientific fields, claimed research findings may often be simply accurate measures of the prevailing bias. The message is to be cautious in interpreting the headline reports about research findings say about new diets.

### 2.3.1 Biased Coin

How do we know that a given coin is fair, meaning the probability of heads/tails is 50/50? We don't know! Some coins are known to have a slight bias toward heads or tails; there is also some chance that the coin lands on its side depending on how it is thrown and on what surface etc. See Diaconis (2004) for an in-depth treatment of coin tossing and gambling problems.

We suppose that the probability $p$ that the coin lands on heads is unknown. We think it is equally likely to be any number between zero and one. This is called the prior distribution and it is an "uninformative" or flat prior, shown in Figure 2.6

Suppose we record a data sequence (i.e., outcomes of tosses of the coin)

$$\{H, T, T, T, T, H\}.$$

What can we now say about $p$? Using independence we have that the probability of observing such a sequence, $f(data|p)$, is

$$f(data|p) = p^2(1-p)^4,$$

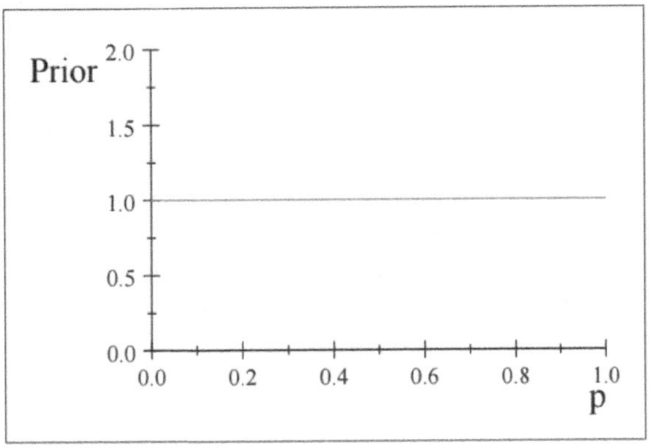


**FIGURE 2.6**
Flat prior

because there were two heads and four tails in six throws. This is called the **Likelihood** and is sometimes denoted $L$. For given $p$ some sequences are more likely than others. Statistics is about inverting that statement to say that given some data what can we say about $p$. The Likelihood is plotted below as a function of $p$ (i.e., we write this as $L(p)$).

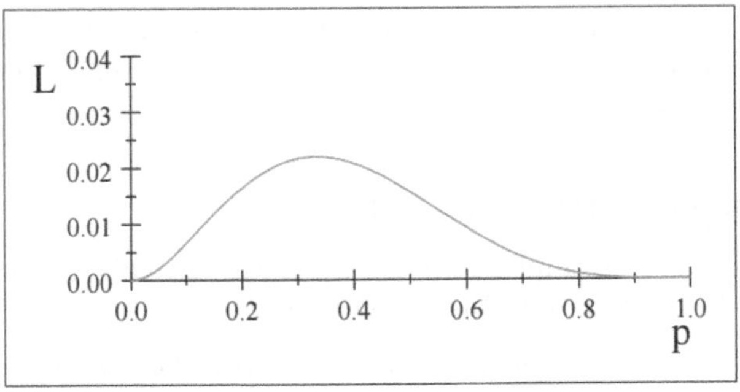


What is our updated guess about $p$ or more precisely, about the distribution of $p$ given the data? Using Bayes Theorem, we have

$$posterior(p) = f(p|data) = \frac{f(data|p)prior(p)}{f(data)},$$

where the posterior is a distribution over the random variable $p$. We already calculated $f(data|p)$ and we specified $prior(p) = 1$ if $p \in [0, 1]$. Therefore, we know that

$$posterior(p) \propto p^2(1-p)^4 = \frac{p^2(1-p)^4}{\int_0^1 p^2(1-p)^4 dp}.$$

The denominator in this expression is arrived at using the property that a density (the posterior is a density for $p$) must integrate to one but it is just a constant. The posterior density for $p$ has a peak (mode) at $p = 1/3$ but has positive probability mass everywhere on $[0, 1]$.

Now suppose that we toss the coin a hundred times and observe a sequence $HTH\ldots$ with exactly 48 heads and 52 tails. Then

$$L = p^{48}(1-p)^{52}.$$

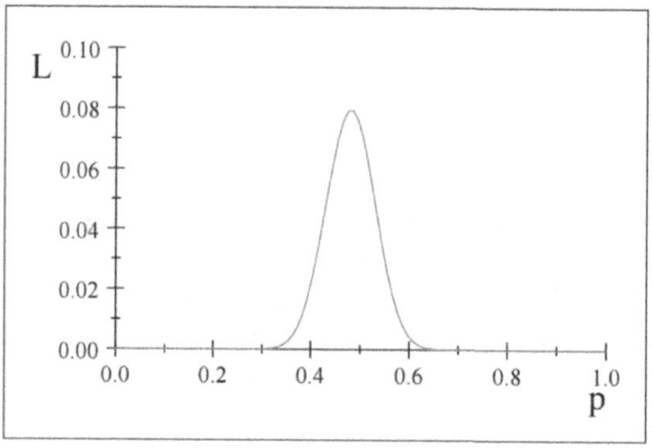


The posterior is concentrating around the unknown value of $p$ as the amount of data increases, i.e., as $n \to \infty$. In this case, it looks like $p$ is pretty close to 0.50.

### 2.3.2 Sequential Trading Model

We next consider an example from economic theory, called the **sequential trading** model (Glosten and Milgrom (1985)).

**Example 30** *The value of a shiny object can take two possible values, high and low with equal probability*

$$V = \begin{cases} V_H & \textit{with prob } \frac{1}{2} \\ V_L & \textit{with prob } \frac{1}{2} \end{cases}, \; V_H > V_L.$$

*For example* $V_H = 1$ *and* $V_L = 0$*. There are two types of traders who may issue buy or sell orders for the object: the Informed, who know what its value* $V$ *is, and the uninformed, who do not know* $V$*. They are chosen randomly (after* $V$ *has been determined) as follows*

$$T = \begin{cases} I & \textit{with prob } \mu \\ U & \textit{with prob } 1-\mu. \end{cases}$$

*Whichever type of trader is chosen issues their order. The strategies of the traders are as follows: The informed traders (I) will issue a buy order if the value is high $V_H$, and issue a sell order if the value is low $V_L$; The uninformed traders (U) issue buy or sell orders randomly with probability 1/2.*

Suppose that a trader arrives in the market. We don't know whether they are uninformed or informed, but we do know whether they issue a buy order or a sell order, i.e., we observe the order flow. Suppose that we receive a buy order, what can we infer from that?

We work backwards. Let

$$A = \{V = V_L\}, \quad B = \{buy\ order\ received\}.$$

We can calculate the probability that we receive a buy order given the underlying value, $P(B|A)$, directly from the knowledge of the traders strategies and the distribution of trader types. That is,

$$P(B|V = V_L) = P(B|A) = \frac{1}{2}(1 - \mu),$$

because if the value is low, the informed trader will not buy and the uninformed trader will buy one half of the time. Likewise

$$P(buy|V = V_H) = P(B|A^c) = (1 - \mu)/2 + \mu = \frac{1 + \mu}{2},$$

because when the value is high, the informed trader will always buy. Finally, $P(B^c|A) = 1 - P(B|A) = (1 + \mu)/2$ and $P(B^c|A^c) = (1 - \mu)/2$.

By Bayes rule, we can calculate the updated distribution (**posterior**) of the value $V$ given the receipt of a buy order:

$$\begin{aligned}
P(A|B) &= \overbrace{P(V = V_L|buy)}^{posterior} \\
&= \frac{\overbrace{P(buy|V = V_L)}^{likelihood}\overbrace{P(V = V_L)}^{prior}}{P(buy)} \\
&= \frac{P(buy|V = V_L)P(V = V_L)}{P(buy|V = V_L)P(V = V_L) + P(buy|V = V_H)P(V = V_H)} \\
&= \frac{\frac{1}{2}(1 - \mu) \times \frac{1}{2}}{\frac{1}{2}} \\
&= \frac{1}{2}(1 - \mu)
\end{aligned}$$

It follows that

$$P(V_L|buy) = \frac{1}{2}(1 - \mu), \quad P(V_H|buy) = \frac{1}{2}(1 + \mu).$$

Our distribution of value is affected by the fact that we received a buy order. In terms of our best guess about the value, we have in the absence of any information $E(V) = (V_L + V_H)/2$, but updated with the order information we have

$$\begin{aligned} E(V \mid \text{buy}) &= \frac{1}{2}(1-\mu)V_L + \frac{1}{2}(1+\mu)V_H \\ &= \frac{V_L + V_H}{2} + \frac{\mu}{2}(V_H - V_L) \\ &= E(V) + \frac{\mu}{2}(V_H - V_L). \end{aligned} \tag{2.11}$$

This means that receiving a buy order will raise our expected value of $V$ by the amount $\mu(V_H - V_L)/2$. Likewise, were we to receive a sell order it will lower our expected value of $V$ by the amount $\mu(V_H - V_L)/2$.

## 2.4 Games of Chance

Games of chance are where probability theory began. Gamblers wanted to know how likely they were to win or lose, and this led to the development of this field. We represent the (potential) outcome of a game (the gain or loss) by the random variable $X$. The outcome itself is not known in advance of the playing itself, although the potential outcomes and their probabilities are known.

**Definition 6** *A Fair game is a gamble that is (actuarially) fair, i.e., is zero in expectation, $E(X) = 0$. On average, you receive what you put in, no more and no less. An unfair game has $E(X) < 0$. The return of a game is measured by $E(X)$.*

Historically, games or chance were evaluated accorded to whether they were fair or not, and the expected outcome was the main focus. More recently, attention has also levelled on risk or uncertainty, i.e., how much variability there is in the random outcome, which we next define.

**Definition 7** *The riskiness of a game is measured by its variance* $\text{var}(X)$ *or standard deviation* $\text{stdev}(X)$.

**Example 31** *Suppose I toss a balanced coin, with outcomes heads I win ($X = +1$), tails I lose ($X = -1$). This is a fair game, i.e., $E(X) = 0$. We have* $\text{var}(X) = E(X^2) - E^2(X) = 1$.

**Example 32** *Consider the national lottery. You pay $1 for a ticket and guess 6 numbers from 1-59 with a prize of $C, which varies depending on how many* *people play ( the prize is divided equally among the n winning tickets). There are exactly*

$$\frac{59!}{6!53!} = 45,057,474$$

*different possible lottery picks. From an individual's point of view, the outcome is a random variable $X$ such that*

$$X = \begin{cases} C/n & \frac{1}{45,057,474} \\ -1 & 1 - \frac{1}{45,057,474}. \end{cases}$$

*The expected payoff is*

$$E(X) = \frac{C}{n} \times \frac{1}{45,057,474} - \left(1 - \frac{1}{45,057,474}\right).$$

It is apparent that the lottery problem is actually quite complicated. The value of $E(X)$ is usually less than zero (unless $C$ is extremely large). Furthermore, $E(X)$ varies with $n$ and $C$, which are not known at the time of purchase, although $C$ is often known approximately or at least a lower bound on $C$ is announced from time to time. The number of people who choose the lottery numbers you have chosen is usually just one (yourself), but it could be two or more, which would shave your winnings.

It turns out that you can improve your expected payoff (but not your probability of winning) by choosing numbers that are not birthdays, or rather downweighting birthdays. This is because many people pick their birthday or their children's birthday or their dog's birthday, and therefore the numbers 1-31 are more heavily represented overall than those numbers from 32-59. Since the winning numbers should be uniformly distributed on $\{1, \ldots, 59\}$ and each six number combination is equally likely to be drawn, by choosing numbers less chosen by other people, you are less likely to have to split your winnings with another person.

**Example 33** *Consider a casino roulette wheel with 37 slots, 18 red, 18 black, and 1 void, all equally likely. Suppose that the customer bets on black. We can describe the gain per play of the customer through the random variable $X$, where*

$$X = \begin{cases} 1 & 18/37 \\ -1 & 19/37. \end{cases}$$

*The expected payoff for the customer is*

$$E(X) = 1 \times \frac{18}{37} - 1 \times \frac{19}{37} = -\frac{1}{37}.$$

*The customer may almost double your money but more likely they will lose their stake. This is not a Fair game for the customer. The payoff for the Casino is $-X$ with expected return per play*

$$E(-X) = 1 \times \frac{19}{37} - 1 \times \frac{18}{37} = \frac{1}{37}.$$

*The risk per play for the Casino is*

$$\text{var}(-X) = 1 - \left(\frac{1}{37}\right)^2 \simeq 1, \quad \text{stdev}(-X) = \sqrt{1 - \left(\frac{1}{37}\right)^2} \simeq 1.$$

Suppose the Casino plays $n$ games per day, what is its risk and the return? The outcomes are the sequence of wins or losses: $+1, -1, +1, \ldots$ Call these outcomes random variables $X_1, X_2, \ldots$ The payoff to Casino at the end of the day is

$$T = X_1 + \cdots + X_n = numberofwins - numberoflosses.$$

For example, $n = 100$ plays, with 53 wins and 47 losses gives $T = +6$. The expected payoff per game and risk per game is

$$E\left(\frac{T}{n}\right) = \frac{1}{37}, \quad \text{var}(\frac{T}{n}) = \frac{1}{n} \times \left(1 - \left(\frac{1}{37}\right)^2\right)$$

$$\text{stdev}(\frac{T}{n}) = \frac{1}{\sqrt{n}}\sqrt{\left(1 - \left(\frac{1}{37}\right)^2\right)}.$$

In this case, the risk per game satisfies

$$\text{stdev}(\frac{T}{n}) \to 0$$

as $n$ gets large. Casino's make lots of money with very little risk.

One useful lesson from this is that **bold play** is optimal for the customer! Meaning, suppose you have to win \$1,000,000 (you borrowed from some gangsters who want the money by tomorrow morning or they will take a pound of flesh). Your best chance of achieving that objective is to bet everything you have every time. If instead you place lots of small bets in sequence, you will have a vanishingly low chance of success. On the other hand, when the odds are in your favor (the Casino), it is better to have lots of small bets placed against you than one big one.

## 2.5 Horse Racing

We next consider gambling on Horse Racing (or equivalently, betting on elections or sports games) as this is quite popular around the world and illustrates some of the probability concepts we have been developing. Of interest to us is the gambling system whereby individuals bet on who will win the race at some **odds**, which determines their potential winnings. We will show the connection between odds and probability. There are several different systems in use.

**Fixed Odds Betting.** In the virtual world, the majority of horse racing betting sites use the fixed odds system. With a fixed odds bet, the payout for a winning wager is agreed at the time a bet is placed and will not change for that transaction, although the rates facing new customers will change over time reflecting supply and demand.

**Parimutuel Betting.** In contrast to the fixed odds system, some sites will also offer the Parimutuel odds method. Common in the USA and Hong Kong but not in Europe. This style of horse race betting is controlled by a "tote" system that takes into account all money in the betting pool and determines the payout odds of winning bets once the house's (the house plus the state plus the Federal government) cut is removed and after all bets are in. Essentially, Parimutuel betting differs from fixed odds betting in that the final payout is not set until the betting pool is closed and can be different from the indicative odds.

In the table below, we show an example, the 11.15am race at Fairview, South Africa. The weight of the rider, the age of the horse, and its name are given along with its odds of winning (these characteristics are considered important factors in the horse's performance). In this case, the three-year-old Peace in our World was the favorite, and its rider weighed in at 9 stone (around 57kg) exactly. The odds given here are so-called UK/Irish odds in which odds of $x/y$ mean that, if the horse wins, you receive $x+y$ if you bet $y$. There are also decimal odds and American odds, which are presented slightly differently.

| **Name of Horse** | **Rider** | **Age** | **Odds** |
|---|---|---|---|
| Herodotus | 9-6 | 6 | 9/4 |
| Peaceful Day | 9-3 | 5 | 12/1 |
| Peace in our World | 9-0 | 3 | 10/11 |
| Safari Blue | 9-0 | 3 | 9/2 |
| En Garde | 8-6 | 4 | 14/1 |

Peace in our World is the strong favorite, whereas En Garde is a long odds outsider.

### 2.5.1 Implied Probability

We next calculate what is called the implied probability of a horse winning derived from the odds the bookmakers give on it. This is calculated on the zero profit assumption, that is, on average, the bettor wins his stake back nothing more and nothing less (and the bookmakers make zero expected profit). The expected return on a dollar bet (with random outcome $X$) on a horse with odds $x/y$ is

$$E(X) = \frac{winnings}{stake} \times \Pr(win) = \frac{x+y}{y} \times p,$$

where $p$ is the probability the horse wins (or the bet pays out). Suppose that the expected return on your dollar is $\pi$ dollars (if $\pi = 1$, you just earn your money back and make zero profit), then it follows that

$$p = \frac{y}{x+y} \times \pi.$$

The case with $\pi = 1$ is called the implied probability (of this horse winning). Note that this is different from the "objective probability" of this horse winning whatever that is. For the race given above, we calculate the implied probabilities.

| Name of Horse | Rider | Age | Odds | Prob |
|---|---|---|---|---|
| Herodotus | 9-6 | 6 | 9/4 | 0.307 |
| Peaceful Day | 9-3 | 5 | 12/1 | 0.077 |
| Peace in our World | 9-0 | 3 | 10/11 | 0.524 |
| Safari Blue | 9-0 | 3 | 9/2 | 0.182 |
| En Garde | 8-6 | 4 | 14/1 | 0.067 |

The implied probabilities sum to 1.157, a number greater than one, what does this mean? Suppose that we require the probabilities to sum upto one by introducing the profit factor $\pi$. This works for the choice $\pi = 1/1.157 \simeq 0.864$. The amount $1 - \pi$ can be interpreted as the bookmaker's average profit rate; since this is a zero-sum game between the customer and the bookmaker, this is also the customer's average loss.

Is it possible to devise a betting scheme (i.e., betting something on all the horses) that is guaranteed to make you money or not? Let us see whether this is possible in this case.

We can state this mathematically as follows: can we find $w_1 \geq 0, \ldots, w_5 \geq 0$ such that $w_1 + \cdots + w_5 = 1$ such that

$$w_1\frac{13}{4} \geq 1, \quad w_2 13 \geq 1, \quad w_3\frac{21}{11} \geq 1, \quad w_4\frac{11}{2} \geq 1, \quad w_5 15 \geq 1,$$

with at least one inequality being strict. If such a weighting vector exists, this would imply that one can make a positive profit with zero risk, which is also called an **arbitrage opportunity**. For example,

$$w_1 = \frac{4}{13}, \; w_2 = \frac{1}{13}, \; w_3 = \frac{11}{21}, \; w_4 = \frac{2}{11}, \; w_5 = \frac{1}{15}$$

satisfies all the inequalities, but this doesn't work because it violates the budget constraint. In fact, it is not possible to make an arbitrage profit here. Bookmakers are not that stupid; in fact, they have built in a profit. If one can find a horse race where the sum of the implied probabilities is less than one, then it would be possible to make an arbitrage profit. We leave this as an exercise.

As we will see later in many contexts, it matters not just what you think is likely to happen, but what other people think is likely to happen, and indeed what you think other people think you think, etc. What do people do in practice? The **favorite-longshot bias**. On average, bettors tend to overvalue "longshots" and relatively undervalue favorites. That is, in a horse race where one horse is given odds of 2-to-1, and another 100-to-1, the true odds might, for example, be 1.5-to-1 and 300-to-1 respectively. Betting on the "longshot" is therefore a much worse proposition than betting on the favorite. Various theories exist to explain why people willingly bet on such losing propositions, such as risk-loving behavior, risk-averse behavior or simply inaccurate estimation.

As we discussed, the weight of the rider and the age of the horse are considered important factors in determining the performance. A lot of work is done trying to model the outcome of horse races or rather the probability that a given horse will win. The following is a more complete list of possible factors that could determine the probability that horse $h$ wins the race:

$LIFE\%WIN_h$- percentage of races won by horse entered in the past two years

$AVESPRAT_h$- an average speed rating for the last four races

$W/RACE_h$- winnings per race in the current year (in \$000s)

$LSPEDRAT_h$- a track-adjusted speed rating for the previous race in which the horse ran

$JOCK\%WIN_h$- percentage of winning rides by Jockey

$IOCK\#WIN_h$- number of winning rides by jockey in last year

$WEIGHT_h$- weight of jockey

$POSTPOS_h$- starting position of horse (inside or outside)

$NEWDIST_h$- equals one if a horse had run three or four of its last four races at distance levels of less than one mile, and zero otherwise.

There are ways of including all these variables into a model. Specifically, one may suppose that

$$\begin{aligned}\Pr(\text{Horse } h \text{ wins}) = \Phi\Big(&\theta_1 LIFE\%WIN_h + \theta_2 AVESPRAT_h + \theta_3 W/RACE_h \\ &+ \theta_4 LSPEDRAT_h + \theta_5 JOCK\%WIN_h \\ &+ \theta_6 JOCK\#WIN_h + \theta_7 WEIGHT_h \\ &+ \theta_8 POSTPOS_h + \theta_9 NEWDIST_h\Big),\end{aligned}$$

where $\Phi$ is the normal c.d.f. and $\theta_1, \ldots, \theta_9$ are unknown parameters, but we leave this for future study. Please gamble responsibly.

## 2.6 Key Points

1. Probability is an essential tool in understanding financial markets, specifically in quantifying uncertainty and giving a guide to decision-making making.
2. Conditional probability tells you the likelihood of something happening given your information, which is a central piece of information necessary to assist in decision-making.
3. The rules of probability are mostly intuitive extensions of counting.

## 2.7 Exercises

1. The ELO rating system in chess is designed to measure the strength of a player and to provide a prediction of when one player will beat another. Even in chess, better players sometimes lose to lower-ranked players, and so we talk about the probability of player $A$ beating player $B$, denoted $P_{A\#B}$. If player $A$ has rating $R_A$ and player $B$ has rating $R_B$, then

$$P_{A\#B} = \frac{Q_A}{Q_A + Q_B}, \quad Q_j = 10^{R_j/400}, \ j = A, B.$$

2. Suppose that the probability that any individual is born on day $i$ is $p_i$ with $\sum_{i=1}^{n} p_i = 1$. For $n = 3$, calculate the probability that out of three people, at least two of them have the same birthday.
3. Suppose that you are offered the following gamble. With probability $p$ you receive 200 and with probability $1 - p$ you receive $-100$. The probability $p$ is unknown to you except that it is equally likely to be any number in $[0, 1]$. How do you compare this gamble with A and B?
4. Show that for any independent random variables $X, Y$,

$$\text{stdev}(X + Y) \leq \text{stdev}(X) + \text{stdev}(Y)$$

because the square of the left hand side is $\text{var}(X) + \text{var}(Y)$ and the square of the right-hand side

$$
\begin{aligned}
&(\operatorname{stdev}(X)+\operatorname{stdev}(Y))^2\\
&=\operatorname{stdev}(X)^2+\operatorname{stdev}(Y)^2+2\operatorname{stdev}(X)\operatorname{stdev}(Y)\\
&=\operatorname{var}(X)+\operatorname{var}(Y)+2\operatorname{stdev}(X)\operatorname{stdev}(Y)\\
&\geq \operatorname{var}(X)+\operatorname{var}(Y)\\
&=(\operatorname{stdev}(X+Y))^2\\
&=\operatorname{var}(X+Y).
\end{aligned}
$$

5. Suppose you receive a coded message in a series of 8 zeros and ones

$$1,1,0,0,0,1,0,1$$

but the device used makes errors, in fact, each bit is reversed ($1 \to 0$ or $0 \to 1$) with probability $p$. What is the probability that the message comes through perfectly? This is

$$(1-p)^8$$

so the probability of an error is

$$1-(1-p)^8.$$

Suppose you can ask the sender to repeat the message twice more (so three times in total).

$$
\begin{aligned}
&1,1,0,0,0,1,0,1\\
&1,1,1,0,0,0,0,1\\
&1,1,0,0,0,0,1,1
\end{aligned}
$$

How do you decode the message with minimum error? How much better do you do than with just one message? Take the majority rule! In this case, the probability you are wrong for any given digit is

$$E_3 = \overbrace{p^3}^{\text{all three wrong}} + \overbrace{3p^2(1-p)}^{\text{two wrong, one right}} = 3p^2 - 2p^3$$

If $p = 0.1$, then $E_3 = 0.028$. For an 8-digit message, the probability of perfectly correct message is

$$(1-E_j)^8,$$

which is 0.43 and 0.80 respectively. By this process, one can reduce the error rate.

# 3

# *Statistics Review*

## Outline

In many real-world settings—financial markets and macroeconomic data among them—the underlying data-generating mechanisms remain unknown. To apply probability theory in such contexts, we build statistical models that embed unknown parameters within a given structure. By collecting sample data, we can then use inferential tools to uncover the underlying regularities.

After reading this chapter, you will be able to:

- Understand how statistics turns sample evidence into reliable knowledge.
- Estimate population parameters using sample statistics.
- Perform hypothesis testing and construct confidence intervals.
- Analyze relationships between variables through correlation and linear regression.
- Apply multiple regression techniques to incorporate multiple predictors.
- Identify and correct survivorship bias and sample selection issues.
- Implement time series analysis to analyze chronologically ordered data.

**Example 34** *An opinion poll company asks two thousand randomly selected voters out of the total of 150 million eligible voters who they will vote for in the coming presidential election.*

**Example 35** *A pharmaceutical company wants to test the effectiveness of a new drug. Volunteers are assigned randomly to one of two groups. The first group will receive the new drug; the second group will receive a placebo. They measure the outcomes for both groups and measure whether the difference in outcomes is significant, from which they may infer that the drug would work on the whole population.*

In the above examples, we knew the rules of the game. In the stock market and the economy, we don't know the rules, so how do we apply the laws of probability? We use a model that allows some unknown quantities but specifies

DOI: 10.1201/9781003543121-3

some structure. We observe a sample of data, and we use statistics to tell us how to fill in the gaps in our knowledge. Statistics says how sampling reveals the truth.

Suppose we have a random variable $X$ with mean $\mu = E(X)$ and variance $\sigma^2 = \text{var}(X)$ (and standard deviation $\sigma = \text{stdev}(X)$). $X$ is called the population. Suppose further that $X$ is normally (or Gaussian) distributed, meaning that the density of $X$ is for any $x \in \mathbb{R}$ defined in (2.6) We say that

$$X \sim N(\mu, \sigma^2).$$

The standard normal random variable $Z$ has $\mu = 0$ and $\sigma^2 = 1$, and for any $X \sim N(\mu, \sigma^2)$ we have $Z = (X - \mu)/\sigma \sim N(0, 1)$.

This is our first statistical model: the unknown quantities or parameters are the mean $\mu$ and the variance $\sigma^2$ of $X$. We suppose that our data $\{X_1, \ldots, X_n\}$ is a randomly drawn sample from this population with sample size $n$, that is, $X_1 \sim N(\mu, \sigma^2)$, $X_2 \sim N(\mu, \sigma^2)$, etc.

**Algorithm 1** *We estimate the unknown parameters $\mu, \sigma^2$ by the sample mean and sample variance*

$$\overline{X} = \frac{1}{n}\sum_{i=1}^{n} X_i = \frac{1}{n}(X_1 + \cdots + X_n), \quad s^2 = \frac{1}{n}\sum_{i=1}^{n}\left(X_i - \overline{X}\right)^2.$$

In Excel, this is @Average and @STDEV so easy to compute. Note that in many books $s^2 = (n-1)^{-1}\sum_{i=1}^{n}\left(X_i - \overline{X}\right)^2$, but we do not make this distinction here because for finance applications $n$ is usually so big that the difference between $n$ and $n-1$ is inconsequential.

We next discuss the properties of the **estimators** $\overline{X}$ and $s^2$ that we will need. We have

$$E(\overline{X}) = \mu$$

by the linearity property of expectation, which says that on average, the estimate is correct. Furthermore,

$$\text{var}(\overline{X}) = \frac{\sigma^2}{n}$$

using the independence of the observations (the variance of the sum is the sum of the variance). It follows that $\text{var}(\overline{X})$ decreases with sample size $n$ and indeed converges to zero, that is $\text{var}(\overline{X}) \to 0$ as $n \to \infty$. Finally, one can show that the distribution of $\overline{X}$ is $N(\mu, \sigma^2/n)$, i.e.,

$$\overline{X} \sim N(\mu, \sigma^2/n).$$

This means that if $n$ is large, $\overline{X}$ is very close to $\mu$. Likewise, we may show that $s^2$ is close to $\sigma^2$ when $n$ is large.

**Algorithm 2** *Define the standard error of the mean*

$$\text{stderr} = \frac{s}{\sqrt{n}}. \tag{3.1}$$

The standard error is the approximate theoretical standard deviation of (in this case) $\overline{X}$ around its true value $\mu$ and it captures the accuracy of our measurement. We will use it below in hypothesis testing and confidence intervals.

## 3.1 Hypothesis Testing and Confidence Intervals

We want to test the hypothesis that $\mu = 0$. A test statistic is formed as the ratio of an estimated value minus its null value to its standard error both constructed from the sample data. It is a numerical representation of the evidence obtained from the data, and is expected to be small when the null hypothesis is true and large otherwise. The precise meaning of small and large is calibrated from an associated probability distribution that describes the random behavior of the test statistics under the null hypothesis. In particular, a critical value is obtained from the null distribution such that test statistics above this value are likely to happen purely by chance with a predetermined probability (called the significance level). If the test statistic is above the critical value, one rejects the null hypothesis, while if it is below the critical value, one does not reject the null hypothesis. The magnitude of the critical value is determined by the significance level. A significance level of 1% can be interpreted as saying that evidence of that strength or stronger could happen by chance with probability 0.01. A significance level of 10% would mean that evidence of that strength or stronger could happen by chance with probability 0.10. The lower the significance level, the stronger the evidence must be to reject the null hypothesis. Consequently, if one does reject the null hypothesis at a low level, i.e., 1%, one should interpret this as powerful evidence against the null hypothesis. It is perhaps common practice to use 5% as the standard. For a two-sided test, the critical values are $\pm 1.96$ for the 5% level and for a one-sided test, the critical values are $+1.645$.

**Algorithm 3** *Student's t statistic is defined as the estimate divided by its standard error,*

$$T = \frac{\overline{X}}{\text{stderr}} = \frac{\overline{X}}{s/\sqrt{n}}. \tag{3.2}$$

Under the null hypothesis that $\mu = 0$, the distribution of $T$ is approximately (for large $n$) equal to $N(0, 1)$. We will make use of such approximations throughout this book. There is a more precise theory based on Student's t distribution that works for any sample size, and this is traditionally the way statistics was taught, but in most financial applications, the sample sizes are so large that this doesn't really affect conclusions much.[1] We reject the null hypothesis if $|T| > z_{\alpha/2}$, where $z_\alpha$ is the normal critical value, when $\alpha = 0.05$, $z_{\alpha/2} = 1.96$. We equivalently reject if $|\overline{X}| > z_{\alpha/2} \times \text{stderr}$. In practice, authors either report $\overline{X}$ along with stderr or they report the Z-score, in this case the value of $T$.

The Type I error (the probability of falsely rejecting a true null hypothesis) is $\alpha$; the Type II error is the probability of falsely accepting a false null hypothesis, which depends on the alternative hypothesis. Both types of errors are inevitable in statistics as in life, what is the appropriate balance? The **Blackstone Ratio,** which originated within the English legal system, is that: *It is better that ten guilty persons escape than that one innocent suffer.* Of course, this was written long before the terms serial killer or suicide bomber were coined. In the statistical context, this amounts to aiming for a Type II error that is ten times higher than the Type I error.

One final way of reporting evidence is to avoid the yes/no nature of hypothesis testing and to provide the so-called p-value, which is in this case either $p = \Phi(T)$ or $p = 1 - \Phi(T)$, whichever is smaller; here, $\Phi(z) = \Pr(Z \leq z)$ is the c.d.f. of the standard normal distribution. The p-value lies between 0 and 1, and it is interpreted as the probability of observing a more extreme value of the test statistic than was observed when the null hypothesis is true. Essentially, the p-value converts the Z-score to a probability value. Of course, to a Bayesian, the p-value is anathema, and mentioning it to one is like discussing the afterlife with an atheist.

**Algorithm 4** *The* ***confidence interval*** *for $\mu$ is denoted*

$$\overline{X} \pm z_{\alpha/2}\text{stderr}, \tag{3.3}$$

*which is shorthand notation for the closed interval* $[\overline{X} - z_{\alpha/2}\text{stderr}, \overline{X} + z_{\alpha/2}\text{stderr}]$.

This (random) interval contains the true value $\mu$ with probability $1 - \alpha$. For example, we are 95% confident that the interval contains the truth. We show in Figure 3.1 the data of sizes $n = 5$, $n = 20$, and $n = 100$ drawn from a standard normal distribution along with the 95% confidence intervals for the mean.

Statistics elaborates these ideas about estimation, hypothesis testing, and confidence intervals. Different contexts, different methods, different assumptions. Sometimes statistics gets it wrong.

**Example 36** *An opinion poll asks two thousand randomly selected voters out of the total 150 million eligible voters who they will vote for in the coming*

[1]What is a large $n$? Well most textbooks suppose that $n > 30$ is large. If $n \leq 30$, then one may use the t distribution, but we shall ignore this case in the sequel. Typically sample sizes are large in financial applications.

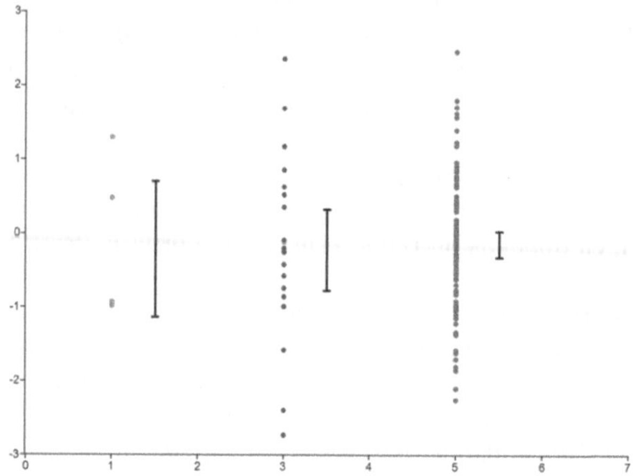


**FIGURE 3.1**
Confidence intervals for normal means

*presidential election. It might say that of all voters 45% ± 3% would vote for President Trump. Here, 45% is an estimate derived from a sample of voters and 3% is the "margin of error." This says that if we were to draw a large number of similar samples and form the interval from them, then the true value (parameter) lies in these intervals with the stated probability, usually 95%.*

What went wrong?

1. We asked the wrong people (not a representative sample). Around 1 in 10 may agree to give their opinion.
2. We asked the right people but:
   (a) they either didn't vote
   (b) they changed their minds about who to vote for
   (c) they lied

We turn to a classic study that is one of the first hypothesis tests conducted. The question is, are boys and girls equally likely to be born? John Arbuthnot used data from 1629-1710 on the number of boy and girl live births in London to answer this question. The data are plotted in Figure 3.2. He reported that in all 82 years, there were more boys born than girls. We naturally think that the ratio should be 1 i.e., boys and girls are equally likely. This would be the statistical null hypothesis, which makes this example like a coin toss, whose outcome is either heads or tails with equal probability. What is the probability that when you toss a fair coin, you get heads 82 times in a

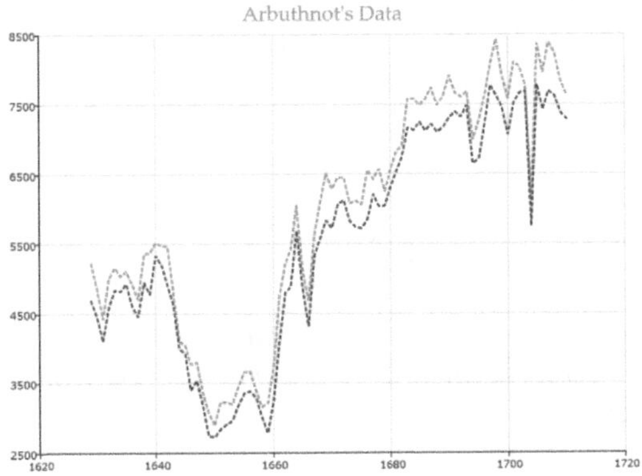


**FIGURE 3.2**
Frequency of live births by sex

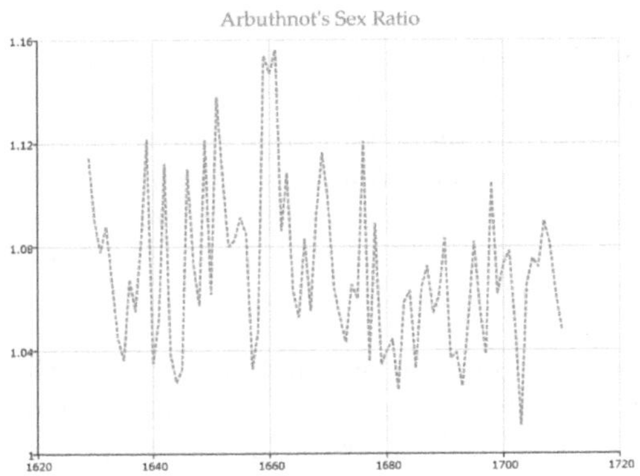


**FIGURE 3.3**
Sex ratio at birth by year

row? This is $1/2^{82}$, which is a very small number (25 zeros). One can conclude from this analysis that boys are more likely to be born than girls, i.e., that the probability of a boy is larger than the probability of a girl. Can we say more?

We calculate the ratio of the number of boys to girls each year $i$, call this $X_i$, which we plot for each year in Figure 3.3. We assume that this ratio is $N(\mu, \sigma^2)$ for each $i$. We wish to test the special value of $\mu = 1$. We have

$$\overline{X} = 1.0708, \quad s = 0.03125, \quad n = 82, \quad \text{stderr} = \frac{s}{\sqrt{n}} = 0.00345.$$

The estimated sex ratio is about 7% in favor of boys with a standard deviation of around 3% per birth. Is this evidence that the sex ratio is not 1? We know that $\overline{X} \sim N(\mu, \sigma^2/n)$. It follows that if we subtract off the value $\mu$ and divide by the standard deviation we get a standard normal distribution $N(0,1)$, that is $(\overline{X} - \mu)/\text{stderr} \sim N(0,1)$. We calculate the value of the test statistic as

$$T = \frac{\overline{X} - 1}{\text{stderr}} = 20.52.$$

This is very strong evidence against the valuc $\mu = 1$.

The confidence interval for $\mu$ is $\overline{X} \pm 1.96 \times \text{stderr}$, which can be described as the closed interval

$$[1.064, 1.078]. \tag{3.4}$$

This is the plausible range of values for $\mu$.

**Example 37** *The UNODC says that worldwide, 90% of murderers (convicted) are male and 80% of murder victims are male. There is some variation across countries, but basically, this is a pretty universal finding that murder is mostly about young men killing other young men. Agatha Christie was a famous British novelist who mostly wrote murder/detective novels; the Guinness World Records lists Christie as the best-selling fiction writer of all time, her novels having sold more than two billion copies. In her books, there were a total of 82 murders. There were 45 male murderers and 36 female murderers. There were 30 male victims and 53 female victims. Test whether the proportion of murderers in Agatha Christie novels is consistent with the worldwide proportion, assuming a Gaussian distribution for the ratio.*

We suppose there are population outcome variables that we denote by $Y$ and $X$. We want to test whether they have the same population mean. Suppose that $X_1, \ldots, X_n$ and $Y_1, \ldots, Y_m$ are two (independent) samples of data drawn from these respective populations.

**Algorithm 5** *Define the sample means and averages as follows:*

$$\overline{X} = \frac{1}{n}(X_1 + \cdots + X_n), \quad \overline{Y} = \frac{1}{m}(Y_1 + \cdots + Y_m)$$

$$s_X^2 = \frac{1}{n}\sum_{i=1}^{n}(X_i - \overline{X})^2, \quad s_Y^2 = \frac{1}{m}\sum_{i=1}^{m}(Y_i - \overline{Y})^2.$$

*Then define the two-sample test statistic*

$$T = \frac{\overline{X} - \overline{Y}}{\sqrt{\frac{s_X^2}{n} + \frac{s_Y^2}{m}}}. \tag{3.5}$$

*Provided $n, m$ are large, we have approximately under the null hypothesis $T \sim N(0,1)$. We compare $T$ with $\pm z_{\alpha/2}$.*

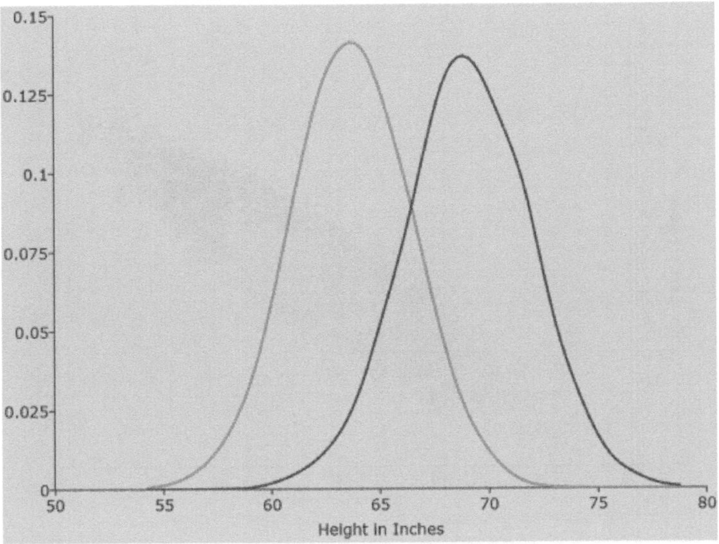


**FIGURE 3.4**
Distribution of male height (blue); distribution of female height (red)

**Example 38** *Are men taller than women? For a sample of data from the USA, we obtain* $\overline{X} = 69.026$, $\overline{Y} = 63.709$, $s_X^2 = 2.863$ *and* $s_Y^2 = 2.696$, *while* $n = m = 5000$. *Therefore,* $T = 159.5$, *which strongly rejects the null hypothesis. However, there is quite a bit of overlap in the distributions as we can see in Figure 3.4.*

## 3.2 Correlation and Linear Regression

We study the relation between outcome variables $X, Y$ by correlation analysis or regression based on a sample of data $\{Y_1, X_1, \ldots, Y_n, X_n\}$. In Figure 3.5 we show height and weight for men (blue) and women (red) from some sample of data from the USA. This shows a positive association between height and weight. Taller people tend to be heavier, and this is true for both the data as a whole and for the two subsets of male and female.

The population correlation and covariance between random variables $Y$ and $X$ are defined as

$$\rho_{YX} = \frac{\text{cov}(Y, X)}{\sqrt{\text{var}(Y)\text{var}(X)}}, \quad \sigma_{YX} = \text{cov}(Y, X) = E\left[(Y - E(Y))(X - E(X))\right]. \tag{3.6}$$

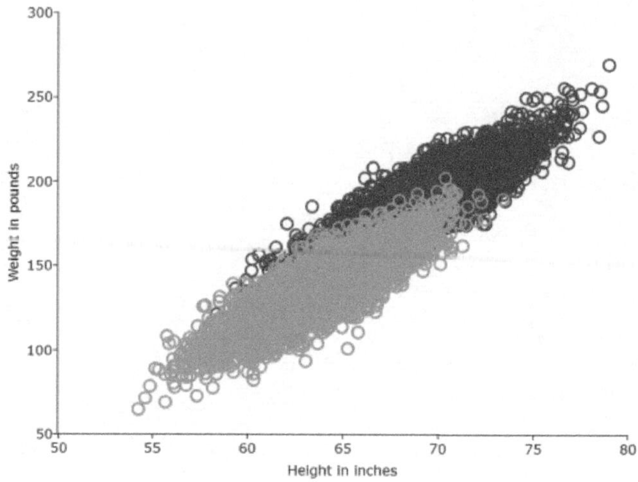


**FIGURE 3.5**
Scatter plot of height and weight

Both measure the degree to which $Y$ and $X$ move together. If $\rho_{YX} > 0$, then $X, Y$ tend to move in the same direction (positive correlation). If $\rho_{YX} < 0$, then $X, Y$ tend to move in the opposite direction (negative correlation). If $\rho_{YX} = 0$, we say that $X, Y$ are uncorrelated. The correlation $\rho_{YX}$ lies between $-1$ and $+1$, whereas the covariance may take any value. The covariance and correlation are both symmetric in $X, Y$ in the sense that $\text{cov}(Y, X) = \text{cov}(X, Y)$.

**Algorithm 6** *For a sample of data* $\{Y_1, X_1, \ldots, Y_n, X_n\}$ *we define:*

$$\widehat{\sigma}_{YX} = \frac{1}{n}\sum_{i=1}^{n}(Y_i - \overline{Y})(X_i - \overline{X}),$$

$$\widehat{\sigma}_{YY} = \frac{1}{n}\sum_{i=1}^{n}(Y_i - \overline{Y})^2,$$

$$\widehat{\sigma}_{XX} = \frac{1}{n}\sum_{i=1}^{n}(X_i - \overline{X})^2.$$

$$\widehat{\rho}_{YX} = \frac{\widehat{\sigma}_{YX}}{\sqrt{\widehat{\sigma}_{YY}\widehat{\sigma}_{XX}}}.$$

Note that we may write

$$\rho_{YX} = E(\widetilde{Y}\widetilde{X}),$$

$$\widetilde{X} = \frac{X - E(X)}{\text{stdev}(X)}, \quad \widetilde{Y} = \frac{Y - E(Y)}{\text{stdev}(Y)}.$$

That is, the correlation between $X$ and $Y$ is the average value of the product of the standardized variables $\widetilde{X}, \widetilde{Y}$.

**Example 39** *Suppose that*

$$\widetilde{X} = \begin{cases} +1 & \frac{1}{2} \\ -1 & \frac{1}{2} \end{cases}, \quad \widetilde{Y} = \begin{cases} +1 & \frac{1}{2} \\ -1 & \frac{1}{2} \end{cases},$$

*so that both random variables have mean zero and variance one. Suppose that for some $p \in [0, 1/2]$*

$$(\widetilde{X}, \widetilde{Y}) = \begin{cases} (+1,+1) & p \\ (+1,-1) & \frac{1}{2} - p \\ (-1,+1) & \frac{1}{2} - p \\ (-1,-1) & p. \end{cases}$$

*Then, we have*

$$\rho_{XY} = E(\widetilde{X}\widetilde{Y}) = 2p - (1 - 2p) = 4p - 1.$$

*The value $p = 1/4$ makes each pair of outcomes equally likely and corresponds to $\rho_{XY} = 0$, whereas the value $p = 1/2$ makes only $(+1,+1)$ or $(-1,-1)$ happen and corresponds to $\rho_{XY} = +1$, while the value $p = 0$ makes only $(+1,-1)$ or $(-1,+1)$ happen and corresponds to $\rho_{XY} = -1$.*

The special values of $0, -1$, and $+1$ are of interest. A correlation of $+1$ says that $X$ and $Y$ move perfectly together, and in fact they satisfy $Y = a + bX$ for some $b > 0$ and some $a$; A correlation of $-1$ says that $X$ and $Y$ satisfy $Y = a + bX$ for some $b < 0$ and some $a$; A correlation of 0 says that $X$ and $Y$ bear no (linear) relation to each other, i.e., there is no $a, b$ for which $Y = a + bX$.

**Example 40** *The number of left-footed socks sold in a store is perfectly correlated (+1) with the number of right-footed socks. The temperature in centigrade is perfectly correlated with the temperature in Fahrenheit. The payoff to the Casino is perfectly negatively correlated with the payoff to the customer.*

**Example 41** *Taller people tend to weigh more, and shorter people tend to weigh less. Height is positively correlated with weight.*

We calculate estimates of the correlations and regression parameters defined below based on the sample dataset, but we do not go into the details here. What do you think is the correlation between human weight and height? The correlation is apparently between 30-50%. You might think that weight is proportional to volume, and so weight should be proportional to the cubic

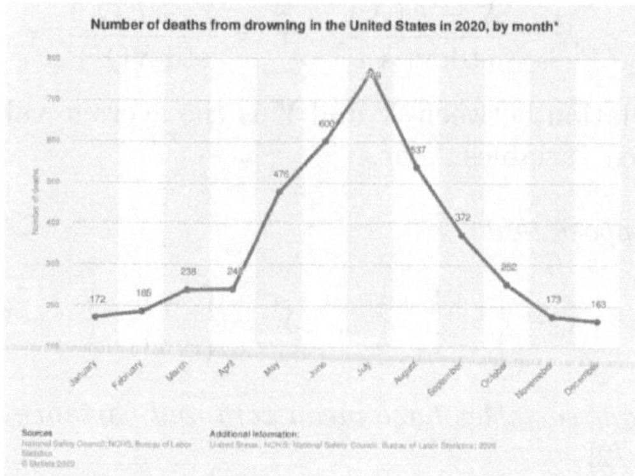


**FIGURE 3.6**
Number of deaths by drowning each calendar month in the USA in 2020

power of height? The so-called Body-Mass-Index is used to identify people who are malnourished or overweight by the WHO and other organizations. This is calculated as $BMI = weight/height^2$, where weight is in $kg$ and height is in $m$. The classifications in common use are: underweight (under 18.5 kg/m2), normal weight (18.5 to 24.9), overweight (25 to 29.9), and obese (30 or more). The medical establishment and statistical community have both highlighted the limitations of BMI, specifically the arbitrariness of the exponent 2 in the denominator, and alternatives have been proposed.

**Example 42** *Grade in high school is positively correlated with grade in university*

This question is of interest to university admissions committees. What do you think is the correlation between these two grades? Cyrenne and Chan (2012) investigated the relationship with Canadian data using multiple regression and found correlations of less than 40%.

Some empirical correlations are negative.

**Example 43** *As the weather gets colder, heating costs increase. Temperature and spending on heating is negatively correlated*

Some correlations are meaningless.

**Example 44** *Death by drowning is positively correlated with ice cream sales.*

Around 235,000 people die each year around the world from drowning, according to the WHO, and in the USA, around 4000 per year die this way, around 80% of whom are male. The peak drowning month in the USA is July, which is also the peak month for the volume of ice cream consumed.

This is an example of a spurious correlation. See Tylervigen (2015) for more examples of spurious correlations.

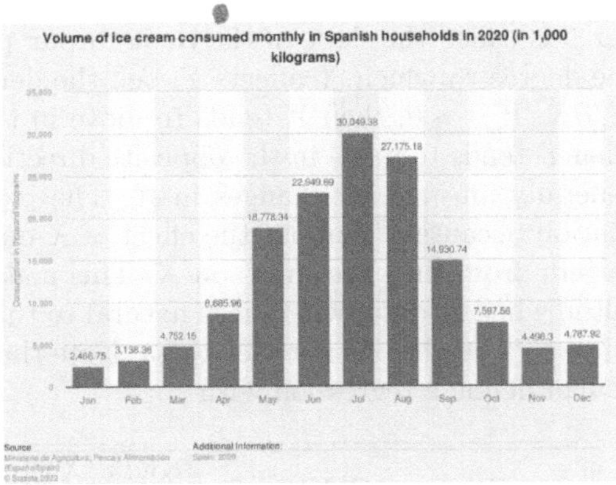


**FIGURE 3.7**
Volume of Ice cream sales each calendar month in Spain in 2020

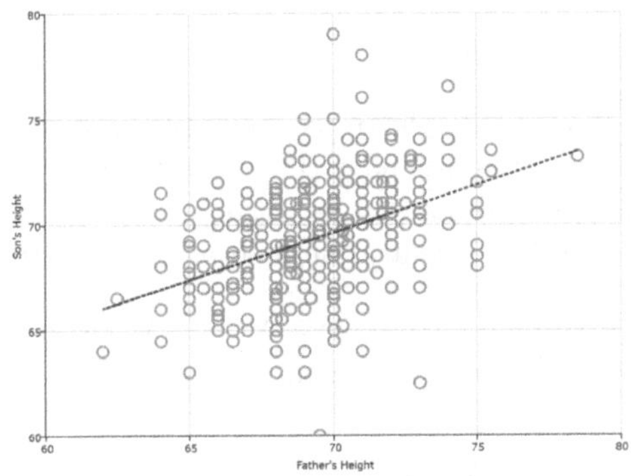


**FIGURE 3.8**
Galton's height data. $Y = 38.25 + 0.448X$, $\rho_{Y,X} = 0.39$

We now turn to regression (sometimes called conditional expectation). We suppose that the random variables $Y, X$ are related through the linear equation

$$Y = \alpha + \beta X + \varepsilon, \tag{3.7}$$

where $\varepsilon$ is a mean zero random variable (a fair game). This model is used to explain $Y$ by $X$. Here, $\alpha$ is called the intercept, $\beta$ is called the slope. The classic example is Galton's height data (in inches). Galton wanted to identify the effect of genetics on inheritance of characteristics such as height and intelligence. He collected a sample of data on the characteristics of British families in the 19th century, in particular, he measured $X$ the father's height and $Y$ the son's height.

The parameter $\beta$ is called the slope of the **best linear predictor** (BLP). This measures the degree to which $X$ affects $Y$, i.e., the derivative of $Y$ with respect to $X$, $\partial Y/\partial X$. If $\beta > 0$, then $Y$ tends to move in the same direction as $X$. If $\beta < 0$, then $Y$ tends to move in the opposite direction to $X$. If $\beta = 0$, then $Y$ is not generally affected by changes in $X$. The $\beta$ is an asymmetric measure of association because it is about the effect of $X$ on $Y$, which may be different in magnitude from the effect of $Y$ on $X$. This makes sense for some examples like Galton's height data, where it is natural to think of the father's height affecting the son's height but not vice versa. Note that for any random variables $Y, X$ we can define a regression with

$$\boxed{\alpha = E(Y) - \beta E(X), \quad \beta = \frac{\text{cov}(Y,X)}{\text{var}(X)}}. \tag{3.8}$$

That is, the slope coefficient is the ratio of the covariance between $Y$ and $X$ to the variance of $X$. We have

$$\text{var}(Y) = \beta^2 \times \text{var}(X) + \text{var}(\varepsilon),$$

where $\beta^2 \times \text{var}(X)$ can be thought of as the explained part of the variance of $Y$, while $\text{var}(\varepsilon)$ is the unexplained part. The regression $R^2$ is usually defined as the ratio of the explained variance to the total variance of the outcome variable $Y$, i.e., $\beta^2 \times \text{var}(X)/\text{var}(Y)$; it is also defined as the squared correlation $\rho_{YX}^2$.

**Algorithm 7** *For a sample of data* $\{Y_1, X_i, \ldots, Y_n, X_n\}$ *we define the Ordinary Least Squares estimators as the values of* $\alpha, \beta$ *that minimize the sum of squared errors*

$$\sum_{i=1}^{n} (Y_i - \alpha - \beta X_i)^2 .$$

*The explicit forms of the estimators are given below*

$$\widehat{\beta} = \frac{\widehat{\sigma}_{YX}}{\widehat{\sigma}_{XX}}, \quad \widehat{\alpha} = \overline{Y} - \widehat{\beta}\overline{X}.$$

We can rewrite $\beta$ as

$$\beta = \frac{\text{cov}(Y,X)}{\text{var}(X)} = \frac{\text{cov}(Y,X)}{\sqrt{\text{var}(X)\text{var}(Y)}} \times \sqrt{\frac{\text{var}(Y)}{\text{var}(X)}} = \rho_{YX} \times \frac{\text{stdev}(Y)}{\text{stdev}(X)}.$$

Therefore, if $Y, X$ have the same standard deviation

$$\beta = \rho_{YX} \in [-1, 1]. \tag{3.9}$$

If $Y, X$ have different standard deviations then although $\beta, \rho$ have the same sign (positive, zero, or negative), their magnitudes can be different and $\beta$ may take any number in $\mathbb{R}$.

Francis Galton introduced the concept of **regression toward the mean.** The regression equation (3.7) can be written in standardized units $\widetilde{Y} = (Y - E(Y))/\text{stdev}(Y)$, $\widetilde{X} = (X - E(X))/\text{stdev}(X)$ as follows

$$\widetilde{Y} = \widetilde{\alpha} + \widetilde{\beta}\widetilde{X} + \widetilde{\varepsilon}, \quad \widetilde{\alpha} = 0, \quad \widetilde{\beta} = \rho_{YX}, \tag{3.10}$$

where $\widetilde{\varepsilon} = \varepsilon/\text{stdev}(X)$ is mean zero. In this transformed regression, the intercept is zero and the slope coefficient is a correlation that necessarily satisfies $|\rho_{YX}| \leq 1$. This says that fathers who are taller than average height tend to have son's who are taller than average $(0 < \rho_{YX})$, but whose height is closer to the average. For example, suppose that

$$\widetilde{X} = \frac{X - E(X)}{\text{stdev}(X)} = +2,$$

then on average, we expect

$$\widetilde{Y} = \frac{Y - E(Y)}{\text{stdev}(Y)} \simeq 0.8.$$

Regression toward the mean is a much-discussed concept and applied to many contexts. If winning involves luck and skill, then winners tend to be less good next time, and losers tend to be better next time. Many examples illustrate this concept. Sports teams, grades on consecutive tests, mutual fund performance, etc.

In practical correlation and regression analysis, it sometimes makes sense to consider other transformations of the data. There are several motivations for doing this. We may find the coefficients more interpretable in the transformed coordinates. The linear regression model may appear to work better after transformation. We next give the two leading cases.

For example, suppose that we transform the $Y$ to $Y^* = a + bY$ for some constants $a, b$, but do not transform the $X$. This arises, for example, if we wish to change the outcome units, say from Centigrade to Fahrenheit, but say $X$ is a binary outcome (either zero or one) whose units it doesn't make sense to change. In this case, we obtain the regression equation

$$Y^* = a + b(\alpha + \beta X + \varepsilon) = \alpha^* + \beta^* X + \varepsilon^*, \tag{3.11}$$

$$\alpha^* = a + b\alpha, \quad \beta^* = b\beta, \quad \varepsilon^* = b\varepsilon.$$

If $b > 0$, then the slope $\beta^*$ has the same sign (positive or negative) as $\beta$, so the direction of the effect of $X$ on $Y^*$ is the same as the direction of $X$ on $Y$, but its magnitude now reflects the transformed dependent variable. A leading case is when $Y^* = (Y - E(Y))/\text{stdev}(Y)$ in which case $b = 1/\text{stdev}(Y)$. In this case, a one unit change in $X$ has the effect $\beta^*$ on $Y$ in standardized units, i.e., in standard deviations.

Suppose instead we transform the $X$ variable so that $X^+ = a + bX$ for some constants $a, b$ (but do not transform the $Y$ variable). Then we have

$$Y = \alpha + \beta\left(\frac{X^+ - a}{b}\right) + \varepsilon = \alpha^+ + \beta^+ X^+ + \varepsilon^+, \tag{3.12}$$

$$\alpha^+ = \alpha - \beta\frac{a}{b}, \quad \beta^* = \frac{\beta}{b}, \quad \varepsilon^+ = \varepsilon.$$

For example $X^+ = (X - E(X))/\text{stdev}(X)$. This transformation is widely applied in machine learning in multiple regression settings because it allows for the comparison of the strength of effects from variables measured on different scales.

## 3.3 Multiple Regression

Galton's dataset also included observations on the mother's height and the number of kids in the family, both of which seem like plausible factors in the development of the son, so we include them in a multiple regression of son's height explained by the father's height, the mother's height, and the number of kids in the family. We obtained the estimates by **Ordinary Least Squares** along with the standard errors and $\text{R}^2$, presented below

$$son = \underset{(4.15)}{20.412} + \underset{(0.047)}{0.403} father + \underset{(0.046)}{0.334} mother - \underset{(0.040)}{0.079} kids, \quad R^2 = 0.25. \tag{3.13}$$

The standard errors are in parentheses below the estimates; the standard error on the coefficient of father is 0.047, so that the confidence interval for that coefficient is $0.403 \pm 1.96 \times 0.047$. This coefficient is significantly greater than zero. This is also true for *mother* and *kids*, these factors both contribute significantly and in the expected way. We can predict a son's height better if we know both the father's height and the mother's height, and how many kids were in the family. We can capture the improvement in performance of the regression by the $R^2$ measure defined above. In this case, the $R^2$ is 0.25, whereas the regression using only the father as the predictor had an $R^2 = 0.40^2 = 0.16$, so a quite substantial improvement is obtained by including these additional variables.

Nowadays, much research is trying to understand how best to include large numbers of predictors in regression, so-called **machine learning**. In financial markets, correlations can be quite low, which makes this complicated.

## 3.4 Survivorship Bias or Sample Selection

There are two further problems with regression and correlation: endogeneity and sample selection.

**Example 45** *We observe the price and quantity sold of watermelons in a market on different days and by different vendors. What correlation would we expect to see between these variables? The problem is that price and quantity are simultaneously determined, and so any correlation is possible and meaningless. Need to model demand and supply separately.*

In finance, we only observe the firms that have survived, and this can create a bias in our calculations (called survivorship bias) that is difficult to take account of. This especially affects long-term studies where a large fraction of the sample firms may fail during the sample period.

**Example 46** *During the Second World War, the Americans were worried that they were losing lots of bombers to enemy fire. They recorded the locations of all hits on returning bombers, as in the graphic below. They proposed to strengthen those areas that had been hit by enemy fire. Abraham Wald, the statistician, argued that this was the wrong policy. Better to strengthen the areas that did not show any hits! He argued this because the hit aircraft had returned successfully whereas the aircraft that had not returned were likely to have been hit elsewhere.*

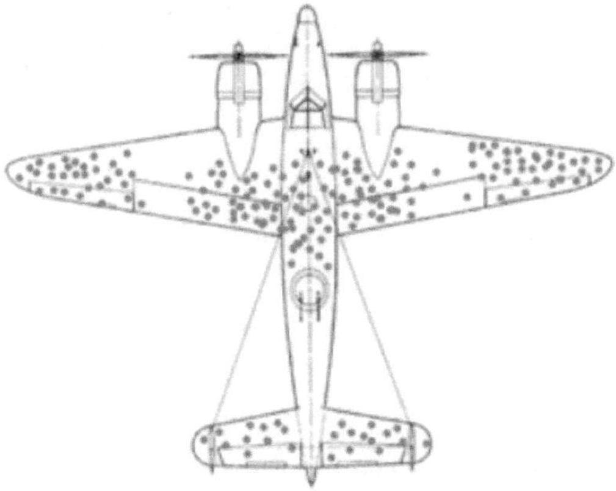

## 3.5 Time Series

A time series is a series of data points indexed in time order. Usually observations taken at successive equally spaced points in time, say $X_1, X_2, \ldots$

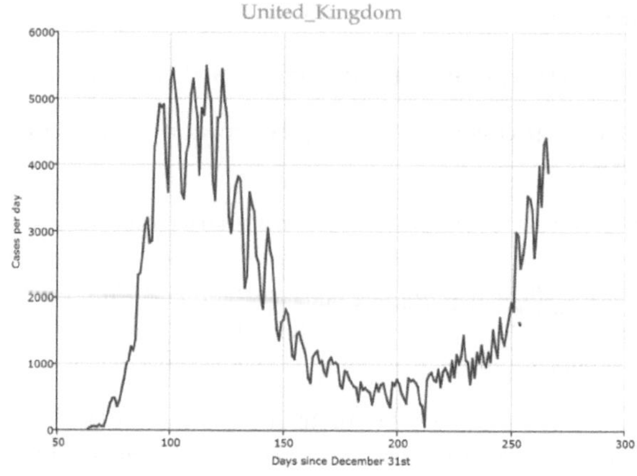


**FIGURE 3.9**
United Kingdom daily new COVID-19 cases

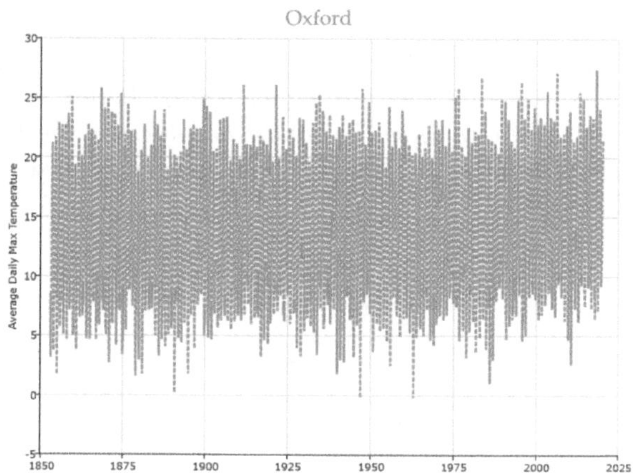


**FIGURE 3.10**
Oxford monthly temperature

Examples of time series include: the monthly average maximum temperature at a specific location; the daily closing values of the S&P500 index; the quarterly value of GNP of the USA; the annual number of births in a country; the daily number of new cases of COVID-19 in country X. We plot a couple of these examples below. In Figure 3.9 we show the time series of new COVID-19 cases in the UK up until September 22nd of 2020. In Figure 3.10 we show monthly average daily maximum temperature at Oxford.

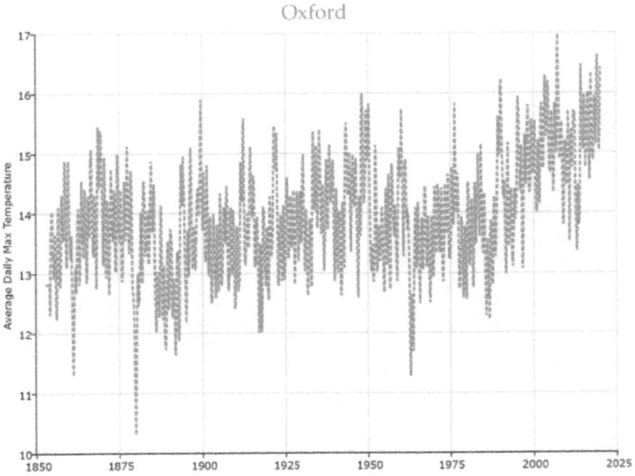


**FIGURE 3.11**
Smoothed monthly max temperature Oxford

This series has a strong seasonal component: January temperature is usually much colder than July temperature. The main question of interest here is whether there is a trend in this series due to climate change. To answer this question, we need to separate the trend from the cycle part. One way to do that is to work with the 12-month average temperatures (these are sometimes called the smooth moving average or $\text{SMA}_{12}$). We can now see the trend at the end of the period. It does seem that there has been an increase in hot air over Oxford.

To remove the trend of a series, a common approach is to take the difference between successive observations, i.e., let

$$Y_t = X_t - X_{t-1}$$

and this often eliminates the trend. A series without trend and seasonal components is called stationary. A lot of time series methodology is concerned with stationary time series. Figure 3.12 shows the difference of the Oxford temperature series.

## 3.6 Key Points

1. Statistics is a discipline that provides tools for analyzing and interpreting data.
2. A statistical model has unknown parameters that describe the distribution of the outcomes we observe. Based on sample data from

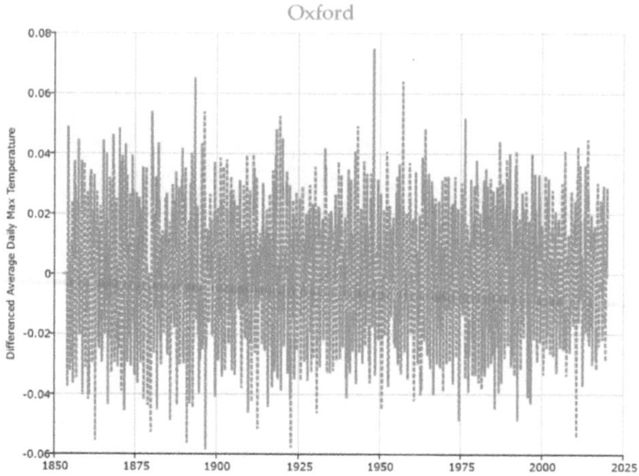


**FIGURE 3.12**
Difference of monthly maximum temperature at Oxford

the model, we can estimate the parameters, and we can also estimate the remaining uncertainty about their true values (confidence intervals). We may also test whether some parameters are equal to hypothesized values based on the data.

# Part II

# Applications in Finance

# 4

# *Economic Behavior Toward Time and Uncertainty*

## Outline

This chapter delves into the foundational assumptions of economic behavior related to time preference, risk, and uncertainty. It shows how individuals weigh present against future cash flows and how they respond to different levels of risk. Core ideas—such as the discount rate, present discounted value, and expected-utility theory—provide a unifying lens for understanding decision-making under uncertainty.

After reading this chapter, you will be able to:

- Understand the baseline behavioral assumptions of economic agents—including a preference for "more," rational choice, and immediacy.
- Analyze time preference and its consequences for valuing future cash flows.
- Calculate the present value of future cash flows using a constant discount rate and understand its role in asset pricing.
- Apply mathematical tools to compute present discounted values and solve related problems.
- Evaluate attitudes toward risk and uncertainty, distinguishing among risk-neutral, risk-averse, and risk-seeking behavior.
- Utilize utility theory to understand how individuals make decisions under risk, illustrated by cases such as the St Petersburg paradox.
- Connect risk preferences to real-world settings—asset pricing, insurance, and investment strategy.

Some fundamental assumptions of human economic behavior are:

1. Individuals prefer more to less
2. They act rationally to achieve the best outcome for themselves
3. They prefer good outcomes now rather than in the future.

DOI: 10.1201/9781003543121-4

Each of these assumptions has been subject to some debate, but these axioms are widely accepted in mainstream economics courses. The attitude to risk or uncertainty is more complex, and we will treat this further below. In the next section, we look at the third axiom that individuals prefer good outcomes now rather than in the future, and we see how this is taken into account in decision making.

## 4.1 The Time Value of Money

Suppose that an asset promises to pay cash flows $C$ at certain times in the future

$$\begin{array}{ccccccccccc} P & & C & & C & & C & & C & & \\ - & -- & - & -- & - & -- & - & -- & - & - & \cdots \\ today & & year{+}1 & & year{+}2 & & year{+}3 & & year{+}4 & & \end{array}$$

How should we determine what the fair price $P$ of the asset today should be, assuming that these cash flows are without risk, i.e., will be paid in full at the precise time indicated? We might just add the cash flows together and say that is the correct price, but this ignores the time value of money. The key assumption we make is that a dollar today is worth more than a dollar tomorrow. The value of future cash flows depends on when they arrive, and in particular, the value decreases with the time until payment. This by itself says that $P < nC$, where $n$ is the total number of periods where cash flows are received. To make further progress, we need to specify precisely how much more $C$ in year one is worth than $C$ in year two, etc.

We suppose that you can invest your money, and for each dollar invested, you will receive a total of $1 + R$ after one year, where $R > 0$ is a certain value (the net return), say 10%. Therefore, one dollar today is not equivalent to one dollar a year from today. If one needs one dollar a year from now, you only need $\$1/(1 + R)$ today, because after investment, it will deliver the one dollar you need in a year's time. We next call $R$ the **discount rate** that determines the relative value of today and tomorrow. Given the discount rate, we can determine the current valuation of future cash flows. How much is $C$ in one year's time worth today? The present value of the known amount $C$ one year in the future is

$$\frac{C}{1+R},$$

because if one currently had $C/(1+R)$ and one invests it at rate $R$, one would receive next year

$$\frac{C}{1+R} \times (1+R) = C.$$

The present value of the amount $C$ two years in the future is, by repeating the same logic, equal to $C/(1 + R)^2$. The present value of the amount $C$ at $i$

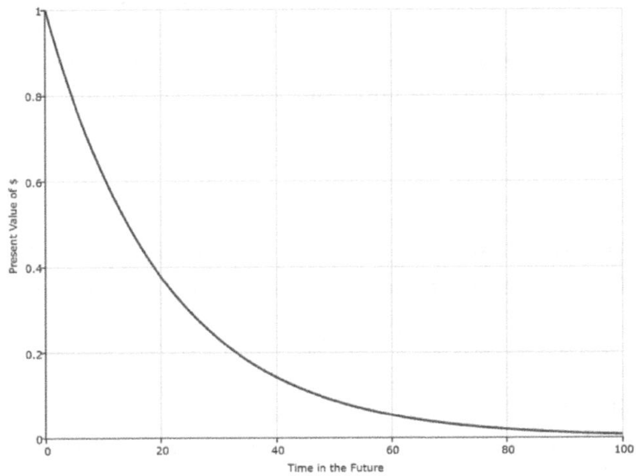


**FIGURE 4.1**
Present value today of \$1 at future times $t = 1, \ldots, 100$ with $R = 0.05$

years in the future is therefore

$$\frac{C}{(1+R)^i}, \quad i = 1, 2, \ldots$$

We show in Figure 4.1 the present value of \$1 by horizon $i$, for a particular choice of $R$, specifically, $R = 0.05$; in this case, the value decays rapidly with $i$. For smaller $R$, the decay rate would be slower, and future values would be worth more today.

Prominent economists in the past considered discounting future pleasures as immoral and/or wrong-headed.

> Pigou (1920): ... "it implies a defective telescopic faculty, ..., and therefore we see future pleasures, as it were, on a diminishing scale."
>
> Ramsey (1928): "...we do not discount later enjoyments in comparison with earlier ones, a practice that is ethically indefensible and arises merely from the weakness of imagination.".
>
> Harrod (1948): "...Pure time preference is a polite expression for rapacity and the conquest of reason by passion."

Nowadays, discounting the future is widely accepted. However, there is always a debate about the appropriate rate to use. In environmental economics in particular, what discount rate should be used when we talk about climate change and the associated cost/benefit calculations? The Stern review, for example, used a discount rate of 1.4%, which leads to a much bigger present value of the costs of climate change than the more usual 4%.

Let us take this one step further. Suppose that an asset is known to receive future cashflows $C_1, C_2, \ldots$ at periods $1, 2, \ldots$ in the future. Then we can calculate the **Present Discounted Value** (PDV) of all future cash flows by discounting all cash flows individually, and then add them up to give

$$\boxed{PDV = \frac{C_1}{1+R} + \frac{C_2}{(1+R)^2} + \cdots},$$

assuming that this sum is finite (in the case of a finite horizon, this is not an issue). We further suppose that the fair price for this asset $P$ satisfies

$$P = PDV. \tag{4.1}$$

This is an assumption, but it seems reasonable. If $P < PDV$, this would mean that to an individual with discount rate $R$, the PDV of the cash flows is worth more than $P$, in which case that individual should buy the asset, which should have the effect of forcing the price up until it is no longer so undervalued. We note that the PDV (and hence the price) depends negatively on $R$. If discount rates go up, asset prices should fall. The PDV depends positively on the cash flows, i.e., $\partial PDV/\partial C_j = 1/(1+R)^j > 0$ for every $j$.

We next consider three examples to illustrate this concept. Before we do that, we outline some elementary mathematical tools we will need. We will use below the sum of a geometric series in $x$,

$$1 + x + x^2 + \ldots + x^n = \sum_{i=0}^{n} x^i = \frac{1 - x^{n+1}}{1 - x},$$

which is valid for any $x \neq 1$ (for $x = 1$, the sum is just $n + 1$). This follows by multiplying out $(1-x)\left(1 + x + x^2 + \ldots + x^n\right) = 1 - x^{n+1}$ and working term by term. When $n$ is very large and $0 < x < 1$, the sum approaches $1/(1-x)$, which can be called the long horizon approximation. Another result we may need is

$$\lim_{n \longrightarrow \infty} \left(1 + \frac{x}{n}\right)^n = e^x = \exp(x) \tag{4.2}$$

for any $x$; the symbol $e$ on the right hand side is Euler's $e = 2.718$.

**Example 47** *A 30-year government bond pays to the bearer an amount \$100 at the end of the first year, the second year, etc. Suppose your discount rate is 4%. How much would you be willing to pay for these cash flows?*

**Solution 1** *The total payout is \$3000, but it is spread out over 30 years. The PDV of those payments is*

$$\begin{aligned} PDV &= \frac{100}{1.04} + \frac{100}{1.04^2} + \ldots + \frac{100}{1.04^{30}} \\ &= \frac{100}{1.04}\left(1 + \frac{1}{1.04} + \cdots + \frac{1}{1.04^{29}}\right) \\ &= \frac{100}{1.04}\frac{1 - \frac{1}{1.04^{30}}}{1 - \frac{1}{1.04}} = 1729. \end{aligned}$$

*The true value based on this discount rate is much less than \$3000. In this case,* $(\frac{1}{1.04})^{30} = 0.308$, *so that the long horizon approximation would give \$2500, which is not so good as an approximation.*

**Example 48** *You buy a house with a 30-year mortgage for* $T =$*\$1,000,000. Suppose that the annual interest rate is 4% and payments are made annually. How much would your payments be? Suppose that payments are made monthly. How much would your payments be? Suppose that payments are made daily. How much would your payments be?*

**Solution 2** *First, annual payments. We suppose, as is quite common, that the bank requires an up-front payment (sometimes this is called an arrangement fee) as well as 30 remaining payments to cover the mortgage. We have 31 payments of* $C$ *at interest rate* 4%. *We suppose that the PDV of our payments is equal to the current value of the cash we receive, in which case we must have*

$$1000000 = C + \frac{C}{1.04} + \ldots + \frac{C}{1.04^{30}}.$$

*Our purpose is to find* $C$. *In general, we have* $n+1$ *payments of* $C$ *at interest rate* $R$ *and we must have*

$$T = C + \frac{C}{1+R} + \ldots + \frac{C}{(1+R)^n}.$$

*This implies that for* $x = 1/(1+R)$

$$T = C \times \frac{1-x^{n+1}}{1-x}, \quad \textit{therefore } C = T \times \frac{1-x}{1-x^{n+1}}. \tag{4.3}$$

*Therefore, in the particular case we require an annual payment of \$54,668. What happens as we pay off the mortgage is that some proportion of our annual payment is going to pay off the principal (the \$1000000 we borrowed), and some is paying off the interest on the remaining principal. An interest-only mortgage would require \$40,000 per year, which is fewer payments each year, but it would not pay off the capital.*

The bank usually calculates the interest rate for a fraction of the year as $R/m$. It follows that we should have

$$\begin{aligned} T &= C + \frac{C}{1+\frac{R}{m}} + \ldots + \frac{C}{\left(1+\frac{R}{m}\right)^{n\times m}} \\ &= C\left(1 + \frac{1}{1+\frac{R}{m}} + \ldots + \frac{1}{\left(1+\frac{R}{m}\right)^{m}} + \ldots + \frac{1}{\left(1+\frac{R}{m}\right)^{n\times m}}\right) \end{aligned}$$

from which we obtain

$$\boxed{C = T \times \frac{1-x}{1-x^{nm+1}}}, \quad x = \frac{1}{1+\frac{R}{m}}. \tag{4.4}$$

Now, consider monthly payments. In this case, we take $m = 12$ and we obtain 361 equal monthly payments of $C = \$4751$, and so annual payments $mC = \$57,012$. Which payment scheme (annual or monthly) results in fewer total payments to the bank?

Now suppose that we take $m \to \infty$ and so $C \to 0$. This corresponds to making more and more frequent payments of correspondingly smaller amounts. We have as $m \to \infty$ for any $R$,

$$\left(1 + \frac{R}{m}\right)^m = \exp(R).$$

Furthermore, we have $m(1 - x) = m(R/m)/(1 + R/m) \to R$, and so

$$mC = T \times \frac{\frac{m\frac{R}{m}}{1+\frac{R}{m}}}{1 - \frac{1}{\left(1+\frac{R}{m}\right)}\left(\frac{1}{\left(1+\frac{R}{m}\right)^m}\right)^n} \to \frac{R}{1 - \exp(-nR)}.$$

In the case with $T$ = \$1,000,000, $R$ = 4%, and $n$ = 30, this gives $mC$ = \$57,240, which are the total annual payments under **continuous compounding**.

**Example 49** *The MegaMillions and PowerBall Jackpots can be paid out in the 30-year installments, with one annual payment being made for each of the 30-year term. The level of payments is calculated such that the payments rise 4% from year to year until the full sum has been paid out, with the first payment being \$1,000,000. Payment can also be offered as a lump sum and will be paid out at 60% of the total cash value of the annuity amount.*

Suppose that your discount rate is $R = 0.04$, should you take the cash or the annual payout? We first calculate the annual payments and their undiscounted sum

$$C_2 = 1.04C_1, C_3 = 1.04C_2, \ldots, C_{30} = 1.04C_{29}$$

$$A = C_1 + C_2 + \ldots C_{30} = C_1 \left(1 + 1.04 + 1.04^2 + \cdots 1.04^{29}\right) = 56.08C_1.$$

We have $C_1$ = 1,000,000, $C_2$ = 1,040,000, etc., then $A$ = 56,080,000. This is the amount that the lottery company would advertise as the winning prize. You value the annual payments with discounting, so that your valuation is

$$C_1 + \frac{C_2}{1.04} + \ldots = 30C_1 = 30{,}000{,}000.$$

Then 60% of $A$ is 33,650,000, which is more than 30,000,000, so you should prefer to take the cash now. In fact, in the US the lottery prize money is taxable, so that unless you offset some expenses (such as mortgage interest) you will have to pay around 40% of the winnings to the Federal government. So in the end, the \$56.08 million is actually more like \$24 million. Isn't this false advertising?

## 4.2 Attitudes to Risk or Uncertainty

We next consider how to take account of risk in our valuation of an uncertain outcome $X$; here we will forget about the time aspect to concentrate purely on risk. Economic theory usually admits three possibilities regarding an individual's attitude to risk:

1. They are indifferent to risk, **risk neutral**. They only care about $E(X)$.
2. They dislike risk per se, i.e., they are **risk averse**. They prefer a certain outcome with $V$ to any uncertain outcome $X$ that has the same (or less) expected value, i.e., $E(X) \leq V$.
3. They like risk, **risk seeking**. They prefer an uncertain outcome $X$ to a certain outcome $V$, whenever $E(X) \geq V$.

So far, we have evaluated a game of chance according only to its expected value and defined a fair game as one whose expected value is zero. This is consistent with risk-neutral behavior, where risk itself is not considered. More recently (since around 1713), it has been acknowledged that human beings have preferences over risk, and this contributes to how they make choices between different uncertain outcomes.

Which of the following do you prefer?

**Algorithm 8** *1. Choice A with +200 with probability 1/2 and −100 with probability 1/2;*
*2. Choice B with +50 for sure;*
*3. Choice C Nothing*

Clearly, choice C is dominated by choice B. For A, the expected value is

$$E(A) = \frac{1}{2}200 + \frac{1}{2}(-100) = 50.$$

For B, it is the same. According to expected value, there is no difference between $A$ and $B$, and a risk-neutral person would be indifferent between them. The only difference between $A$ and $B$ is that $A$ is risky, whereas $B$ is not. A risk averse person should prefer $B$ over $A$ and a risk seeking person should prefer $A$ over $B$.

Now what about

**Algorithm 9** *1. Choice D with +200000 with probability 1/2 and −100000 with probability 1/2;*
*2. Choice E +50000 for sure*

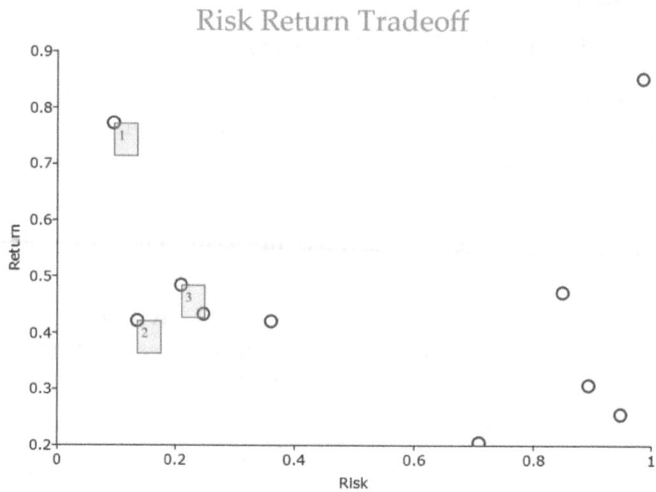


**FIGURE 4.2**
Risk return trade-off

For D, the expected value is

$$E(D) = \frac{1}{2}200000 + \frac{1}{2}(-100000) = 50000.$$

For E, it is the same. So the only difference between $D$ and $E$ is that $D$ is risky, whereas $E$ is not. A risk-averse person should prefer $E$ over $D$ and a risk-seeking person should prefer $D$ over $E$.

In practice, many people prefer $A$ over $B$ but $E$ over $D$, which violates the usual organization of behavior into these three categories. Nevertheless, we will maintain this classification.

To summarize. A risk-averse person dislikes risk, but a risk seeker likes it, everything else being equal. In general, risk-averse individuals like insurance, like hedging, dislike lotteries, they need compensation for taking on risk. Risk-seeking individuals: dislike insurance, like speculating and gambling, like rock climbing, bungee jumping, and swimming in Australia. A risk seeker might accept a negative return in order to have risk. A risk-averse person might accept risk if they receive a positive return. However, the more risk they face, the higher return they need in compensation. For large amounts, we are all risk-averse. Financial markets are the most studied place for evaluating individuals' preferences over risk and return. We usually assume risk aversion is the dominant behavior in financial markets.

In Figure 4.2, we show several options according to their risk and return. This graphic is a standard way to present the performance characteristics of different assets with risk (usually measured here by standard deviation) on

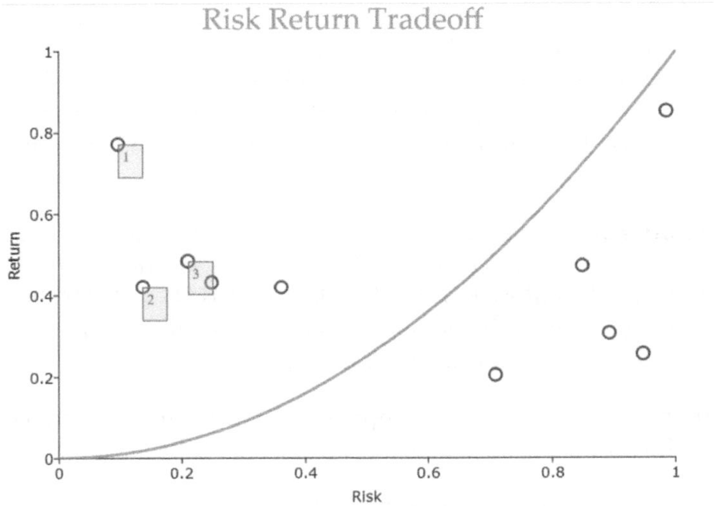


**FIGURE 4.3**
Risk return trade-off with indifference curve

the horizontal axis and return (usually measured by the mean) on the vertical axis. Suppose that you are risk-averse. Then you prefer 1 over 2 below, no matter what. However, regarding the choice between 2 and 3, the answer will depend on your precise degree of risk aversion. Some risk-averse persons will prefer 2 over 3, and some will prefer 3 over 2. The fundamental issue here is how to rank different alternatives when one has two characteristics (risk and return) to take account of, and when the rankings implied by the individual characteristics are different.

The red line below in Figure 4.3 is the **indifference curve** of a particular individual that defines the set of risk/return values that the individual is indifferent among, it is a simple way to characterize his preferences. The line contains points with high risk and high return, and other points with low risk and low return. Points above the line to the northwest for this individual are preferred to points below the line, as the preferred direction of travel is northwest. We next define a framework for defining preferences between risk and return that is widely used in economics.

How does a risk-averse person trade off risk against return in general? How does a risk-averse person choose between investments with different risk/return profiles?

One approach is based on the **Sharpe Ratio** (return per unit of risk), which is defined as the return per unit of risk

$$\boxed{SR = \frac{E(X)}{\text{stdev}(X)} = \frac{\mu}{\sigma}}, \tag{4.5}$$

(in the usual definition of the Sharpe Ratio, one subtracts the risk-free rate from $E(X)$, but we ignore this here). This quantity is a single number that is therefore ordered, meaning that for any given pairs $(\mu, \sigma^2)$ and $(\mu', \sigma'^2)$ we have either $SR = SR(\mu, \sigma^2) \geq SR(\mu', \sigma'^2) = SR'$ or $SR' \geq SR$; this gives us a basis to choose between these two investments provided the variances are positive.

**Example 50** *For option A, we have* $E(A) = 50$ *and* $\text{var}(A) = 22{,}500$ *and so* $SR = 50/150 = 1/3$. *For option D, the payoff is exactly 1000 times the payoff of option A, and so* $E(D) = 50{,}000$ *and* $\text{var}(D) = 22{,}500{,}000{,}000$ *and so* $SR = 1/3$, *the same. For options B and E, since the variance is zero, the SR is undefined and so we can't rank them.*

An alternative, more general approach is to maximize so-called **Mean-Variance Utility**

$$U = E(X) - \gamma \text{var}(X) = \mu - \gamma\sigma^2. \tag{4.6}$$

Here, $\gamma$ is a parameter that measures the degree of risk aversion: (a) $\gamma > 0$ is risk averse; (b) $\gamma = 0$ is risk neutral; (c) $\gamma < 0$ is risk seeking. The value $U$ is a single number that is therefore ordered, meaning that for any given pairs $(\mu, \sigma^2)$ and $(\mu', \sigma'^2)$ we have either $U = U(\mu, \sigma^2) \geq U(\mu', \sigma'^2) = U'$ or $U' \geq U$; this gives us a basis to choose between these two investments. The indifference curve is defined as the set of risk-return combinations that give the same payoff in utility, i.e., $\{(\text{stdev}(X), E(X)) : U = u\}$.

**Example 51** *For options A-E, we have*

$$\begin{aligned} U(A) &= 50 - \gamma 22{,}500, \;\; U(B) = 50, \;\; U(C) = 0 \\ U(D) &= 50{,}000 - \gamma 22{,}500{,}000{,}000, \;\; U(E) = 50{,}000. \end{aligned}$$

*Clearly, for any* $\gamma > 0$, $U(B) > U(A)$, $U(C)$ *and* $U(E) > U(D)$. *Clearly, for some values of* $\gamma > 0$, $U(A) > U(C)$, *whereas for others* $U(A) < U(C)$. *In the comparison between* $A, D$ *it also depends on the value of* $\gamma$.

## 4.3 The Birth of Utility Theory

We next discuss this historical example, which leads to the development of expected utility theory and an understanding of how risk aversion matters.

**Example 52** *St Petersburg Paradox. Consider the following game of chance: you pay a fixed fee to enter and then a fair coin is tossed repeatedly until a tail appears, ending the game. The pot starts at 1 dollar and is doubled every time a head appears. You win whatever is in the pot after the game ends. Thus,* *you win 1 dollar if a tail appears on the first toss, 2 dollars if a head appears on the first toss and a tail on the second, 4 dollars if a head appears on the first two tosses and a tail on the third, etc. What would be a fair price $P$, to pay for playing the game?*

The expected value of the game payoff is

$$E(X) = \frac{1}{2} \times 1 + \frac{1}{4} \times 2 + \frac{1}{8} \times 4 + \ldots = \infty.$$

Note also that $\text{var}(X) = \infty$. If we just evaluate this game according to its expected return, we should have an infinite price, i.e., $P = \infty$. This seems counterintuitive, if not silly. Certainly, no one is going to pay this amount to play the game, even if they had such a bank account in the first place.

Bernoulli solved this problem by computing the logarithm of earnings, which is now called a utility function $U(x)$, instead, and taking its expectation

$$\begin{aligned} E(\log(X)) &= \frac{1}{2} \times \log 1 + \frac{1}{4} \times \log 2 + \frac{1}{8} \times \log 4 + \ldots \\ &= \frac{1}{2} \sum_{k=1}^{\infty} \frac{\log(2^k)}{2^k} = \log(2) \times \sum_{k=1}^{\infty} \frac{k}{2^{k+1}} = \log 2 < \infty. \end{aligned}$$

This says that an individual who likes expected logarithmic utility has a finite valuation of the game, and in particular, the correct price is $P = 2$, because $\log(2) = E(\log(X))$. This is the fair price for this individual, and the answer seems reasonable overall.

The logarithm is a popular utility function, but nowadays others are usually used instead. One can assume a general utility function $U(x)$ as describing behavior provided it possesses certain properties. The function $U$ should be increasing in $x$ to comply with the first axiom of behavior that more is preferred to less. In addition to being consistent with risk aversion, the marginal utility should be concave, i.e., decreasing with $x$, i.e., $U'(x) = 1/x \to 0$ as $x \to \infty$, that is, the value of a further dollar once one has a trillion dollars in the bank is much less than when one has nothing. This property is necessary for the expectation to exist for $X$ in the St. Petersburg paradox. Decreasing marginal utility is necessary but not sufficient. One also has, in this case, to guarantee that $E(U(X)) < \infty$, which requires that marginal utility decreases fast enough. Specifically, one can find a payoff scheme $X$ for which $E(\log(X)) = \infty$, and to value this game would require a utility function that had an even faster decay of marginal utility than the logarithm. Nevertheless, Bernoulli's argument makes sense for any payoff scheme for which expected utility is finite. It captures the notion of risk aversion.

An alternative approach to reconciling the St. Petersburg game with rational decision making is to consider the bankruptcy issue. Specifically, if one assumes that there is a finite amount of capital, then it is not credible that the other side could pay you more than that limit. In that case, the maximum payoff is finite, and so expected utility would be finite, and the fair price would be finite.

We next investigate the utility function in more detail. Suppose that $U(x)$ is a concave function, which is consistent with risk aversion in the sense that

$$\overbrace{E(U(X))}^{\text{mean of utility}} < \overbrace{U(E(X))}^{\text{utility of mean}}$$

for any random variable $X$. A risk-averse person prefers to receive the mean value with no risk of receiving the uncertain value whose mean is the same. We give a little longer explanation. Suppose that $X$ is a random outcome with mean $\mu = E(X)$ and variance $\sigma^2 = \text{var}(X)$. Let $Y$ be a certain outcome with outcome $\mu$ (and zero variance). Any risk averse person would prefer $Y$ to $X$ and strictly so, i.e.,

$$E(U(X)) < E(U(Y)) = U(Y) = U(\mu) = U(E(X)).$$

A risk-seeking person would have a (convex) utility function $U$ with $E(U(X)) > U(E(X))$, whereas a risk neutral person would have a (linear) utility function $U$ with $E(U(X)) = U(E(X))$.

The certainty equivalent of $X$ is defined as the value $CE$ such that

$$E(U(X)) = U(CE). \tag{4.7}$$

For a risk-averse person, $CE < E(X)$. The certainty equivalent depends on the distribution of $X$ and on preferences, i.e. on $U$. For example, suppose that $X$ is the St. Petersburg game outcome, then we have already calculated the certainty equivalent and called it the fair price.

Expected utility theory is at the heart of decision-making theory, but it is quite complicated to work with. We next consider a simplification of this. Note that by a second order **Taylor expansion** of $\log(X)$ about $\log(E(X))$ we can obtain

$$\begin{aligned} E(\log(X)) &\simeq \log(E(X)) + \frac{1}{E(X)}E(X - E(X)) \\ &\quad - \frac{1}{2E^2(X)}E\left((X - E(X))^2\right) \\ &= \log(\mu) - \frac{1}{2\mu^2}\sigma^2. \end{aligned}$$

The approximation here is widely used but is not well grounded.

We interpret this to say that the expected utility function approximately depends just on the mean $\mu$ (in an increasing way) and on the variance $\sigma^2$ (in a decreasing way). Mean variance preferences are those for which $E(U(X)) = f(\mu, \sigma^2)$, for some function $f$ with $f$ increasing in $\mu$ and decreasing in $\sigma^2$. We will work with a special case of this.

In economics more generally, it is usual practice to define utility over consumption or consumption streams, whereas in finance, the end purpose of investment and speculation are usually ignored. In some cases, one considers wealth as the value that enters the utility function, and then the wealth level interacts with the risk aversion, but this leads to a more complicated analysis, which we eschew here.

## 4.4 Key Points

1. The time value of money is a key concept in evaluating the benefits of cash flows received at different times, such as mortgage payments and bond coupons.
2. Attitude to risk is a key assumption that we need to determine in evaluating uncertain outcomes. Risk aversion is the dominant assumption that we believe humans obey; they prefer to take on less risk everything else being equal. They also prefer more return; usually risk and return are in conflict, hence the risk return tradeoff.

## 4.5 Exercises

1. You buy a house with a 30-year mortgage for $T$ =\$1,000,000. Suppose that the annual interest rate is 4% and payments are made annually. Calculate for each year the remaining principal on the mortgage.
2. Calculate the indifference curve for mean variance utility with $\gamma = 5$, meaning give different values of $\mu, \sigma^2$ for which $U = \mu - 5\sigma^2$ is the same.
3. Suppose that you are offered two scenarios
   (a) Facing a 1% chance of losing \$20,000 you can
      i. buy a full insurance policy for \$90 or
      ii. buy an insurance policy with a \$500 deductible for \$20.
   (b) Facing a 1% chance of losing \$500 you can buy a full insurance policy for \$70 or not.
   Write down the expected mean variance utility for all these choices and compare.

# 5

# *Financial Markets*

## Outline

This chapter provides an in-depth overview of financial markets, highlighting how they foster economic efficiency and growth by channeling funds from savers to borrowers. It surveys the main market types and instruments and explains the forces that govern their behavior. The chapter also examines risk-management mechanisms, the structure of financial markets, and the challenges they face.

After reading this chapter, you will be able to:

- Understand the fundamental purpose of financial markets in channeling funds and promoting economic efficiency and growth.
- Recognize the importance of risk management and the role of speculators in providing liquidity and enabling risk transfer.
- Identify the different types of financial markets, including fixed income, stock, foreign exchange, cryptocurrency, derivatives, commodity, and betting markets.
- Analyze the structure and functioning of fixed income markets, with emphasis on the money market, bond market, and the yield curve.
- Examine the operation of stock markets, the concept of stock indexes, and the statistical properties of daily returns.
- Explore other asset classes such as commodities, foreign exchange, cryptocurrencies, and real estate.
- Evaluate the time series variation in yield curves and understand the implications of yield curves for economic forecasting.
- Understand the key features and challenges of financial markets, including market manipulation, bubbles, crashes, and the impact of regulation.

One purpose of financial markets is to channel funds from savers to borrowers. There is economic efficiency and growth if entrepreneurs with productive ideas borrow capital from savers, who may have inferior investment

DOI: 10.1201/9781003543121-5 

opportunities of their own, to implement their projects. Another purpose of financial markets is **risk transfer**—the transfer of risk from one group who would rather not bear the risk to parties more willing to bear them. The word **speculator** (or speculation) often has negative connotations. However, it is important to realize that to provide the **insurance** or **hedging** demanded by some requires that someone else, you might call speculators, to take the other side of the trade. Ultimately, these transactions can increase the overall welfare of society, so that financial markets are not necessarily in total a **zero-sum game**.

A key feature of security markets is that they allow the separation of ownership and management. A small business can be owner-managed, but a large corporation has capital requirements that exceed the possibilities of a single individual. As companies grow beyond a certain point, they may opt to go public, i.e., to be listed on a stock exchange. This process involves an Initial Public Offering, where shares in the company are sold to investors, who then become shareholders. These shares can then be traded in the secondary market (the stock exchange) between those who want to buy and those who want to sell. The shareholders elect the board of directors, which hires the managers who run the business (and in principle maximize its value for the shareholders). This separation of powers in principle leads to an improvement of economic efficiency and welfare. However, conflicts of interests can arise, and this can lead to negative outcomes. The financial crisis of the late 2000s demonstrated a range of weaknesses in the architecture of financial markets, including **Moral hazard**. Executives faced incentives to take excessive risks—big profits yield big bonuses, but big losses do not result in negative bonuses. Government bailouts were needed to stabilize the system with large future fiscal consequences. Additional regulation and supervision were introduced. Many fines were issued to investment banks for misconduct.

We can classify financial markets, or rather financial securities, into the following:

- **Fixed Income Markets**
  - **Money Markets**—debt instruments with maturity $\leq 1$ year;
  - **Bond Markets**—debt instruments with maturity $\geq 1$ years;
- **Stock/Equity Markets**—shares of listed companies; NYSE, NASDAQ, SSE;
- **Foreign Exchange Markets**—currency pairs;
- **Crypto currencies**—Bitcoin, Ethereum, Binance;
- **Derivatives Markets**—futures contracts, options;
- **Commodity Markets**—pork bellies, copper, fine wines, etc.;
- **Betting markets**—horse racing, sports, politics.

We will discuss some of these markets and the instruments that they trade below. According to the Bank of America, in 2024, the value of global stock market and fixed income markets is \$255 trillion; the fixed income market composes \$130 trillion of that, whereas the stock market represents \$125 trillion. So they are a big deal.

## 5.1 Fixed Income Markets

Governments and companies borrow money to fund their expenditure. They issue fixed-income contracts that specify fixed payments of cash at specific future dates. The assumption here is that these payments are not subject to risk, at least the nominal payments are guaranteed, so that an investor who buys the bond and holds it to maturity can expect to receive exactly what is promised. We may distinguish between instruments issued by the US Federal Government and other organizations, such as companies or other countries, where there may be a risk of default (credit risk). We mostly focus on the US market here in terms of terminology.

### 5.1.1 Money Market

The money market is a subsector of the fixed-income market with a short horizon or term. The main instruments are as follows.

**Treasury bills** (T-bills). Short-term US government debt was introduced in 1929. They are sold in terms ranging from a few days to 52 weeks. Bills are typically sold by the Treasury auction on a periodic basis and then bought and sold by investors in the Secondary market. The auction price is typically at a discount from the par amount (par amount is also called face value); rarely, they have sold at a price equal to or greater than the par amount (1938). When a bill matures, you are paid its par amount. The difference between the par amount and the purchase price is essentially your interest. These assets are highly liquid, i.e., they are easy to buy and sell.

**Federal Funds**. A bank without enough cash on hand to meet the requirement will borrow from other banks. The Federal Funds rate is the interest banks charge each other to borrow Fed funds. The current Fed Funds rate dictates all other short-term interest rates. This rate is set (in a target range) by the monetary policy committee of the Federal Reserve Board. The effective federal funds rate (EFFR) is calculated as a volume-weighted median of overnight Federal Funds transactions reported in the FR 2420 Report of Selected Money Market Rates.

There are some other notable instruments. **Commercial Paper**. Large companies with impeccable credit can simply issue short-term unsecured promissory notes to raise cash (IOU's). **Repos**. Repurchase agreements, or repos, are a form of short-term borrowing used in the money markets, which involve the purchase of securities with the agreement to sell them back at a specific date, usually for a higher price.

### 5.1.2 Bond Market

The Government Bond market is huge: US Treasury Securities $\$21\times10^{12}$ outstanding in 2017, Japanese securities $\$10.46\times10^{12}$ outstanding in 2013. This market is used by the government to fund its spending beyond its tax revenue. It is used by investors as a source of guaranteed income, at least in the case of reliable sovereign lenders such as the USA.

**Coupon Bonds** have coupon payments $c$ expressed as a percentage of redemption or face value or principal (which may be say $1000). A coupon is paid every six months (or year) until maturity, at which date the holder receives the face value. Most long-term government bonds are issued in this form in the primary market by auction to registered participants and then traded between participants in the secondary markets.

**Zero Coupon Bonds**, which make a single payment at a specified future time, also known as zeros. T-bills with original maturities of less than a year are zeros; longer maturity zeros can be constructed by "stripping" coupon bonds by investment banks, i.e., a form of financial engineering, and then resold to investors. Suppose you have to pay a big bill in 17 months time, then buy and hold a 17-month zero, that will exactly match one's assets with one's liabilities.

**Treasury Inflation-Protected Securities** (TIPS) in the US and Index-linked Gilts in the UK are both designed to deliver returns protected against inflation and are usually linked to the consumer price index, CPI. Can be short maturity or long maturity. In times of high inflation, these add to the debt burden of the issuer.

**Municipal bonds**. Issued by states, cities, counties, or other local governments. They have a tax-exempt status, and so high-tax-bracket investors often hold Muni bonds. Higher risk of default.

**Corporate bonds**. Companies can raise funds by issuing bonds with similar structure to government bonds. There is a wide spectrum of **credit quality**; the default risk is typically higher than for government bonds. Secured bonds are those with specific collateral. Unsecured bonds—also known as debentures in the US (in the UK, debentures are often secured). Junior (subordinated) bonds/debentures—lower-priority claim to the firm's assets than existing senior debt (bonds/debentures or loans), and hence, riskier.

Moody's and S&P rates corporate and sovereign (nation state) bonds on a scale from: Aaa (highest quality, minimal chance of default) to C (currently in default). In 2008, there were many defaults, including in the Aaa category. Over the years, there have been many defaults by sovereign states such as Argentina, but not by the USA, Germany, China, Japan, UK, for example.

**TABLE 5.1**
Interest rates across countries as of July 2024

| Country | Rate | Previous |
|---|---|---|
| Japan | 0.1 | 0.1 |
| Switzerland | 1.25 | 1.5 |
| China | 3.35 | 3.45 |
| Singapore | 3.42 | 3.53 |
| South Korea | 3.5 | 3.5 |
| Euro Area | 4.25 | 4.25 |
| Australia | 4.35 | 4.35 |
| Canada | 4.5 | 4.75 |
| United Kingdom | 5.25 | 5.25 |
| United States | 5.5 | 5.5 |
| Saudi Arabia | 6 | 6 |
| Indonesia | 6.25 | 6.25 |
| India | 6.5 | 6.5 |
| South Africa | 8.25 | 8.25 |
| Brazil | 10.5 | 10.5 |
| Mexico | 11 | 11 |
| Russia | 18 | 16 |
| Argentina | 40 | 40 |
| Turkey | 50 | 50 |

Table 5.1 shows interest rates for a sample of countries in June 2024. There is considerable variation in the level of interest rates.

## 5.2 Yield Curve and Discount Function

We next look in more detail at government bonds. These bonds are of different maturity or horizon. At the short end is the 1-month T-bill, at the long end is the 30-year bond. The longer-term bonds are typically issued as coupon bonds, that is, they pay a coupon \$c every six months until maturity, when it returns its principal. These are traded in very big markets at prices determined by different investors coming together in a consensual way. We now turn the logic around. Given the prices of these bonds, what is the implied discount rate for each horizon? Here, we allow the implied discount rate to vary with horizon, and use the market prices of such bonds (which are observed every day) to figure out what the corresponding discount rate is for each horizon. Theoretically, two different zero bonds at the same horizon should have the same implied discount rate (but not necessarily the same price if the payouts are different). Two bonds with the same horizon and same payout should have exactly the same price.

We suppose that we have a **zero bond** that pays a fixed amount (the principal) at some specified date in the future (the maturity). Let $n$ denote the horizon of the zero.

**Definition 8** *The spot rate is the yield or discount rate $R_n$ on an $n$ period zero with payoff $C$ (at $n$ periods in the future) and price $P$ that satisfies*

$$P = \frac{C}{(1 + R_n)^n}. \tag{5.1}$$

*This equation can be inverted to obtain*

$$R_n = \left(\frac{C}{P}\right)^{1/n} - 1.$$

*If we observe $P$ and we know $(C, n)$, then $R_n$ is determined.*

**Definition 9** *The discount factor $d_n$ is the standardized price for a unit payoff in the $n-$period future, and is defined as*

$$d_n = \frac{1}{(1 + R_n)^n}.$$

This is a decreasing function of $n$, reflecting the time value of money. The **discount function** is just the set of points $d_1, \ldots, d_n$ or rather the function $d(n)$. The zero coupon **yield curve** is just the set of points $R_1, \ldots, R_n$ or rather the function $R(n)$. This is also called the **term structure** of interest rates. For a typical coupon bond with coupon $c$ every period and principal $M$ at maturity $n$, we should have

$$P = \sum_{j=1}^{n} \frac{c}{(1 + R_j)^j} + \frac{M}{(1 + R_n)^n},$$

which involves all the discount rates $R_1, \ldots, R_n$.

One can calculate the yield curve and the discount function from a sample of Government coupon bonds with observed prices $P_1, P_2, \ldots$ knowing their coupon payments and maturities. The current US yield curve is shown in Figure 5.1 along with its implied discount curve in Figure 5.2. The US yield curve during 2022 is shown in Figure 5.3.

The **yield to maturity** of a coupon bond is the annual rate of return $R$ for the bond, assuming that the investor holds the asset until its maturity date and reinvests all the interim payments at the same constant rate $R$. This varies across bonds because of different maturities and payments. It is sort of like an average over the maturity-specific discount rates. Suppose that a bond

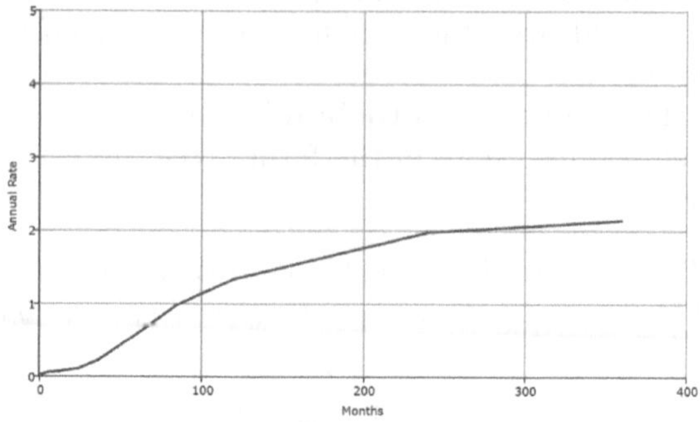


**FIGURE 5.1**
Current US yield curve

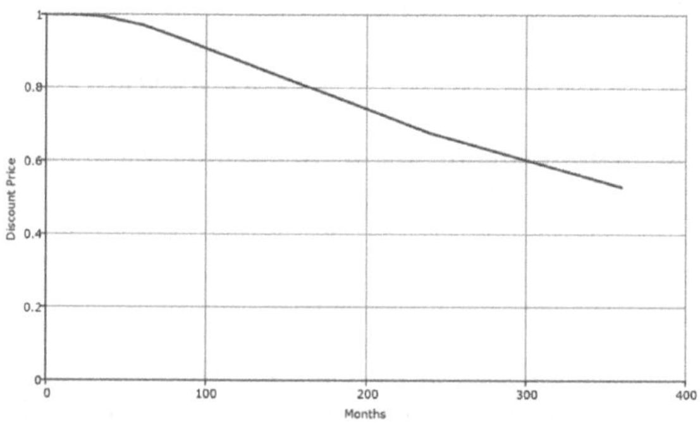


**FIGURE 5.2**
Current US discount function

pays a coupon of \$5 every year for 19 years and then pays \$100 at maturity (after 20 years). What is $R$ if $P = 120$? We have the following equation

$$
\begin{aligned}
120 &= \sum_{j=1}^{19} \frac{5}{(1+R)^j} + \frac{100}{(1+R)^{20}} \\
&= \frac{5}{1+R} \sum_{j=0}^{18} \frac{1}{(1+R)^j} + \frac{100}{(1+R)^{20}} \\
&= \frac{5}{1+R} \frac{1 - \left(\frac{1}{1+R}\right)^{19}}{1 - \left(\frac{1}{1+R}\right)} + \frac{100}{(1+R)^{20}} \\
&= \frac{5}{R}\left(1 - \left(\frac{1}{1+R}\right)^{19}\right) + \frac{100}{(1+R)^{20}}.
\end{aligned}
$$

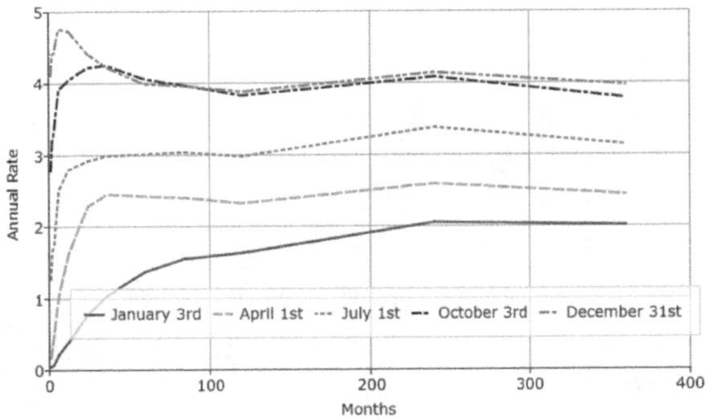


**FIGURE 5.3**
Yield curves during 2022

This is a complicated equation in $R$, but can easily be solved by computer algorithms. The solution is around 3.45%.

We can use a given yield curve to price any asset with guaranteed cash flows. Suppose that a new asset is issued that pays guaranteed amounts $c_j$ (coupons plus redemption value) at times $\tau_j$, $j = 1, \ldots, m$ in the future

$$\begin{array}{cccccc} P & c_1 & c_2 & c_3 & & c_m \\ - & - - - & - - - - - & - - - & \cdots\cdots - - & - \\ today & \tau_1 & \tau_2 & \tau_3 & & \tau_m \end{array}.$$

What is the correct price for this bond? The absence of arbitrage yields the linear pricing rule

$$P = \sum_{j=1}^{m} \frac{c_j}{(1+R_j)^{\tau_j}} = \sum_{j=1}^{m} c_j d_j, \tag{5.2}$$

where the price is equal to the present discounted value of future cash flows. Perhaps the asset is already trading at some price $P^*$, we might use the above pricing formula to determine whether this asset is overpriced or underpriced, and thereby enact a trading strategy.

Fixed income mathematics de-emphasizes risk. Although Government bonds are nominally risk-free, many investment strategies involving them are far from riskless. For example, one may buy a 10-year bond with a coupon 4%, hold it for a year, and then sell it again. You will have made 4% income over the year, but the price you sold your 9-year bond at may be above or below the price you initially paid, and you may experience a capital gain or loss. The current price is related to the discount rates: if the discount rates go up, this implies that the price goes down. Recently, as central banks raised interest rates, this led to dramatic falls in the prices of bonds, and investors holding bond portfolios experienced losses on paper and were forced in many cases to realize those losses because of margin calls, etc.

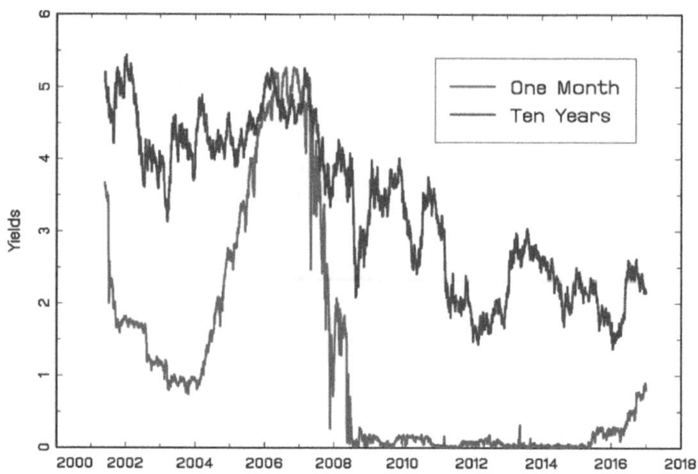


**FIGURE 5.4**
Time series of one-month and ten-year yields since 2000

### 5.2.1 Time Series Variation in Yield Curve

Yields vary over country and over time. We work with the US Treasury zero coupon yields as provided on the US Treasury website, see the data sources page. This gives yields for 1,3,6,12,24,36,50,84,120,240, and 360 months over the period 1990-2016, although there is some missing data. For example, the one-month yield is only available after 2000, and the thirty-year yield was missing for the period 2002-2006. We plot the one-month and 120-month yields in Figure 5.4. The behavior of yields in the more recent period is obviously very different in terms of the level and trend as compared with the period 1952-1991 covered by their graph. In particular, at the short rate of one month, the level was very close to zero from 2008-2016, and obviously approaching what came to be called the **zero lower bound**.

The mean (over time) yield curve is upward sloping, i.e., on average, interest rates increase with maturity. Furthermore, the average yield curve is concave. However, on any given day, one can find quite different patterns: upward sloping, downward sloping, and hump shaped. We give the summary statistics of the daily yields in the Table, which shows the upward sloping average yield curve. The average one-month rate over this period is 1.25% and the average 30-year rate is 5.3%. The variability (the stdev) seems to peak in the middle at around 2.4 and is less at the short end and at the long end.

Macroeconomists use some variables derived from the yield curve and other interest rates to predict future recessions. We list the main ones below:

**Term spread**. The difference between long-term interest rate and short-term interest rate (10-year minus three-month rate).

**TABLE 5.2**
Summary statistics of daily yields (mean and standard deviation)

| | 1 | 3 | 6 | 12 | 24 |
|---|---|---|---|---|---|
| mean | 1.2488 | 2.8712 | 3.0002 | 3.1330 | 3.4597 |
| stdev | 1.5804 | 2.3632 | 2.3977 | 2.3920 | 2.3966 |
| | 36 | 60 | 120 | 240 | 360 |
| mean | 3.6945 | 4.1198 | 4.6965 | 4.8131 | 5.2964 |
| stdev | 2.3266 | 2.1700 | 1.9040 | 1.5439 | 1.7906 |

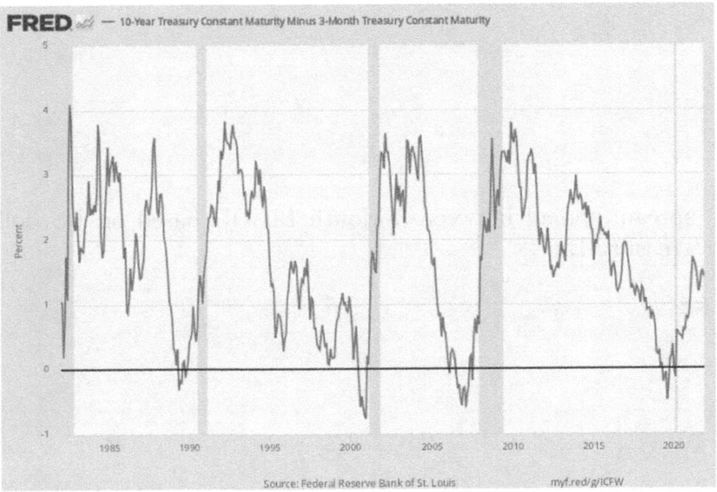


**FIGURE 5.5**
Term spread, 10 year - 3 month

**Ted spread.** The TED spread is the difference between the three-month Treasury bill and the three-month LIBOR based in U.S. dollars. The LIBOR (London Interbank Offer Rate) was the interest rate on interbank uncollateralized loans (until its extinction in October 2024)[1], and reflected the risk that banks may not be able to pay off their loans. The TED Spread represents a quantifiable measure of monetary policy as well as perceived credit risk within the economy. When banks charge each other higher rates of interest, it reflects an increase in the risk of default.

**Junk spread.** (High Yield) A high-yield bond spread is the percentage difference in current yields of various classes of high-yield bonds compared against Treasury bonds. Measures similar thing to the Ted spread, but focuses more on the extreme end of the bond market.

[1]LIBOR was the reference rate for hundreds of trillions of dollars of derivative contracts, which is why it was so difficult to replace after it emerged that the rate was being manipulated by some unscrupulous traders.

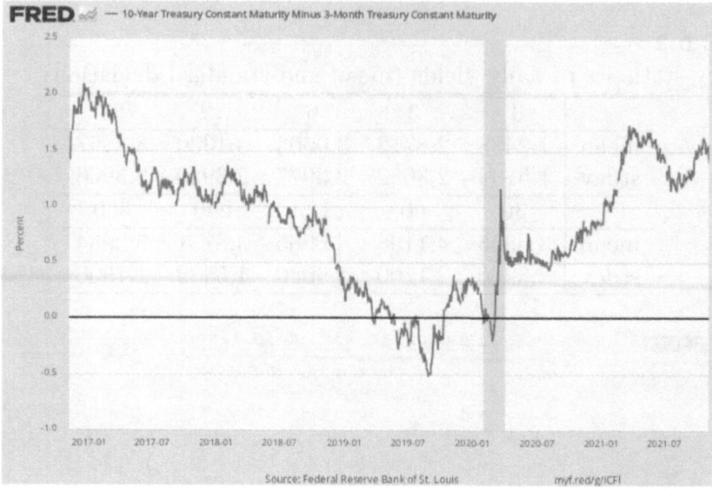


TED spread: spread between 3-Month LIBOR based on US dollars and 3-month Treasury Bill

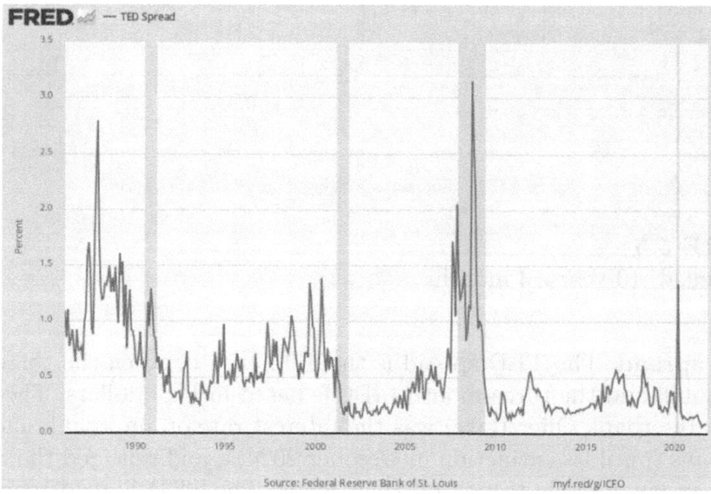

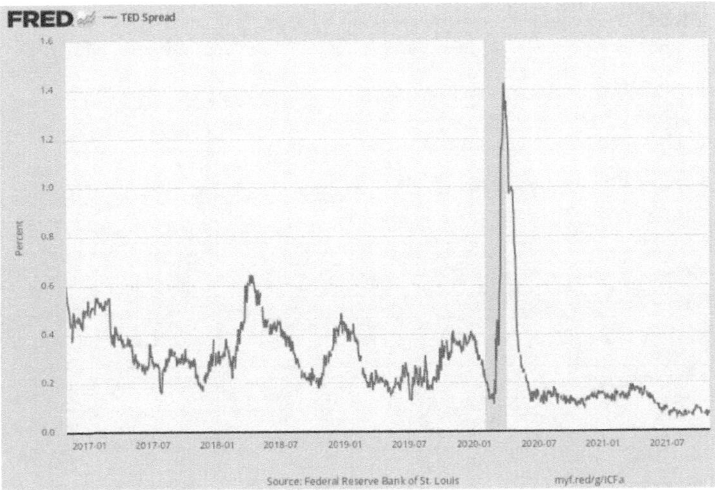
FRED
— TED Spread
Percent
1.6
1.4
1.2
1.0
0.8
0.6
0.4
0.2
0.0
2017-01
2017-07
2018-01
2018-07
2019-01
2019-07
2020-01
2020-07
2021-01
2021-07
Source: Federal Reserve Bank of St. Louis
myf.red/g/ICFa

Junk spread

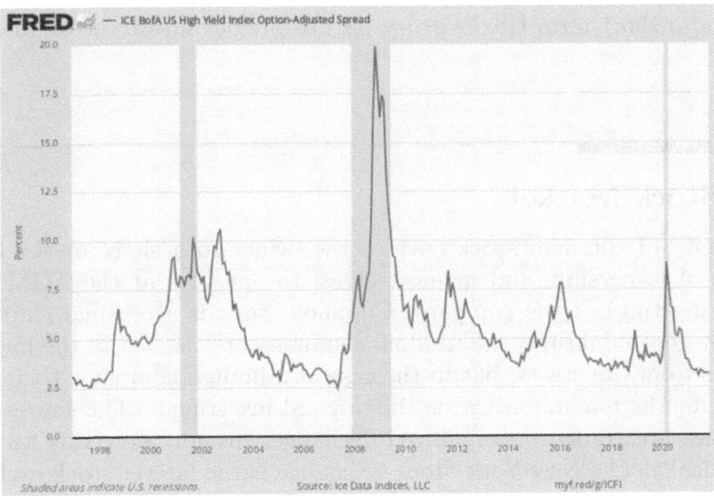
FRED
— ICE BofA US High Yield Index Option-Adjusted Spread
Percent
20.0
17.5
15.0
12.5
10.0
7.5
5.0
2.5
0.0
1998
2000
2002
2004
2006
2008
2010
2012
2014
2016
2018
2020
Shaded areas indicate U.S. recessions.
Source: Ice Data Indices, LLC
myf.red/g/ICFI

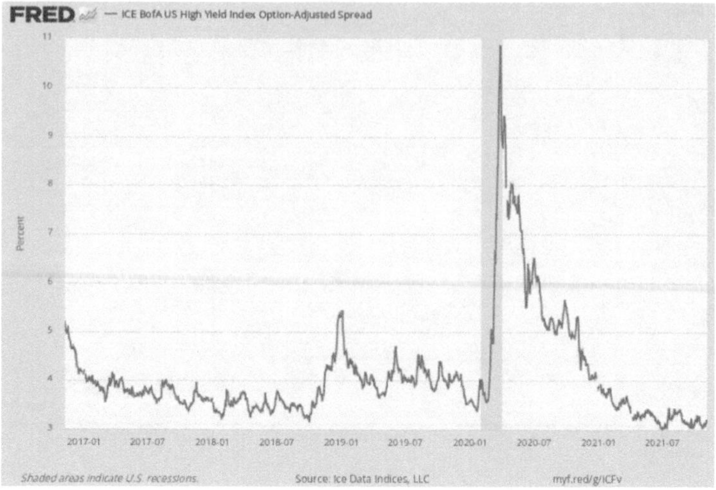


Numerous studies document the ability of the slope of the yield curve (often measured as the difference between the yields on a long-term US Treasury bond and a short-term US Treasury bill) to predict future recessions.

## 5.3 Stock Market

Each share of common stock entitles the owner to a share in the financial benefits of ownership, and in most cases, to one vote at the AGM (annual general meeting) of the company. Common stock is a residual claim: if the company goes bankrupt, the residual claimants are the last in the line for the proceeds from the assets, but in the case of a limited company, their liability is limited—the maximum loss is the original investment. The shares of large companies are traded on organized exchanges, usually now this takes place electronically. The New York Stock Exchange is the largest stock exchange in the world, and around 1.5 billion shares in 2800 companies' are traded there every day. According to the World Federation of Stock Exchanges (FESE), the 10 biggest stock markets in the world by market capitalization in (US$ millions) at the end of 1999 and 2022 are shown below.

Stock exchanges generally have opening hours similar to regular office hours, for the NYSE that is currently 9.30am-4pm. They are also closed on weekends and during holidays so that on average the NYSE is open for 250-255 days per year. That is, stock markets are only open for roughly 20% of

**TABLE 5.3**
Stock exchanges ranked by value traded

| Rank | Exchange 1999 | Value | Exchange 2022 | Value |
|---|---|---|---|---|
| 1 | NYSE | 11.44 | NYSE (US) | 24.68 |
| 2 | Nasdaq | 5.20 | NASDAQ OMX | 19.50 |
| 3 | Tokyo | 4.46 | Shanghai SE | 7.05 |
| 4 | London | 2.86 | NYSE Euronext (Europe) | 5.90 |
| 5 | Paris | 1.50 | Shenzhen SE | 5.31 |
| 6 | Deutsche Börse | 1.43 | Tokyo SE Group | 5.15 |
| 7 | Toronto | 0.79 | Hong Kong Exchanges | 4.57 |
| 8 | Italy | 0.73 | India SE | 3.32 |
| 9 | Amsterdam | 0.70 | London SE Group | 3.17 |
| 10 | Switzerland | 693,133.0 | Saudi Stock Exchange | 3.15 |

the available time (whereas crypto currency exchanges are open 24/365 so 100% of the time). Transactions happen throughout the trading day in stock markets and are executed at different prices. We denote the price at time $t$ of a one share of a company by $P_t$.

Stock Indexes reflect broader market movements as they are the average prices of underlying stocks at a point in time, similar to the way that the general price level is measured by the CPI or RPI.

**Definition 10** *Stock Index values. For some weights $w_{jt}$, $j = 1, \ldots, J$, the index value at time $t$ is the weighted sum of the prices of the $J$ individual stocks that are members of the index*

$$I_t = \sum_{j=1}^{J} w_{jt} P_{jt}.$$

*Different types: Price weighted (Dow Jones, Nikkei225) $w_{jt} = 1/J$, Value weighted (S&P500, SSEC, STOXX, Hang Seng), $w_{jt} = MCap_{jt} / \sum_{j=1}^{J} MCap_{jt}$, Equal weighted (in terms of value invested) (S&P500 Equal Weighted).*

In calculating the index, there are some adjustments for stock splits and new entrants, etc. The adjustments are necessary to preserve the continuity of the level of the stock index with respect to these events.

**Example 53** *The S&P500 index contains 505 large-cap stocks traded on NYSE, NASDAQ, Cboe BZX Exchanges. Market cap is US\$23.7 trillion (as of April 30, 2018). Foundation March 4, 1957. Figure 5.6 shows the level of this index since 1927.*

**Example 54** *The SSE Composite Index (SSEC) is a stock market index of all stocks (around 1500 A shares and B shares) that are traded on the Shanghai Stock Exchange. Foundation 15 July 1991. Market cap CN¥32.697 trillion (September 2017). CN¥12.727 trillion (free-float adjusted, September 2017).*

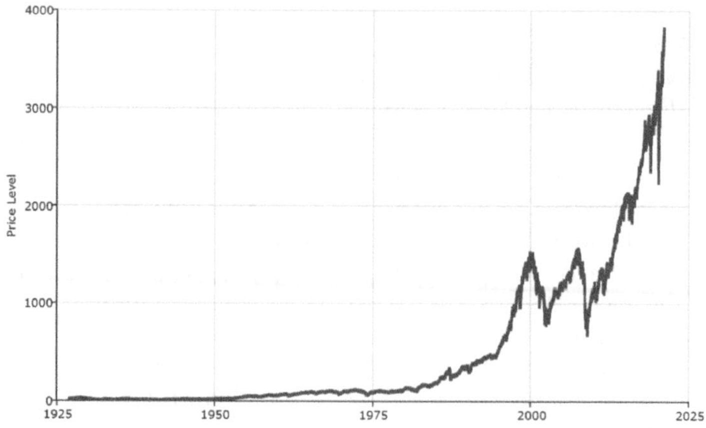


**FIGURE 5.6**
S&P500 price level since 1927

**Example 55** *The EURO STOXX 50 is a stock index of Eurozone stocks designed by STOXX, an index provider owned by Deutsche Börse Group. It is made up of fifty of the largest and most liquid stocks in the eurozone. Market cap €1.962 trillion (March 2016).*

**Example 56** *The Hang Seng Index is a freefloat-adjusted market-capitalization-weighted stock-market index in Hong Kong.50 constituent companies represent about 58% of the capitalization of the Hong Kong Stock Exchange. HSI was started on November 24, 1969.*

**Example 57** *The Nikkei 225. Tokyo Stock Exchange (TSE). Foundation 7 September 1950.*

Figure 5.7 shows the level of the S&P500, the SSEC, and the STOXX since 1991, where we have normalized each index to one at the beginning of the sample period. Over this period, the SSEC did very well in comparison with the others. Figure 5.8 shows the same comparison but from 2010 onwards. Over this period, the SSEC did very poorly in comparison with the others.

### 5.3.1 Returns

Investors (or speculators or traders as they may also be called) buy a stock at the prevailing price at time $t$, say, and hold it for a certain length of time, called the holding period

$$\underset{t}{\overset{buy}{+}} \rightarrow\rightarrow\rightarrow\rightarrow \overset{hold}{\rightarrow} \rightarrow\rightarrow\rightarrow\rightarrow\rightarrow \underset{t+s}{\overset{sell}{-}},$$

and then sell it at time $t+s$, say, at the prevailing price. The holding period could be milliseconds for High Frequency Trading firms, or it could be several

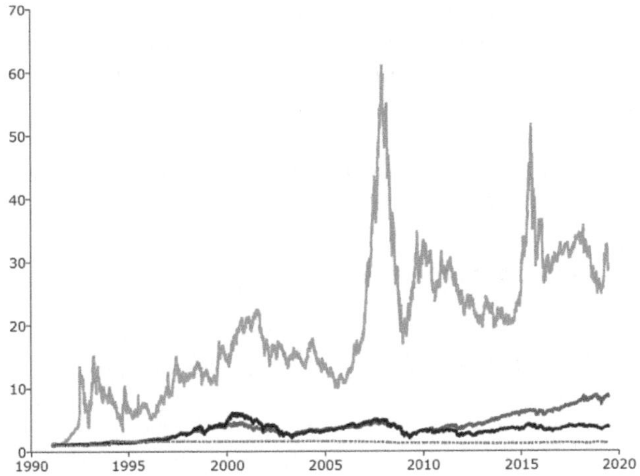


**FIGURE 5.7**
SSEC (Red), S&P500 (Blue), EStoxx (Black), and Dollar/RMB Xrate (Green) normalized to 1 in 1992

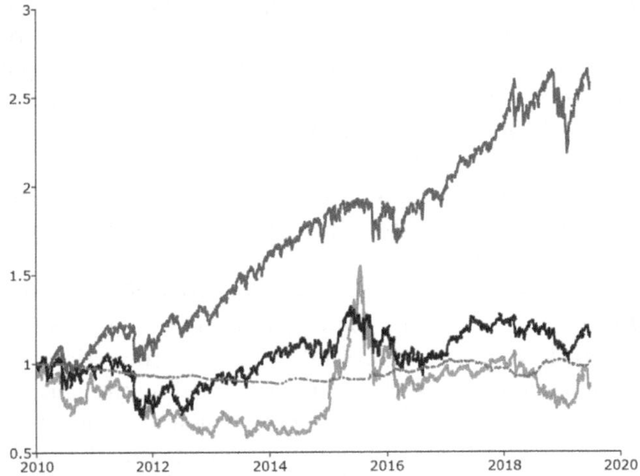


**FIGURE 5.8**
SSEC (Dark Red), S&P500 (Blue), EStoxx (Black), and Dollar/RMB Xrate (Light Red) normalized to 1 in 2010

centuries for say the Duke of Westminster trust. We suppose that investors care about the profit they make from their investments, which we call their returns. Unlike a TV, there is no consumption value to stocks and shares, and so it seems reasonable to assume here that investors only care about their profit (rather than the boasting value or some other possible benefits from holding share certificates). They may be investing in many stocks and other assets at the same time, and of course, they ultimately care about their lifetime consumption, but we will just focus here on their returns. Here, we define what the return on a stock investment is.

**Definition 11** *The (realized) return associated with a price process* $\{P_t\}$, *over the holding period from* $t$ *to* $t+s$ *is:*

$$\text{Gross Return} \qquad \mathcal{R}_{t:t+s} = \frac{P_{t+s}}{P_t} = 1 + R_{t:t+s}$$

$$\text{Net Return} \qquad R_{t:t+s} = \frac{P_{t+s} - P_t}{P_t} = \frac{P_{t+s}}{P_t} - 1.$$

*This is the dollar amount you gain at time* $t+s$ *relative to your investment at time* $t$, *and is defined for any times* $t, t+s$. *In particular, the one-period gross and net return* $(t = 1, s = 1)$ *are denoted:*

$$\mathcal{R}_2 = \frac{P_2}{P_1}, \quad R_2 = \frac{P_2 - P_1}{P_1}.$$

Return is often quoted (net) in percentages and **annualized** (converted so that the holding period is one year, see below) for easy comparison with bank accounts. Here, we are ignoring the possibility of a dividend payout, which does arise for many stocks on a regular basis, so the return defined above could also be called the **Capital Gain** (or Loss). We will later consider the issue of dividends in more detail. In practice, data providers like Yahoo usually provide an Adjusted Closing Price that takes account of dividends and other adjustments, so one can calculate adjusted returns using this price sequence to take account of interim income payments.

Note that the gross return is always non negative $\mathcal{R}_{t:t+s} \geq 0$, whereas the net return $R_{t:t+s}$ can be positive or negative, although it is bounded from below by $-1$, which says that with limited liability (investing in public companies) since you cannot lose more than your initial investment. Well ok, your dignity also. The realized return is of interest when you come to evaluate the performance of an investment or a potential investment. For some purposes, we like to work with standardized holding periods like daily, weekly, monthly, or annual. Daily returns are calculated from the closing price today and the closing price yesterday (or the last closing price in the event of a holiday or weekend). Weekly returns are usually calculated from Wednesday close to Wednesday close to minimize holiday closings. Monthly returns are usually calendar month from first trading day close to the last trading day close. Annual returns are calculated from the first trading day to last trading day of the year. We usually think in terms of annual returns and in percentages, to help in comparing investments with our standard bank account, which is usually quoted in this way. For most people, 10% per year is a pretty good annual rate of return.

The stock price is denominated in a certain currency, dollars, RMB, etc. If you are investing in foreign stocks, you may want to calculate the price and hence return in your own currency. In that case, you calculate your domestic price equal to the foreign price divided by the exchange rate, before then calculating the return. Alternatively, you can multiply the foreign gross return by the exchange rate growth, i.e., home stock return $\mathcal{R}^H_{t:t+s}$

$$\mathcal{R}^H_{t:t+s} = \frac{E_{t+s}}{E_t} \times \mathcal{R}^F_{t:t+s},$$

where $E_t$ is the exchange rate at time $t$ and $\mathcal{R}^F_{t:t+s}$ is the foreign stock return.

**Example 58** *On January 2nd 2024, the S&P500 index was 4742.83 and on December 30th 2024 it was 5906.94. The sterling dollar rate was 1.2729 on January 2nd and 1.2549 on December 30th. Calculate the return to a UK investor from investing in S&P500 over this time period.*

According to the time value of money, future payments must be discounted back to the present, or past payments should be inflated to the present to make the two prices comparable. For the purposes of comparing returns over different periods, a common practice is to adjust for the **inflation** that has occurred. A simple way of doing this is to divide the nominal stock price by the level of the CPI index to give a real price and then calculate returns using the real stock price. See the exercises for an example calculation.

Finally, taxes are important considerations for investors when realizing their profits. In most countries, capital gains are taxed at a different rate from dividends and other income, and indeed, the rate may vary across individuals. An investor typically cares about the after-tax return unless they also derive some satisfaction from their donated tax dollars.

It is important to emphasize that we are talking here about the realized return observed at time $t + s$. From the investor's point of view at time $t$, this return is uncertain and will occur in the future. In fact, the timing of the future sale is also often not known with certainty, either—for example, you may lose your job and have to cash in your investments to live on. We will consider this issue later.

Finally, we introduce another type of return, which is widely used because of various mathematical advantages.

**Definition 12** *Logarithmic returns (aka continuously compounded returns) are defined as:*

$$r_{t:t+s} = \log(\mathcal{R}_{t:t+s}) = \log(1 + R_{t:t+s}) = \log(P_{t+s}) - \log(P_t) = p_{t+s} - p_t,$$

*where lower-case letters denote logarithmic variables. In particular, the one period logarithmic return is*

$$r_2 = \log\left(1 + R_2\right) = \log\left(\frac{P_2}{P_1}\right) = \log(P_2) - \log(P_1) = p_2 - p_1.$$

Logarithmic returns can take any value in $\mathbb{R}$, whereas returns are bounded away from minus one. Also, logarithmic returns are time additive in the sense that $r_{t:t+s} = r_{t:t+1} + r_{t+1:t+2} + \ldots + r_{t+s-1:t+s}$. Notice that if $R$ is small, $\log(1+R) \simeq R$, and so logarithmic returns $r$ and returns $R$ are approximately the same. On the other hand, when $R$ is big (such as over a long horizon), the two numbers can be quite different. Exercise asks you to compute daily returns and daily logarithmic returns.

### 5.3.2 Compounding

We next consider the issue of compounding of return over multiple periods. We are considering here certain return values, or rather ex post outcomes, so abstracting from the question of uncertainty.

Suppose the (net) return is $R_1$ in period 1 and $R_2$ in period 2. If you invest \$1 at the beginning of period 1, then your capital (gross return) after two periods is

$$(1+R_1)(1+R_2) = 1 + (R_1 + R_2) + \overbrace{R_1 R_2}^{\text{interest on the interest}}.$$

If $R_1 = 5\%$ and $R_2 = 4\%$, then you have after two periods

$$1.05 \times 1.04 = 1 + 0.09 + 0.002 = 1.092.$$

We can define an equivalent single-period rate $R$ that satisfies

$$(1+R)^2 = 1.092.$$

In this case, $R = 1.04498$, which is only slightly less than the average return $(R_1 + R_2)/2 = 4.5\%$, that is, the interest on the interest is very small in this case. You may know 1.04498 as the **geometric mean** of 1.05 and 1.04, that is, $1.04498 = (1.05 \times 1.04)^{1/2}$; know this, that the geometric mean is always lower than the arithmetic mean.

Suppose that we invest for $k$ periods. Then the total return is

$$(1+R_1) \times \cdots \times (1+R_k) = 1 + (R_1 + \cdots + R_k) + R_1 R_2 + \ldots + R_1 \times \cdots \times R_k,$$

and the interest on the interest terms starts to mount up. Suppose that the net return is $R$ every period, then after $k$ periods you have $(1+R)^k$. Your capital grows rapidly with $k$; this is called **compound growth** (or exponential growth). If $R = 0.05$ and $k = 5$, we have

$$(1+R)^k = 1.276,$$

which is a little higher than the sum of returns (linear growth) $1 + (k \times R) = 1.25$. But if $k = 100$,

$$(1+R)^k = 131.501,$$

which is much higher than the sum of returns $1 + (k \times R) = 6$. That is, over the long horizon, the interest on the interest matters a lot and swamps the interest on the original capital.

**Example 59** *How long does it take to double your money? The question is, how big is $k$ such that*

$$(1 + R)^k = 2.$$

*This can be solved by taking logarithms, in which case we have*

$$k = \frac{\ln(2)}{\ln(1 + R)} \simeq \frac{70}{100 \times R}.$$

*If $R = 0.05$, then $k = 14.2$, so it takes slightly more than 14 periods to double your money. If $R = 0.10$, then $k = 7.27$, so doubling takes slightly more than 7 periods.*

**Example 60** *What happens when $R < 0$? For example, suppose that $R = -0.05$, i.e., each period you lose 5% of your capital. Does that mean that after 20 periods, you are bankrupt? This would be the implication of the linear approximation. Not at all, since $0.95^{20} = 0.358$. The losses are compounding on smaller and smaller capitals, so they shrink each period.*

What is long horizon, i.e., when does compounding start to make a big difference? We give an answer based on the so-called **binomial expansion**. This is an exact expression that says for any $R$ and any integer $k$,

$$(1 + R)^k = 1 + kR + \frac{k(k-1)}{2}R^2 + \frac{k(k-1)(k-2)}{3 \times 2}R^3 + \cdots + R^k. \quad (5.3)$$

Roughly speaking, if $kR < 1$ we can approximate $(1 + R)^k$ by $1 + kR$ with reasonable accuracy, but if $kR > 1$, then not. The case $Rk = 1$ is interesting, because then $(1 + 1/k)^k \to e \simeq 2.718$ (Eulers e) as $k \to \infty$.

#### 5.3.2.1 Exponential Versus Linear Growth

We give an aside about Exponential growth and its well-known economic implications over the long term, which were noted in the classic essay of Thomas Malthus (1798). In this essay, he predicted a catastrophe based on the observed exponential growth of population compared with the apparent linear growth of food production during his lifetime. In Figure 5.9 we show an example to illustrate the disparity. This argument was repeated in Robert Ehrlich (1969), where he argued that we were heading for mass famine and war. None of this ever happened, or did it? The point here is the far-reaching implication of exponential (or compound) growth over a long period of time unless there is some attenuation.

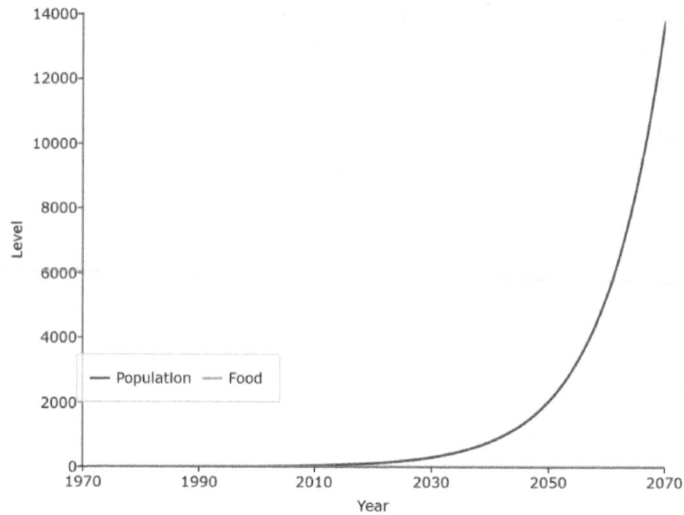


**FIGURE 5.9**
Exponential (compound) versus linear growth

### 5.3.3 Converting Returns Over Different Horizons

We next consider two tasks that are useful for the purpose of comparison and description. (1) Convert a daily return to an annual return; (2) Convert a longer-horizon return to an annual return.

Suppose we have a daily return $R_{daily}$, we convert to an annual return $R_{annual}$ by the following formula

$$1 + R_{annual} = (1 + R_{daily})^{255},$$

where 255 is the approximate number of trading days minus one in a year (some authors use 252 or 250). This is just compounding the daily return over the longer horizon.

Suppose that we have some multiperiod return and we want to convert it to the single-period return that is consistent with it, then we just reverse the process. For example, converting an annual return to a daily return proceeds as follows

$$1 + R_{daily} = (1 + R_{annual})^{1/255}.$$

Suppose that we have daily returns $R_1, R_2, \ldots, R_{255}$ observed in a year, then the annual return can be explicitly defined as

$$\mathcal{R}_{year} = (1 + R_1)(1 + R_2) \times \cdots \times (1 + R_{255}).$$

This is the same as the direct definition $P_{255}/P_0$, since

$$\frac{P_{255}}{P_0} = \frac{P_1}{P_0} \times \frac{P_2}{P_1} \times \cdots \times \frac{P_{255}}{P_{254}} = \mathcal{R}_{year} = 1 + R_{year}.$$

That is, the two definitions are identical. There are 255 one-day returns and only one yearly return.

For logarithmic returns, we have

$$r_{annual} = \log(1+R_{annual}) = \log((1+R_{daily})^{255}) = 255\times\log(1+R_{daily}) = 255\times r_{daily}$$

$$r_{daily} = \frac{r_{annual}}{255}.$$

Conversion is much simpler for logarithmic returns because of their time additivity.

**Example 61** *The S&P500 index was 17.03 on 19500110 and was 1842.37 on 20140110*

$$\mathcal{R}_{19500110:20140110} = \frac{1842.37}{17.03} = 108.18$$

$$R_{19500110:20140110} = \frac{1842.37 - 17.03}{17.03} = 107.18,$$

*which delivers an annual return of 7.6%, since*

$$108.18^{1/64} - 1 = 0.076.$$

*For comparison, the long horizon logarithmic returns,*

$$r_{19500110:20140110} = \log(1842.37) - \log(17.03) = 4.684$$

*are quite different, but they deliver a very similar annual return of 7.3%, since* $4.684/64 = 0.073$. *The current level of S&P500 4544.90 (22/10/2021).*

**Example 62** *The Argentinian stock market index MERVAL was 590 on 19961008 and was 1796920 on 20240904, yielding a gross return of 3045.63 over the 28 years, which corresponds to 33% annual net return.*

### 5.3.4 Statistical Properties of Daily Returns

We mostly consider daily returns when it comes to statistical calculations because there are many of them! Each day we observe (closing) prices $P_1, P_2, \ldots$ and from that we calculate the daily net returns $R_1, R_2, \ldots$ (we simplify the notation here), which forms a time series. We next show the time series of daily returns on the S&P500 over the period 1927-2021. The key feature is that daily returns are almost equally likely to be negative as to be positive, that is, you are almost equally likely to lose money on a daily horizon as you are to gain. Also note the main episodes here, the stock market boom and crash of the 1920s and 1930s, the October 1987 crash, which is the single worst day in the stock market, the Global Financial Crisis of 2008/2009, and the COVID-19 spike in March of 2020.

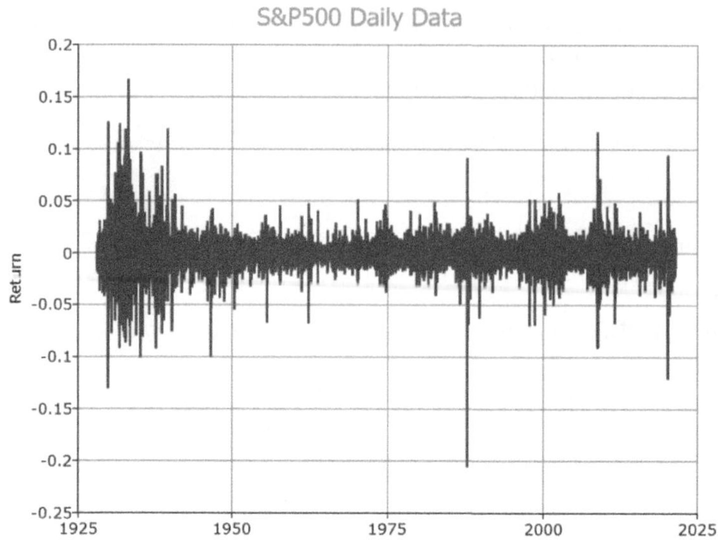


**FIGURE 5.10**
S&P500 daily returns

#### 5.3.4.1 What is the Expected Daily Return on the Market?

Suppose that we treat daily returns as normally distributed with unknown $\mu$ and variance $\sigma^2$. That is, each daily return is a random draw from this population. We have a sample of daily returns $\{R_1, \ldots, R_n\}$ on the S&P500 index from 1927-2020. We estimate $\mu, \sigma^2$ from the sample of data. We obtain:

$$\overline{R} = 0.00037152345, \quad s = 0.011332722, \quad \text{stderr} = \frac{s}{\sqrt{n}}.$$

So the 95% confidence interval for $\mu$ is

$$\overline{R} \pm 1.96 \times \text{stderr} = [0.000126, 0.000617].$$

This interval does not include zero. This says that the population expected return $\mu$ is positive with high confidence, which is what we expect if people are risk-averse.

Daily returns are small and hard to interpret, which is why we prefer to convert to an annualized figure. To annualize the returns, we may compute the annualized average daily mean as

$$(1.00037152345)^{255} = 1.099,$$

which is around 10% per year. It seems that linear approximation works pretty well in this case because the average daily return is small and the condition $kR < 1$ is easily satisfied. Note that for logarithmic returns, mean annual returns are exactly 255 times mean daily returns, and the variance of annual

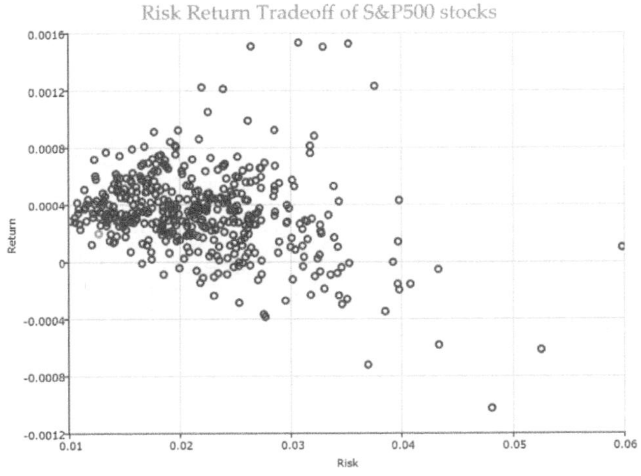


**FIGURE 5.11**
Risk return tradeoff for individual S&P500 stocks from 2005 to 2015

returns is exactly 255 times the variance of daily returns. As a result, it is common practice to multiply $\mu$ and $\sigma^2$ by 255, then we obtain the means and standard deviations in annualized percentage units

$$\text{mean} = (1.00037152345 - 1) \times 255 \times 100 = 9.48\%$$

$$\text{stdev} = 0.011332722 \times \sqrt{255} \times 100 = 18.1\%.$$

This has been called the 10 and 20 rule for stock returns. We can push this argument further by calculating the confidence interval for annual percentage returns as follows

$$(25500 \times \overline{R}) \pm 1.96 \times \sqrt{25500} \times \text{stderr} = \; [5.8\%, 13.1\%].$$

#### 5.3.4.2 What is the Expected Daily Return on Individual Stocks?

We next consider the risk-return trade-off for individual stocks, for 441 stocks from the S&P500 over the period 2005-2015. This was not a good period for the US stock market, and many of these stocks had negative returns over this period as we see in Figure 5.11. The red dot is the S&P5000 index, which has relatively low risk, but is not the least risky of the assets on display over that period.

In practice, we use historical information (sample of data) about returns to measure the risk-return trade-off. How confident are we in our measurements of risk and return? We next show in Figure 5.12 the confidence intervals for the mean daily return for all 441 stocks. The stocks are ordered by sample mean, with the largest mean stocks first and the smallest mean stocks last. The figure shows that for many stocks the confidence interval includes zero, so that the answer to the question above is—not very!

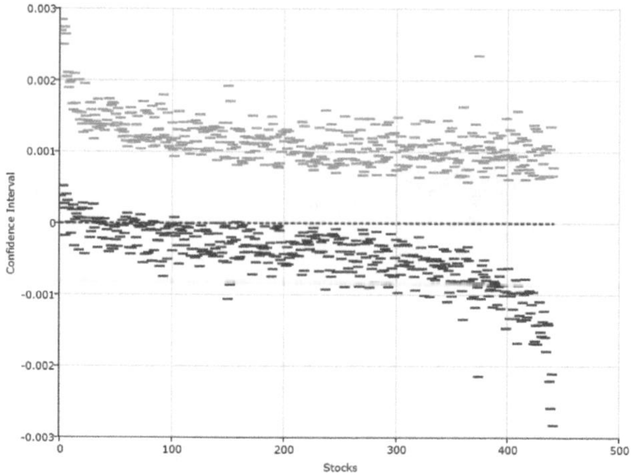


**FIGURE 5.12**
Confidence intervals for the mean of individual stocks

This calculation was based on 2005-2015 data. As an investor, we care about future performance. Will the future performance be roughly the same as the past performance? This is what an investor cares about, or at least about being able to predict future performance. Can we do better in terms of predicting future performance than just looking at the historical average? We will consider this issue in a later chapter.

We next consider some different asset classes beyond the stock market.

**Example 63** *We show the risk-return trade-off for some well-known tech stocks since their initial listing. There is a significant positive relationship.*

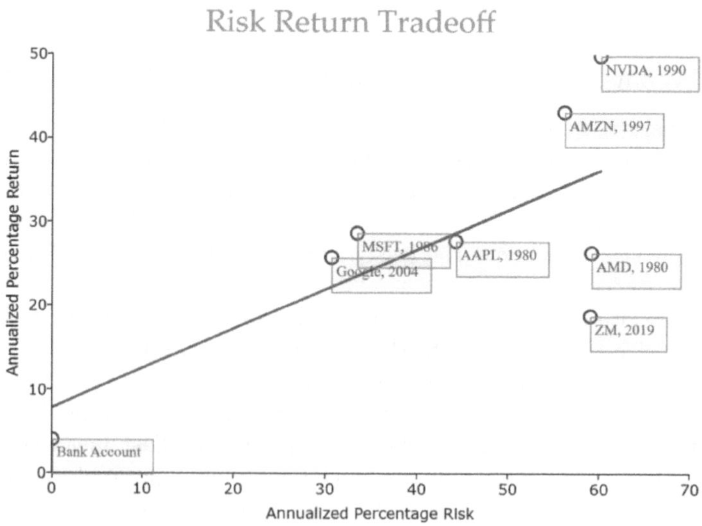

**FIGURE 5.13**
Monthly wheat price

## 5.4 Other Asset Classes

### 5.4.1 Commodities

Commodities play an important role in manufacturing and agriculture. Commodity trading in the US takes place primarily in Chicago at the CME. There are also specialized metal exchanges such as London Metal Exchange, etc. There are some special features of commodity markets due to storage issues (if you buy 100 tons of copper, you better be able to store it somewhere). The wheat price on a monthly basis is shown in Figure 5.13. From prices, we can calculate their percentage change, returns, as we call them. This commodity has monthly average returns and standard deviation: $\overline{R} = 0.0038984119$ and $s = 0.067318926$. On an annual basis, the mean return is around 2% per year increase, which is low compared with the stock market.

### 5.4.2 Foreign Exchange

The wholesale market for foreign exchange (FX) is dominated by big banks and big traders. A lot of the market is OTC (over the counter), involving human-to-human trading on behalf of large banks. There are also electronic trading venues, rather like stock exchanges (albeit with longer hours). The US dollar represents 88.3% of all foreign exchange transactions. The behavior of exchange rates is somewhat different from stock prices. For example, the Yen/dollar exchange rate is shown in Figure 5.14 over the period 1996-2022. Exchange rates are relative prices, and typically they do not show strong trends (except currencies like the Argentinian Peso, where inflation is high),

**FIGURE 5.14**
Daily yen/dollar exchange rate

and technically one can almost say that the rate itself is stationary. Nevertheless, we usually work with their percentage changes or returns.

In this case, we find:

$$\overline{R} = 0.000005203, \quad s = 0.00737, \quad \text{stderr} = \frac{s}{\sqrt{n}}.$$

The mean daily return is much smaller than the stock market index and indeed the 95% confidence interval for $\mu$ is

$$\overline{R} \pm 1.96 \times \text{stderr} = [-0.00012474677, 0.00022880481].$$

This does include zero, so we cannot reject the hypothesis that the true mean is actually zero. For this currency, over this time period, the mean annual percentage return is around 0.133% with a standard deviation around 11.77%.

### 5.4.3 Cryptocurrencies

There are many organized exchanges that allow registered users to trade Bitcoin, Ethereum, and other cryptocurrencies. These exchanges are generally open 24/365, i.e., open over the weekends, national holidays, and so on. Partly this is because the market for Bitcoin is global and does not respect New York office hours. It is also the case that settlement of trades in Bitcoin is at the speed of the internet (or, in the case of FTX, the speed of the US legal system), whereas stock market settlement takes days.

The Bitcoin price was \$457.33 on 20140917 and was \$64071.57 on 20240506, which gives an annual return of around 63.9%. For Bitcoin from 2014-2024 the average daily return and standard deviation were

$$\overline{R} = 0.00209, \quad s = 0.0368.$$

The mean daily return is larger than on the stock market index but the standard deviation is also three times larger. The 95% confidence interval for $\mu$ in percentage terms is

$$\overline{R} \pm 1.96 \times \text{stderr} = [-0.070038, 0.074218],$$

which does not include zero. Returns on crypto have been higher but also bear more risk than the stock market index. For crypto, we have 365 trading days per year so the mean annual percentage return is around 76.29% (remember 365 trading days per year for Bitcoin) with a standard deviation around 70.31%.

### 5.4.4 UK House Prices

Houses are the primary component of household wealth in many countries, and so are important assets. They also deliver a flow of services to families that occupy them. We show the quarterly house prices series for the UK from 1952 to 2021 in Figure 5.15. This shows a substantial upward trend just like the stock market index. We may calculate return on the index as we do for other assets, shown in Figure 5.16. In this case, we find

$$\overline{R} = 0.0154, \quad s = 0.0212,$$

and a confidence interval for the mean quarterly return is

$$[0.0154, 0.0212],$$

which does not include zero. On an annualized percentage basis, the mean is 6.16% and the standard deviation 4.24%.

## 5.5 Key Points

1. In fixed income markets, the key concept is present discounted value, which allows you to calculate the cumulative value of all future cash flows and hence determine the appropriate price of an asset with future promises.
2. Compound growth is a very powerful force for long-term investing.
3. In the stock market, the additional issue of uncertainty/risk enters into consideration. The stock market makes a higher return on average than the bond market, but with higher risk.

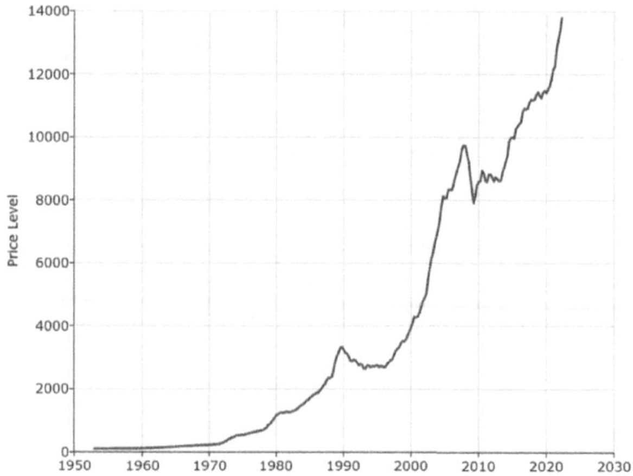


**FIGURE 5.15**
Quarterly house price index

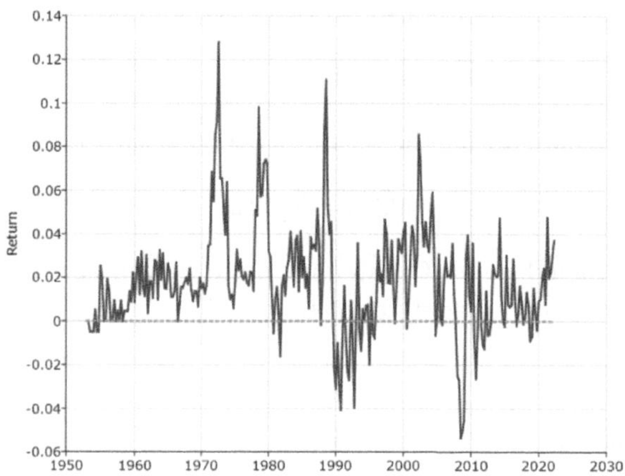


**FIGURE 5.16**
Quarterly return on house prices

## 5.6 Exercises

1. Suppose that in the first period I earn (net) return $R$ and the second period, I earn $-R$, then derive the compounded return and show that I have lost money. Now repeat this $k$ times and show that as $k \to \infty$ I lose all my capital.

2. Suppose that a bond pays a coupon of \$5 every year for 19 years and then pays \$100 at maturity (after 20 years). Recall that when $P = 120$ the yield to maturity $R$ must satisfy

$$120 = \frac{5}{R}\left(1 - \left(\frac{1}{1+R}\right)^{19}\right) + \frac{100}{(1+R)^{20}}.$$

Write this equation as a 20th-order polynomial in $R$, i.e., an equation of the form $f(R) = 0$. Solve this equation numerically by the Newton-Raphson method.

3. The **carry trade** is defined as follows: buy foreign currency and put it in a foreign bank to earn interest (at the foreign rate $r_{ft}^A$) and then at the end of the period convert the total back to domestic. This can be compared with leaving money in a domestic bank and earning domestic interest $r_{ft}^H$. For example. I borrow \$1000 at 5% in the US and convert to Foreign currency at 100:1 rate so F10,000. I earn 10% on a foreign bank account, so capital grows to F11,000. If the exchange rate stays the same, my F11,000 is converted to \$1100, and I have to pay \$1050 back to the US bank for a profit of \$50. If the exchange rate goes up to 110:1, then my F11,000 is converted to \$1000, and I have to pay \$1050 back to the US bank for a loss of \$50. If the exchange rate goes down to 50:1, then my F11,000 is converted to \$5500, and I have to pay \$1050 back to the US bank for a gain of \$4450. Discuss the risks involved with the carry trade.

4. For daily S&P500 stock data calculate returns $R_t$ and logarithmic returns $r_t$ and compare the two series.

5. Suppose that $P(t)$ is the stock market level in the US at time $t$, $I_{US}(t)$ is the level of the consumer price index in the US at time $t$, $E(t)$ is the exchange rate between US dollars and pounds sterling at time $t$, and $I_{UK}(t)$ is the level of the consumer price index in the UK at time $t$. Calculate: (a) The real stock market return in US dollars between $t$ and $t+s$; (b) The US nominal stock market return in UK pounds dollars between $t$ and $t+s$; (c) The real stock market return in UK pounds between $t$ and $t+s$.

6. Suppose that a stock has price $P_0 = 100$ at the beginning of the year, $P_1 = 105$ at the end of the first quarter, $P_2 = 110$ at the end of the second quarter, $P_3 = 115$ at the end of the third quarter, and $P_4 = 115$ at the end of the year. The stock pays a quarterly dividend of 1% (of the price at the beginning of the quarter) at the end of each quarter, e.g., it pays out \$1 at the end of the first quarter. Calculate the capital gain of the stock over the whole year. Calculate the total return over the whole year using the ladder method, that is, calculate the total return for each quarter separately and then

multiply out. For example, the total return for the first quarter is

$$\frac{P_1 + D_1}{P_0} = 1.06.$$

7. Suppose that we have gross returns $\mathcal{R}_1, \mathcal{R}_2 \ldots, \mathcal{R}_n$. We may define the average return as either the Geometric mean, the Arithmetic mean, or the Harmonic mean:

$$\overline{\mathcal{R}}_G = \left( \prod_{i=1}^{n} \mathcal{R}_i \right)^{1/n}, \tag{5.4}$$

$$\overline{\mathcal{R}} = \frac{1}{n} \sum_{i=1}^{n} \mathcal{R}_i. \tag{5.5}$$

$$\overline{\mathcal{R}}_H = \frac{n}{\sum_{i=1}^{n} \frac{1}{\mathcal{R}_i}}. \tag{5.6}$$

In fact it can be proved that

$$\overline{\mathcal{R}}_H \leq \overline{\mathcal{R}}_G \leq \overline{\mathcal{R}}$$

for any data series where $\mathcal{R}_i \geq 0$ for all $i$ (just try a few numbers to convince yourself). Calculate the three different averages for daily stock returns.

# 6

# *Portfolio Choice*

## Outline

This chapter focuses on the principles and techniques of portfolio construction and management. It addresses key questions related to investment choices, risk-return trade-offs, and the optimization of portfolios to maximize utility based on individual risk preferences. The chapter introduces the mean-variance analysis framework and explores various portfolio strategies.

After reading this chapter, you will be able to:

- Grasp the concept of portfolio choice and its role in investment management.
- Apply mean-variance analysis to evaluate and optimize investment portfolios.
- Construct and analyze portfolios with one risky and one riskless asset, two risky assets, and multiple risky assets.
- Understand the market portfolio and its significance within modern portfolio theory.
- Implement practical aspects of portfolio construction, including rebalancing and transaction costs.
- Measure and evaluate portfolio performance using time series data and various performance metrics.

There are many traded stocks as well as fixed income investments with different risk/return profiles, which investment should you choose? How should we combine investments into a portfolio to improve our risk/return trade-off? We address these questions in this chapter.

We assume that investors like return (or rather expected return) and dislike risk (measured by variance or standard deviation). Often, these objectives are in conflict, and one has to trade off one against the other. One approach is to work with a utility function $U$ that reflects our preferences over risk and return and choose the combination of investments that gives us the best utility payoff. It is very convenient, in fact, to work with the so-called mean variance preferences, which are defined over a random outcome $X$ as

$$U = E(X) - \gamma \text{var}(X), \tag{6.1}$$

DOI: 10.1201/9781003543121-6

where $\gamma$ is a parameter representing the degree of risk aversion (some authors replace $\gamma$ by $\gamma/2$).[1] Utility $U$ increases with $E(X)$ and decreases with $\mathrm{var}(X)$; the parameter $\gamma$ controls the degree of risk aversion: larger $\gamma$ denotes more risk averse, $\gamma = 0$ is risk neutral. Since $U$ is a scalar, it can be used to rank individual stocks. The utility function defines indifference curves that represent a personal risk-return trade-off in terms of $\mu, \sigma$. Specifically, the indifference curve $I_u$ at some level of utility $U = u$ is defined as a set of points that give equal utility

$$I_u = \left\{(\mu, \sigma^2) : \mu = \gamma\sigma^2 + u\right\}. \tag{6.2}$$

This set of points can be represented in mean-variance space as a straight line, but in mean/standard deviation space, it is a shifted quadratic curve. One could be indifferent between a high return and high-risk investment and a low-return but low-risk investment. The ranking of assets depends on $\gamma$ of course. In practice, we don't know $\mu, \sigma$ and we rely on estimates of these quantities from historical data, the sample mean $\overline{X}$ and the sample standard deviation $s$. In the sequel, we will ignore this issue.

In Figure 6.1, we plot the risk-return scatter for the sample mean and standard deviations calculated over 2020 for the 5 largest tech stocks, called the Fab5.

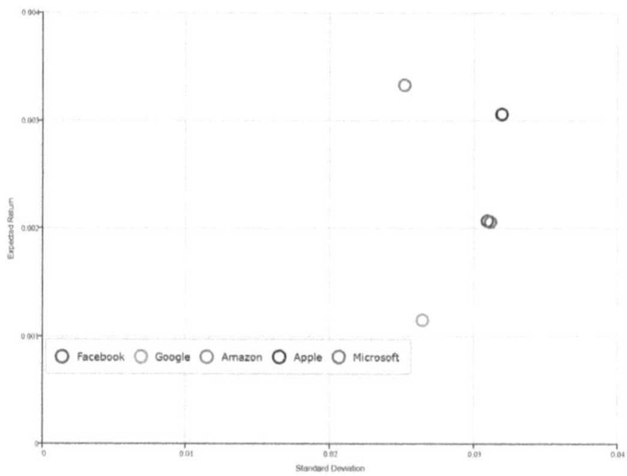


**FIGURE 6.1**
Risk/return trade-off for daily returns on five tech stocks in 2020

We next show the value of $U = E(R) - \gamma\mathrm{var}(R)$ for the Fab5 during 2020 for different values of $\gamma$. Clearly, Amazon is the best for all $\gamma$, but who is second best depends on the attitude to risk. For high risk tolerance (low $\gamma$) Apple comes second, while for low risk tolerance (high $\gamma$) Google comes second.

[1]Note that the units of $U$ are irrelevant. One can add any constant to $U$ or multiply by a positive constant without changing any ranking it delivers.

| Company/$\gamma$ | 0 | 1 | 2 | 5 | 10 |
|---|---|---|---|---|---|
| **Facebook** | 0.00207 | 0.00111 | 0.00016 | −0.00272 | −0.00750 |
| **Google** | 0.00115 | 0.00045 | −0.00025 | −0.00235 | −0.00584 |
| **Amazon** | 0.00333 | 0.00269 | 0.00206 | 0.00016 | −0.00301 |
| **Apple** | 0.00306 | 0.00204 | 0.00102 | −0.00204 | −0.00714 |
| **Microsoft** | 0.00206 | 0.00109 | 0.00012 | −0.00279 | −0.00764 |

An alternative popular approach to portfolio choice is to choose $X$ to

$$\min \text{var}(X) \quad s.t. \; E(X) \geq T, \tag{6.3}$$

where $T$ is some given target return. In this particular case, since Amazon has the highest mean and the smallest variance, it would be chosen in any case where the level of $T$ makes the choice feasible.

We show that one can do better by combining stocks into portfolios, i.e., by putting some capital in each stock. Specifically, diversification improves the risk-return trade-off, meaning that for any given level of risk, one can obtain a higher return, or conversely, for any given level of return, one can obtain lower risk. This allows one to achieve higher utility than by investing in single stocks.

## 6.1 Mean Variance Analysis

Suppose that we have two assets whose future payoffs are uncertain, i.e., they are random variables. Let $X, Y$ denote the payoffs and let $\mu_X = E(X)$, $\mu_Y = E(Y)$, $\sigma_X^2 = \text{var}(X)$, and $\sigma_Y^2 = \text{var}(Y)$.We suppose that $X$ and $Y$ are independent random variables or at least are uncorrelated. Mathematically, there are two general cases: we may have a dominant asset where $\mu_X > \mu_Y$ and $\sigma_X^2 < \sigma_Y^2$, or not, i.e., we may have $\mu_X > \mu_Y$ and $\sigma_X^2 > \sigma_Y^2$. In 2020, Amazon was the dominant asset among all the Fab5. It had a higher mean return and lower variance, but this has not been so in 2021, as the following table shows. If one had to choose one of these five stocks to invest in, then clearly, for this period, Amazon is the best. Who is second and third, etc., depends on the risk-return trade-off.

| Company | $\mu$ | $\sigma$ |
|---|---|---|
| **Facebook** | 0.0011924235 | 0.018668071 |
| **Google** | 0.0022408756 | 0.015002493 |
| **Amazon** | 0.00039256421 | 0.015205556 |
| **Apple** | 0.0014404513 | 0.015845015 |
| **Microsoft** | 0.0019017518 | 0.013259819 |

We will show how to construct a portfolio of $X$ and $Y$ that has higher mean and lower variance than the individual stocks. For calculation, it is simpler to work with some special cases to start with (two assets only is a major simplification, we also relax that later). The special case where $\mu_X = \mu_Y$ is of interest. The special case where $\sigma_X^2 = \sigma_Y^2$ is of interest. The special case where $\sigma_Y^2 = 0$ (i.e., where one asset is riskless) is of interest.

A portfolio of assets $X$ and $Y$ has a payoff that is a linear combination of the payoffs of the underlying assets, i.e.,

$$\mathcal{P} = w_X X + w_Y Y, \tag{6.4}$$

where $w_X$ is the amount invested in asset $X$ and $w_Y$ is the amount invested in asset $Y$. Here, $\mathcal{P}$ is the random payoff of the portfolio. We suppose that

$$w_X + w_Y = 1,$$

that is, the total amount available is one unit, and it is divided into $X$ and $Y$ with no leftovers. For example, $w_X = 1/2$ and $w_Y = 1/2$ is called the equally weighted portfolio. We consider how to choose the weights. We substitute out $w_Y$ and write

$$\mathcal{P} = wX + (1 - w)Y \tag{6.5}$$

where $w = w_X$ is the weighting on asset $X$. Note that $w \in \mathbb{R}$. If $w \in (0, 1)$ i.e., $0 < w < 1$, then a positive fractional weight is put on each asset. On the other hand, if $w > 1$, then $1 - w < 0$. In this case, the asset $Y$ is **shorted**, that is, it is sold, whereas asset $X$ is overbought relative to initial capital. In practice, shorting can be difficult or expensive, or illegal to carry out.

### 6.1.1 One Risky and One Riskless Asset

We first consider the case where $Y$ is the riskless asset and has certain payoff $r_f$, while $X$ is a risky asset with random payoff whose mean is $\mu$ and whose variance is $\sigma^2$. We suppose that $\mu > r_f$. It follows by direct calculation using the properties of mean and variance that:

$$\mu_{\mathcal{P}} = E(\mathcal{P}) = w\mu + (1 - w)r_f = r_f + w \overbrace{(\mu - r_f)}^{\text{risk premium}}$$

$$\sigma_{\mathcal{P}}^2 = \text{var}(\mathcal{P}) = w^2\sigma^2, \quad \sigma_{\mathcal{P}} = \text{stdev}(\mathcal{P}) = |w|\sigma.$$

The portfolio mean is a linear function of $w$, and the portfolio variance is a quadratic function of $w$. If $w \in (0, 1)$ i.e., $0 < w < 1$, then a positive fractional weight is put on each asset, and the variance of the portfolio is less than the variance of the risky asset. On the other hand, if $w > 1$, then $1 - w < 0$. In this case, you are borrowing at the riskless rate to put extra investment into the risky asset, which is called a leveraged position, which would have higher risk and higher return than the risky asset itself.

**Example 64** *If $w = 1$ (100% invested in risky asset), then $\mu_{\mathcal{P}} = \mu$ and $\sigma^2_{\mathcal{P}} = \sigma^2$, if $w = 2$ (borrow 100% and invest 200% in risky asset), then $\mu_{\mathcal{P}} = 2\mu - r_f$ and $\sigma^2_{\mathcal{P}} = 4\sigma^2$, while if $w = 3$ (borrow 200% and invest 300% in risky asset), then $\mu_{\mathcal{P}} = 3\mu - 2r_f$ and $\sigma^2_{\mathcal{P}} = 9\sigma^2$.*

The mean variance utility is a quadratic function of $w$

$$U = r_f + w(\mu - r_f) - \frac{1}{2}\gamma w^2 \sigma^2.$$

To maximize with respect to $w$ we compute the first order condition and set it to zero

$$\frac{\partial U}{\partial w} = (\mu - r_f) - \gamma w \sigma^2.$$

The second order condition is satisfied here because $\partial^2 U/\partial w^2 = -\gamma\sigma^2 < 0$ provided $\gamma > 0$. The first order condition solves for

$$\boxed{w_{opt} = \frac{1}{\gamma}\frac{\mu - r_f}{\sigma^2} = \frac{1}{\gamma\sigma}\frac{\mu - r_f}{\sigma}}.$$

**Example 65** *For S&P500 daily data:* $\mu = 0.00030575$, $\sigma = 0.011979$

$$w_{opt} = \frac{1}{\gamma} \times 2.8928$$

*Therefore, if* $\gamma = 5$, *then you should put approximately* 60% *in the stock market and* 40% *in the bond market.*

Note that if $w > 1$, the portfolio involves borrowing at the riskless rate, making it a leveraged investment. This happens when $\gamma < (\mu - r_f)/\sigma^2$.

In Figure 6.2 we show the feasible set of risk/return outcomes that can be achieved, which is a straight line in mean/standard deviation space.

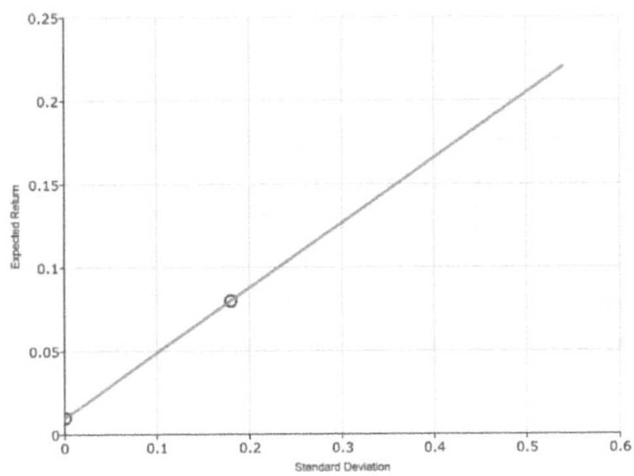


**FIGURE 6.2**
Feasible set of portfolios with one risky asset and one riskless. S&P500 plus riskless asset (annual returns)

The final portfolio has a mean and a variance

$$\mu_{\mathcal{P}} = r_f + \frac{1}{\gamma}\frac{(\mu - r_f)^2}{\sigma^2}, \quad \sigma^2_{\mathcal{P}} = \frac{1}{\gamma^2}\left(\frac{\mu - r_f}{\sigma^2}\right)^2 \sigma^2.$$

Note that the mean and the standard deviation of the portfolio are related in a quadratic way, i.e., we have $\mu_{\mathcal{P}} = r_f + \gamma\sigma^2_{\mathcal{P}}$.

A lot of investors work with the Sharpe Ratio criterion function instead of the mean variance utility function, which we may define here as

$$\boxed{SR = \frac{E(\mathcal{P}) - r_f}{\text{stdev}(\mathcal{P})}}. \tag{6.6}$$

In this case, regardless of $w$, $SR = (\mu - r_f)/\sigma$. The Sharpe Ratio is not useful in this case for distinguishing between $w$. Nevertheless, it can be interpreted as the risk-adjusted return of the portfolio to make further comparisons.

### 6.1.2 Portfolio of Two Risky Assets

We now suppose that both $X, Y$ are risky, i.e., both asset payoffs have a positive variance. We calculate the mean and variance of the portfolio whose outcome is $\mathcal{P}$. This calculation uses the properties of mean and variance we discussed earlier.

**Calculation of the Mean.** We have

$$\mu_{\mathcal{P}} = E(\mathcal{P}) = w\mu_X + (1 - w)\mu_Y$$

If $\mu_X = \mu_Y$, then $\mu_{\mathcal{P}} = \mu_X = \mu_Y$, the portfolio has the same mean as the individual assets no matter what value $w$ takes. If $\mu_X \neq \mu_Y$, then by changing $w$ we can obtain $\mu_{\mathcal{P}}$ equal to any value in $\mathbb{R}$ if $w$ varies over all $\mathbb{R}$. If $\mu_X > \mu_Y$, then we can write

$$\mu_{\mathcal{P}} = \mu_Y + w(\mu_X - \mu_Y)$$

and the mean of the portfolio increases linearly with the weight $w$. If $w \to \infty$, then $\mu_{\mathcal{P}} \to \infty$. On the other hand, if $\mu_X < \mu_Y$, then we can write $\mu_{\mathcal{P}} = \mu_X + (1 - w)(\mu_Y - \mu_X)$, and the mean of the portfolio increases linearly with $1 - w$ i.e., decreases linearly with $w$. If $w \to -\infty$, then $\mu_{\mathcal{P}} \to \infty$. This is a mathematical promise that is hard to realize.

**Calculation of the variance.** We have (because $\text{var}(cX) = c^2\text{var}(X)$ and independence)

$$\sigma^2_{\mathcal{P}} = \text{var}(\mathcal{P}) = w^2\sigma^2_X + (1 - w)^2\sigma^2_Y = w^2(\sigma^2_X + \sigma^2_Y) + \sigma^2_Y - 2w\sigma^2_Y.$$

This is a quadratic function of $w$. In the special case $\sigma^2_X = \sigma^2_Y = \sigma^2$, we have

$$\sigma^2_{\mathcal{P}} = \sigma^2(w^2 + (1 - w)^2).$$

What happens to $\sigma_{\mathcal{P}}^2$ as we vary $w$? We plot below the case $\sigma^2 = 1$ only showing $w \in [0, 1]$

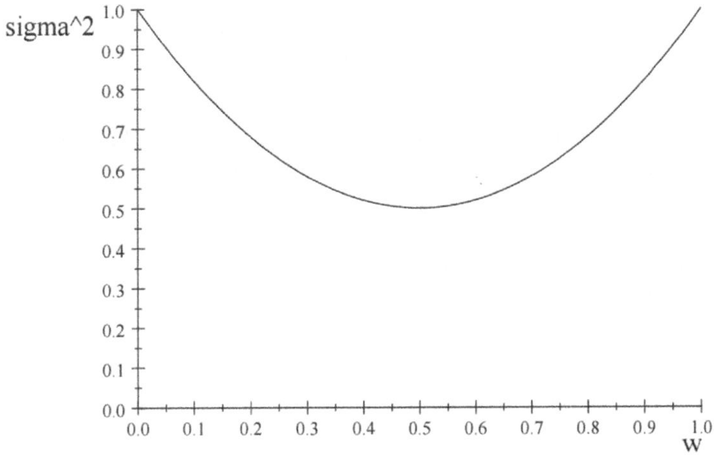


For any $w > 1$ or $w < 0$, the variance of the portfolio is greater than the variance of the individual assets. For any $w$ such that $0 \leq w \leq 1$, the portfolio variance is reduced. There is a unique minimum at the point $w = 1/2$ in which case

$$\sigma_{\mathcal{P}}^2 = \frac{\sigma^2}{2}.$$

That is, by allocating 50/50 you reduce the variance by one half. If the means are the same, $\mu_X = \mu_Y$, then the portfolio with $w = 1/2$ should be strictly preferred by any risk-averse investor over $w = 0$ or $w = 1$. This is the **benefit of diversification**. "Let every man divide his money into three parts, and invest a third in land, a third in business, and a third let him keep by him in reserve." Talmud.

In general, both the mean and the variance of $\mathcal{P}$ are affected by the choice of $w$, the mean is affected linearly, and the variance is affected quadratically, we repeat:

$$\mu_{\mathcal{P}} = \mu_Y + w(\mu_X - \mu_Y) \tag{6.7}$$

$$\sigma_{\mathcal{P}}^2 = (\sigma_X^2 + \sigma_Y^2)w^2 - 2w\sigma_Y^2 + \sigma_Y^2. \tag{6.8}$$

The value of $w$ uniquely determines $\mu_{\mathcal{P}}$ and $\sigma_{\mathcal{P}}^2$, so implicitly there is a one to one relationship between $\sigma_{\mathcal{P}}^2, \mu_{\mathcal{P}}$. As $w$ varies, we obtain different portfolios with implied means and variances.

How to choose which portfolio to invest in? Suppose that we take the mean variance objective function $U(\mathcal{P}) = E(\mathcal{P}) - \gamma \text{var}(\mathcal{P})$ for some parameter $\gamma$. Since the portfolio is defined by the weight $w$, in this case we maximize

$$U(w) = \mu_Y + w(\mu_X - \mu_Y) - \frac{1}{2}\gamma\left((\sigma_X^2 + \sigma_Y^2)w^2 - 2w\sigma_Y^2 + \sigma_Y^2\right)$$

with respect to $w \in \mathbb{R}$. This can be found from the first order condition

$$\frac{\partial U(w)}{\partial w} = (\mu_X - \mu_Y) - \gamma\left((\sigma_X^2 + \sigma_Y^2)w - \sigma_Y^2\right) = 0,$$

$$\boxed{w_{opt} = \frac{\mu_X - \mu_Y}{\gamma(\sigma_X^2 + \sigma_Y^2)} + \frac{\sigma_Y^2}{\sigma_X^2 + \sigma_Y^2}}.$$

The second order condition is satisfied provided $\gamma > 0$. The optimal weight increases with $\mu_X - \mu_Y$, decreases with $\gamma$ (provided $\mu_X > \mu_Y$), and decreases with $\sigma_X^2$.

The feasible set of portfolios is the set of implied portfolio means and portfolio standard deviations as $w$ varies throughout $\mathbb{R}$. In particular, this is a curve or set in $\mathbb{R}^2$

$$\text{Feasible Set}: \quad \{(\sigma_{\mathcal{P}}, \mu_{\mathcal{P}}) : w \in \mathbb{R}\} \subset \mathbb{R}^2.$$

This is clearly a strict subset of $\mathbb{R}^2$.

**Example 66** *Lets suppose that* $\mu_X = 2$, $\mu_Y = 1$, $\sigma_X^2 = 2$, $\sigma_Y^2 = 1$, *then*

$$\mu_{\mathcal{P}} = 1 + w, \quad \sigma_{\mathcal{P}}^2 = 3w^2 + 1 - 2w.$$

*The feasible set is* $\{(\sigma_{\mathcal{P}}, \mu_{\mathcal{P}}) : w \in \mathbb{R}\}$, *which can be drawn as a parabola in* $(\sigma_{\mathcal{P}}, \mu_{\mathcal{P}})$, *i.e.,*

$$\sigma_{\mathcal{P}}^2 - 3(\mu_{\mathcal{P}} - 1)^2 - 1 + 2(\mu_{\mathcal{P}} - 1) = 0.$$

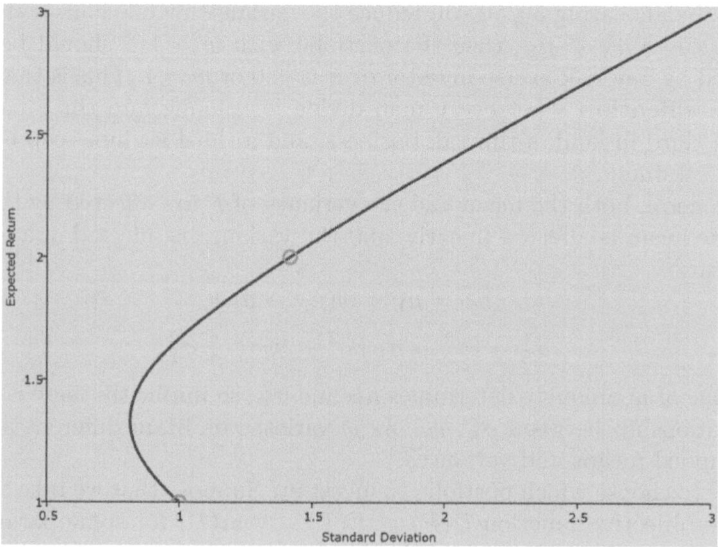


**FIGURE 6.3**
The feasible set

The utility of the portfolio in the example is

$$U(w) = 1 + w - \gamma\left(3w^2 + 1 - 2w\right)$$

for any $w \in \mathbb{R}$. In the special cases ($w = 1$ and $w = 0$) we have $U(X) = 2 - 2\gamma, U(Y) = 1 - \gamma$. For this case $X$ is preferred to $Y$ if and only if $2 - 2\gamma > 1 - \gamma$, i.e., $\gamma < 1$. For individuals with $\gamma = 1$, these two assets yield identical utility, zero. Recall that $w = 0$ corresponds to $Y$ and $w = 1$ corresponds to $X$. The fundamental property of optimization is that you can do better with more choice (this does not apply to subway sandwiches). That is, we must be able to choose $w$ that delivers higher $U$ than either $w = 0$ or $w = 1$ since we are allowed to choose these cases if they are truly the best.

We effectively have to choose a point on the feasible set drawn above that maximizes the utility. The first order condition is

$$1 - 6\gamma w + 2\gamma = 0 \Longrightarrow \boxed{w_{opt} = \frac{1 + 2\gamma}{6\gamma} = \frac{1}{3} + \frac{1}{6\gamma}} \tag{6.9}$$

and the second order condition is $-6\gamma < 0$, so that $w_{opt}$ is a point of maximum. The solution depends on $\gamma$, as $\gamma \to 0$ (risk neutral), $w_{opt} \to \infty$ (long $X$ short $Y$), as $\gamma \to \infty$ (very risk averse), $w_{opt} \to 1/3$ (minimize variance). Note that for $\gamma = 1/4$, $w = 1$, and it is optimal to invest only in $X$; however there is no $\gamma$ such that it is optimal to invest only in $Y$.

We have

$$\mu_{\mathcal{P}} = 1 + \frac{1 + 2\gamma}{6\gamma}, \quad \sigma^2_{\mathcal{P}} = 3\left(\frac{1 + 2\gamma}{6\gamma}\right)^2 + 1 - 2\frac{1 + 2\gamma}{6\gamma}$$

$$U(\mathcal{P}) = 1 + \frac{1 + 2\gamma}{6\gamma} - 2\left(3\left(\frac{1 + 2\gamma}{6\gamma}\right)^2 + 1 - 2\frac{1 + 2\gamma}{6\gamma}\right) \geq U(X), U(Y).$$

There are several cases. If $\gamma = 0$ (risk neutral): $\mu_{\mathcal{P}} = \infty$, $\sigma^2_{\mathcal{P}} = \infty$, $U(\mathcal{P}) = \infty$. If $\gamma = 1 :$ $\mu_{\mathcal{P}} = 3/2$, $\sigma^2_{\mathcal{P}} = 3/4$, and $U(\mathcal{P}) = 3/4$. If $\gamma = \infty$ (more risk averse than your grandma): $\mu_{\mathcal{P}} = 4/3$, $\sigma^2_{\mathcal{P}} = 2/3$, and $U(\mathcal{P}) = -\infty$.

A lot of investors work with the Sharpe Ratio criterion function instead of the mean variance utility function, which we may define here as

$$SR = \frac{E(\mathcal{P}) - r_f}{\mathrm{stdev}(\mathcal{P})}, \tag{6.10}$$

where $r_f$ is the risk free rate. Note that this formulation is different from earlier stated in (4.5) by including the risk-free rate into consideration. One can rank stocks and portfolios uniquely according to the value of $SR(w)$.

In the example, we have

$$SR(w) = \frac{1 + w - r_f}{\sqrt{3w^2 + 1 - 2w}}, \tag{6.11}$$

which is shown below (for the case $r_f = 0$) on the range $w \in [-1, 2]$. It is a nonlinear function of $w$ but has a well-defined peak.

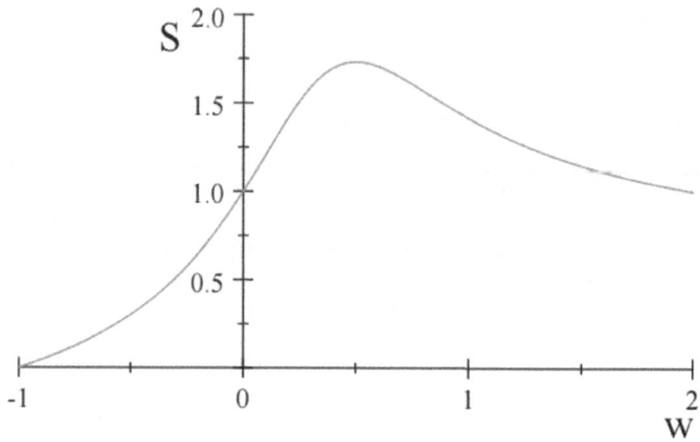


The first order condition of (6.11) is

$$\frac{1}{\sqrt{3w^2+1-2w}} - \frac{1+w-r_f}{2\left(3w^2+1-2w\right)^{3/2}} \times (6w-2) = 0.$$

By multiplying through by $(3w^2+1-2w)^{3/2}$ one obtains the quadratic equation

$$(3w^2+1-2w) - \left(\frac{1+w-r_f}{2}\right) \times (6w-2) = 0,$$

which has the solution

$$w_{sharpe} = \frac{2-r_f}{4-3r_f},$$

provided $r_f \neq 4/3$. By equating with $w_{opt} = \frac{1+2\gamma}{6\gamma}$, we see that this corresponds to what is optimal for the mean variance utility in the special case that $\gamma = 1-3r_f/4$. In particular, when $r_f = 0$, $w_{opt} = 1/2$ and Sharpe ratio maximizing is equivalent to maximizing $U$ with $\gamma = 1$.

Finally, we could just care about minimizing risk or variance. The value $w = 1/3$ achieves this objective (sets the first order condition to zero). In this case $\mu_{\mathcal{P}} = 4/3$, and $\sigma^2_{\mathcal{P}} = 2/3$. This is called the **Global Minimum Variance Portfolio** and is optimal for $\gamma = \infty$. The utility of this portfolio is $U(\mathcal{P}) = (4-2\gamma)/3$.

Consider the general two-asset case. The MV utility is

$$U = \mu_Y + w(\mu_X - \mu_Y) - \gamma\left((\sigma^2_X + \sigma^2_Y)w^2 - 2w\sigma^2_Y + \sigma^2_Y\right).$$

The first order condition is

$$(\mu_X - \mu_Y) - 2\gamma(\sigma^2_X + \sigma^2_Y)w + 2\gamma\sigma^2_Y = 0,$$

which solves to give

$$w_{opt} = \frac{\mu_X - \mu_Y + 2\gamma\sigma_Y^2}{2\gamma(\sigma_X^2 + \sigma_Y^2)} = \frac{\mu_X - \mu_Y}{2\gamma(\sigma_X^2 + \sigma_Y^2)} + \frac{\sigma_Y^2}{\sigma_X^2 + \sigma_Y^2}.$$

Suppose that $\mu_X = \mu_Y$. Then, we have $w_{opt} = \sigma_Y^2/(\sigma_X^2 + \sigma_Y^2)$ no matter what value $\gamma$ takes since, in that case, the mean is not affected by the choice of weighting at all, and so the portfolio choice comes down to minimizing risk.

Suppose that $\gamma = 1$. Then the optimal weighting is in general

$$w_{opt} = \frac{\mu_X - \mu_Y + 2\sigma_Y^2}{2(\sigma_X^2 + \sigma_Y^2)}.$$

In this case, we have

$$0 \le w_{opt} \le 1 \iff \mu_Y - 2\sigma_X^2 \le \mu_X \le \mu_Y + 2\sigma_X^2.$$

That is, provided there is not too much of a difference in the mean values it is optimal to place a positive fraction of your wealth in both assets.

We next calculate some Sharpe Ratios of the Fab5 stocks:

20120518-20211231

| Company | $\mu$ | $\sigma$ | Sharpe |
|---|---|---|---|
| **Facebook** | 0.0011627108 | 0.023107453 | 0.050317567 |
| **Google** | 0.0010634542 | 0.015900998 | 0.066879711 |
| **Amazon** | 0.0013105516 | 0.018773434 | 0.069808839 |
| **Apple** | 0.0010839393 | 0.017819557 | 0.060828634 |
| **Microsoft** | 0.0011399421 | 0.016184170 | 0.070435627 |

### 6.1.3 Portfolio of Three Risky Assets

We next consider the case with three risky assets, which has some differences features from the two asset case, and is essentially as general as can be. A portfolio of assets $X, Y, Z$ is a linear combination of the payoffs, so let

$$\mathcal{P} = w_X X + w_Y Y + w_Z Z,$$

where $w_X$ is the amount invested in asset $X$ and $w_Y$ is the amount invested in asset $Y$ and $w_Z$ is the amount invested in asset $Z$. We suppose that

$$w_X + w_Y + w_Z = 1,$$

that is, the total amount available is one unit, and it is divided into $X, Y, Z$ with no leftovers.

We calculate the mean and variance of the portfolio whose outcome is $\mathcal{P}$. This follows from the properties of mean and variance. We have

$$\mu_{\mathcal{P}} = E(\mathcal{P}) = w_X\mu_X + w_Y\mu_Y + w_Z\mu_Z$$

$$\sigma_{\mathcal{P}}^2 = \text{var}(\mathcal{P}) = w_X^2\sigma_X^2 + w_Y^2\sigma_Y^2 + w_Z^2\sigma_Z^2.$$

Imposing the budget constraint we obtain $w_Z = 1 - w_X - w_Y$, and we can eliminate $w_Z$ from the above formulae, i.e.,

$$\mu_{\mathcal{P}} = \mu_Z + w_X(\mu_X - \mu_Z) + w_Y(\mu_Y - \mu_Z)$$

$$\sigma^2_{\mathcal{P}} = w_X^2\sigma_X^2 + w_Y^2\sigma_Y^2 + (1 - w_X - w_Y)^2\sigma_Z^2,$$

which only involves two choice variables $w_X, w_Y$. As $w_X, w_Y$ vary so does $\mu_{\mathcal{P}}, \sigma^2_{\mathcal{P}}$. We note that there are different combinations of $w_X, w_Y$ that give the same $\mu_{\mathcal{P}}$ and likewise there are different combinations of $w_X, w_Y$ that give the same $\sigma^2_{\mathcal{P}}$. This is different from the two-asset case. The feasible set is now a two-dimensional set, not a curve.

**Example 67** $\mu_X = 3, \mu_Y = 2, \mu_Z = 1, \sigma_X^2 = 3, \sigma_Y^2 = 2, \sigma_Z^2 = 1$. *We show below the feasible set* $\{(\sigma_{\mathcal{P}}, \mu_{\mathcal{P}}) : w_X, w_Y \in \mathbb{R}, w_Z = 1 - w_X - w_Y\}$.

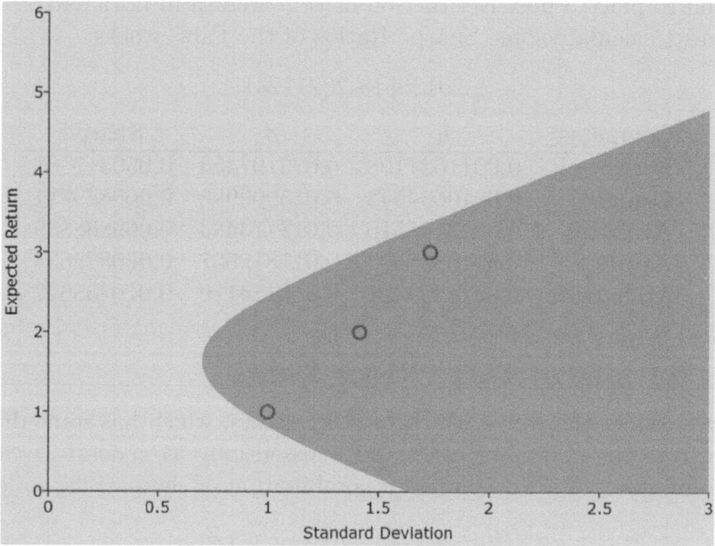


The interior of the red shape, although feasible, is dominated, meaning one can always improve utility by moving to the Northwest. The boundary on the Northwest frontier is called the **Mean Variance Efficient Frontier** and contains the set of portfolios that are undominated, i.e., cannot be unambiguously improved.

**Definition 13** *A feasible portfolio* $\mathcal{P}$ *is on the Mean Variance Efficient Frontier if there does not exist another feasible portfolio* $\mathcal{P}^*$ *for which both*

$$E(\mathcal{P}^*) \geq E(\mathcal{P}), \quad \text{var}(\mathcal{P}^*) \leq \text{var}(\mathcal{P}).$$

This is where any risk-averse investor would want to be, on the frontier. But precisely which one of these points will depend on her preferences. Note that three individual assets are in the interior, and hence, are dominated. One can do better by combining them into portfolios to achieve a better risk-return trade-off.

We next consider how to find or define the efficient frontier. Suppose we fix a target value of expected return $\mu_{\mathcal{P}}$ and find the combination of $w_X, w_Y$ that give the smallest $\sigma^2_{\mathcal{P}}$ while giving $\mu_{\mathcal{P}}$. The interpretation is that we find the portfolio that minimizes variance for a given mean $\mu_{\mathcal{P}}$ and hence will be on the efficient frontier. There are a number of steps in this argument. First, suppose that $\mu_Y \neq \mu_Z$, then we can uniquely determine $w_Y$ as

$$w_Y = \frac{\mu_{\mathcal{P}} - \mu_Z - w_X(\mu_X - \mu_Z)}{\mu_Y - \mu_Z},$$

and we can replace $w_Y$ in the mean and variance formulae. In this case we just have one choice variable $w_X$. We have

$$\begin{aligned}\sigma^2_{\mathcal{P}} &= w_X^2\sigma_X^2 + \left(\frac{\mu_{\mathcal{P}} - \mu_Z - w_X(\mu_X - \mu_Z)}{\mu_Y - \mu_Z}\right)^2 \sigma_Y^2 \\ &\quad + \left(1 - w_X - \frac{\mu_{\mathcal{P}} - \mu_Z - w_X(\mu_X - \mu_Z)}{\mu_Y - \mu_Z}\right)^2 \sigma_Z^2 \\ &= a + bw_X + cw_X^2.\end{aligned}$$

for some $a, b, c$, where

$$c = \sigma_X^2 + \left(\frac{\mu_X - \mu_Z}{\mu_Y - \mu_Z}\right)^2 \sigma_Y^2 + \left(1 + \left(\frac{\mu_X - \mu_Z}{\mu_Y - \mu_Z}\right)\right)^2 \sigma_Z^2 > 0.$$

That is, the portfolio variance is a quadratic function of the choice variable $w_X$ with coefficients that are complicated functions of the assets means and variances. Importantly, $c > 0$, which implies that there will be a global minimum. We have to minimize

$$\sigma^2_{\mathcal{P}}(w) = a + bw + cw^2$$

with respect to $w \in \mathbb{R}$. This has a unique solution with

$$w_{opt} = \frac{-b}{2c}, \quad \sigma^2_{\mathcal{P}}(w_{opt}) = a - \frac{b^2}{4c} \leq a.$$

Since $c > 0$ this is a global minimum rather than a maximum (the second derivative of $\sigma^2_{\mathcal{P}}(w)$ is positive). The minimum depends on $\mu_X, \mu_Y, \mu_Z, \sigma_X^2, \sigma_Y^2, \sigma_Z^2$ and $\mu_{\mathcal{P}}$. We can do this calculation for every value of $\mu_{\mathcal{P}}$ and draw the solutions as a parabola in the space $\sigma_{\mathcal{P}}, \mu_{\mathcal{P}}$, that is, $\sigma_{\mathcal{P}}(w_{opt}), \mu_{\mathcal{P}}$ is a curve, called the **Mean Variance Efficient Frontier.**

KEY POINT. *With three or more assets, the frontier is strictly to the north-west of the three individual assets, meaning that diversification improves our performance unambiguously for any risk-averse investor.*

We now consider which point on the frontier should be chosen, which depends on the utility function $U$. The problem is to maximize

$$\begin{aligned} U(w_X, w_Y) &= \mu_Z + w_X(\mu_X - \mu_Z) + w_Y(\mu_Y - \mu_Z) \\ &\quad - \frac{1}{2}\gamma\left(w_X^2\sigma_X^2 + w_Y^2\sigma_Y^2 + (1 - w_X - w_Y)^2\sigma_Z^2\right) \end{aligned}$$

with respect to $w_X, w_Y \in \mathbb{R}$, where $w_Z = 1 - w_X - w_Y$. This can be found from the two first-order conditions

$$\frac{\partial U(w_X, w_Y)}{\partial w_X} = 0, \qquad \frac{\partial U(w_X, w_Y)}{\partial w_Y} = 0. \tag{6.12}$$

We end up with two equations in two unknowns

$$(\mu_X - \mu_Z) - \gamma w_X\sigma_X^2 + \gamma(1 - w_X - w_Y)\sigma_Z^2 = 0$$

$$(\mu_Y - \mu_Z) - \gamma w_Y\sigma_Y^2 + \gamma(1 - w_X - w_Y)\sigma_Z^2 = 0$$

$$\begin{pmatrix} \sigma_X^2 + \sigma_Z^2 & \sigma_Z^2 \\ \sigma_Z^2 & \sigma_Y^2 + \sigma_Z^2 \end{pmatrix}\begin{pmatrix} w_X \\ w_Y \end{pmatrix} = \frac{1}{\gamma}\begin{pmatrix} \mu_X - \mu_Z + \gamma\sigma_Z^2 \\ \mu_Y - \mu_Z + \gamma\sigma_Z^2 \end{pmatrix}, \tag{6.13}$$

which uniquely determines $w_X$ and $w_Y$.

**Example 68** *Consider the special case that $\mu_X = \mu_Y = \mu_Z$. In this case*

$$\begin{pmatrix} w_X \\ w_Y \end{pmatrix} = \begin{pmatrix} \frac{\sigma_Y^2\sigma_Z^2}{\sigma_X^2\sigma_Y^2 + \sigma_X^2\sigma_Z^2 + \sigma_Y^2\sigma_Z^2} \\ \frac{\sigma_X^2\sigma_Z^2}{\sigma_X^2\sigma_Y^2 + \sigma_X^2\sigma_Z^2 + \sigma_Y^2\sigma_Z^2} \end{pmatrix},$$

*and when $\sigma_X^2 = \sigma_Y^2 = \sigma_Z^2$, we have $w_X = w_Y = w_Z = 1/3$.*

#### 6.1.3.1 Correlation Matters

Suppose that $X, Y$ have same mean and equal variance $\sigma^2$ with correlation $\rho \in [-1, 1]$. Then the mean of the portfolio is not affected by $\rho$ but the variance is, specifically

$$\begin{aligned} \sigma_{\mathcal{P}}^2 &= \mathrm{var}(wX + (1 - w)Y) \\ &= w^2\sigma^2 + (1 - w)^2\sigma^2 + 2w(1 - w)\sigma^2\rho \\ &= \sigma^2\left(w^2 + (1 - w)^2 + 2w(1 - w)\rho\right). \end{aligned}$$

Suppose we minimize the portfolio variance $\sigma_{\mathcal{P}}^2$ with respect to $w$. The first order condition does not depend on $\sigma^2$, i.e.,

$$2w - 2(1 - w) + 2(1 - 2w)\rho = 0$$

and is solved at $w = 1/2$ for any $\rho$. The second order condition for a minimum is satisfied at $w_{opt} = 1/2$. The variance of the optimal portfolio is then

$$\sigma_{\mathcal{P}}^2(w_{opt}) = \frac{1}{2}(1 + \rho).$$

We have several special cases: If $\rho = 0$, then $\sigma^2_{\mathcal{P}}(w_{opt}) = 1/2$, the case we have already seen; If $\rho = +1$, then $\sigma^2_{\mathcal{P}}(w_{opt}) = 1$ (in this case there are no benefits of diversification); If $\rho = -1$, then $\sigma^2_{\mathcal{P}}(w_{opt}) = 0$ (perfect hedging, i.e., diversification completely eliminates all risk). In practice, we expect positive but not unit correlation, which reduces (but does not eliminate) the benefits of diversification relative to the case where $\rho = 0$.

We next show the sample Correlation Matrix between Fab5 returns over the period 20120518-20211231. All the pairwise correlations are positive.

20120518-20211231 Annualized percentage means and stdevs Fab5 returns

| | Mean | stdev |
|---|---|---|
| **Facebook** | 29.30 | 36.67 |
| **Google** | 26.80 | 25.24 |
| **Amazon** | 33.03 | 29.80 |
| **Apple** | 27.32 | 28.28 |
| **Microsoft** | 28.73 | 25.69 |

20120518-20211231 Correlation Matrix between Fab5 returns

| | **Facebook** | **Google** | **Amazon** | **Apple** | **Microsoft** |
|---|---|---|---|---|---|
| **Facebook** | 1 | 0.501 | 0.456 | 0.402 | 0.422 |
| **Google** | | 1 | 0.598 | 0.521 | 0.651 |
| **Amazon** | | | 1 | 0.461 | 0.557 |
| **Apple** | | | | 1 | 0.575 |
| **Microsoft** | | | | | 1 |

The optimal portfolio according to $U = E(R) - \gamma \text{var}(R)$ for the Fab5 20120518-20211231

| $w/\gamma$ | 0 | 1 | 2 | 5 | 10 |
|---|---|---|---|---|---|
| **Mean** | $\infty$ | 31.68 | 30.01 | 29.01 | 28.68 |
| **Stdev** | $\infty$ | 25.55 | 22.97 | 22.19 | 22.08 |
| **U** | $\infty$ | 0.2516 | 0.1946 | 0.0439 | $-0.2006$ |
| **wfb** | -$\infty$ | 0.0846 | 0.0687 | 0.0592 | 0.0560 |
| **wg** | -$\infty$ | $-0.1443$ | 0.0893 | 0.2294 | 0.2761 |
| **wam** | $\infty$ | 0.6366 | 0.3798 | 0.2257 | 0.1744 |
| **wap** | -$\infty$ | 0.0758 | 0.1511 | 0.1962 | 0.2113 |
| **wms** | -$\infty$ | 0.3473 | 0.3111 | 0.2894 | 0.2822 |

### 6.1.4 The General Case

We next consider the general multivariate case $n$ assets with risky payoffs $X_1, \ldots, X_n$. For weights $w_1, \ldots, w_n$ with $w_1 + \ldots + w_n = 1$ the portfolio payoff is

$$\mathcal{P} = w_1 X_1 + \ldots + w_n X_n.$$

We discussed above the effect of the correlation between assets on diversification. Optimal portfolio choice in general depends on all the means, all the variances, and all the covariances:

$$\mu_j = E(X_j), \quad \sigma_j^2 = \text{var}(X_j), \quad \sigma_{ij} = \text{cov}(X_i, X_j).$$

The Mean-Variance Efficient frontier is the set of all portfolios that have the smallest variance for a given expected return, which traces out a parabola in mean/standard deviation space as we have shown for the three-asset case. The solution is known explicitly in terms of these moments, but this involves matrix algebra, so we shall not present the general solution here. Markowitz started this project in the 1950's.

In the case where the number of assets is large, one can show that a diversified portfolio can reduce risk, but not completely eliminate it if there are common factors that affect all stock returns.

**Example 69** *Suppose that* $\sigma_j^2 = \sigma^2$, *and* $\sigma_{ij} = \rho\sigma^2$ *for all* $i \neq j$. *Let* $\mathcal{P}$ *be the portfolio with weights* $w_i$, *where* $\sum_{i=1}^N w_i = 1$. *Then*

$$\begin{aligned}
\text{var}(\mathcal{P}) &= \text{var}\left(\sum_{i=1}^N w_i R_i\right) = \left(\sum_{i=1}^N w_i^2 \text{var}(R_i) + \sum_{\substack{i=1 \\ i\neq j}}^N \sum_{j=1}^N w_i w_j \text{cov}(R_i, R_j)\right) \\
&= \sigma^2 \sum_{i=1}^N w_i^2 + \rho\sigma^2 \sum_{\substack{i=1 \\ i\neq j}}^N \sum_{j=1}^N w_i w_j \\
&= \sigma^2 \sum_{i=1}^N w_i^2 + \rho\sigma^2 \left(1 - \sum_{i=1}^N w_i^2\right).
\end{aligned}$$

A **well-diversified portfolio** satisfies $\sum_{i=1}^N w_i^2 \to 0$ as $N$ is large. For example this holds if $w_i = 1/N$, in which case

$$\text{var}(\mathcal{P}) = \frac{\sigma^2}{N} + \rho\sigma^2 \left(1 - \frac{1}{N}\right) = \rho\sigma^2 + \frac{\sigma^2(1-\rho)}{N}.$$

For such portfolios var($\mathcal{P}$) approaches $\rho\sigma^2$, which is a lower bound. If $\rho = 0$, then the lower bound is zero, meaning that all risk can be diversified away. On the other hand, when $\rho > 0$, some but not all risks can be diversified away.

### 6.1.5 The General Case with Riskless Asset

The **market portfolio** is the value-weighted portfolio of all risky assets. It has a return denoted by

$$R_m = \sum_{i=1}^n w_i R_i, \tag{6.14}$$

where $R_1, \ldots, R_n$ are the returns on all the risky assets in the economy and $w_i$ are the market capitalization weights (that vary across company and may also change over time as prices go up and down).

Now suppose that we can invest in these $n$ risky assets and a riskless asset with payoff $r_f$. How do we choose the weights $w_0, w_1, \ldots, w_n$ with $w_0$ invested in the riskless asset and $w_1, \ldots, w_n$ allocated to the risky assets such that $\sum_{i=0}^{n} w_i = 1$? The solution is complicated, but basically it boils down to drawing the tangent line from the riskless payoff to the MV efficient frontier i.e. tangent to a feasible portfolio of risky assets (called the tangency portfolio). The riskless asset improves the available outcomes. The optimal thing to do is to choose a portfolio that combines the riskless asset with the so-called tangency portfolio. Therefore, economic theory says: choose a portfolio that combines the riskless asset with the market portfolio (S&P500) according to your risk preference $\gamma$.

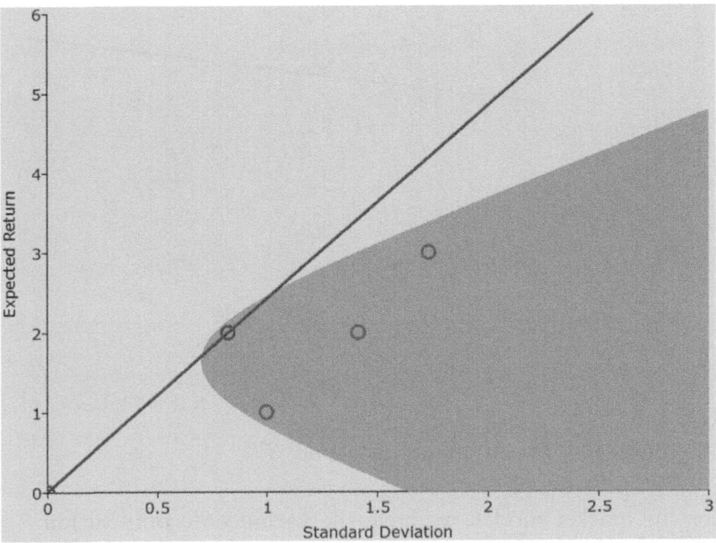


**FIGURE 6.4**
Riskless asset combined with risky assets efficient frontier

The Capital Asset Pricing Model (CAPM, Sharpe (1964)) says that the tangency portfolio is the market portfolio. We may also express the CAPM in terms of its implication for the expected return on assets. Specifically, we should have

$$\boxed{E(R_i) = r_f + \beta_i \left(E(R_m) - r_f\right)}, \tag{6.15}$$

where $\beta_i$ is the slope of the market model regression, specifically,

$$\boxed{\beta_i = \frac{\operatorname{cov}(R_i, R_m)}{\operatorname{var}(R_m)}}.$$

The quantity $\pi_i = E(R_i) - r_f$ is the risk premium on asset $i$, while $\pi_m = E(R_m) - r_f$ is the market risk premium. The CAPM says that the appropriate measure of risk for stock $i$ is its $\beta_i$ not its overall variance. The higher the value of $\beta_i$, the higher we should see $\pi_i$. An asset with $\beta_i = 1$ should have the same excess return on average as the market portfolio. An asset with $\beta_i = 2$ should have twice the excess return on average as the market portfolio. An asset with $\beta_i = 0$, which is called a **market neutral** portfolio should have zero excess return on average.

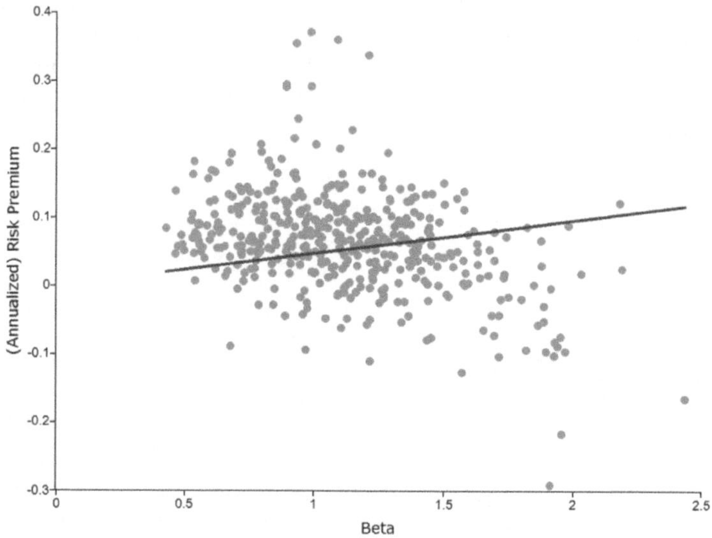


**FIGURE 6.5**
S&P 500 stocks' risk premium against their $\beta$'s.

Under the market model, we have the variance decomposition

$$\|\sigma_{ii} = \mathrm{var}(R_i) = \beta_i^2 \sigma_m^2 + \sigma_{\varepsilon i}^2\|,$$

into the common component and the idiosyncratic component to total variance. We also have

$$\sigma_{ij} = \mathrm{cov}(R_i, R_j) = \beta_i \beta_j \sigma_m^2,$$

$$\rho_{ij} = \frac{\beta_i \beta_j \sigma_m^2}{\sqrt{\beta_i^2 \sigma_m^2 + \sigma_{\varepsilon i}^2}\sqrt{\beta_j^2 \sigma_m^2 + \sigma_{\varepsilon j}^2}}.$$

In general, $0 < \rho_{ij} < 1$, because $\sigma_{\varepsilon i}^2, \sigma_{\varepsilon j}^2 > 0$.

### 6.1.6 Practical Aspects

We have presented the portfolio choice argument without explicit reference to a time frame. So, how does the holding period affect the results? The usual scaling law says that the mean and the variance of a k-period random return should be exactly k times the mean and the variance of a one-period return. Therefore, the mean variance utility defined for k-period returns is exactly k times the mean variance utility for the one-period return, and the precise choice of optimal portfolio is invariant to the time horizon.

How do you implement the portfolio? You have to buy or sell shares in each company. We next demonstrate how this is consistent with our mathematical framework that has focused on returns. Let $n_i$ be the number of shares purchased in asset $i = 1, 2$ at prices $P_j$, and let $V$ be the total amount invested, where

$$V = n_1 P_1 + n_2 P_2.$$

Without loss of generality, we suppose that $V = 1$ (1 could be \$1 trillion). Then let

$$w_i = \frac{n_i P_i}{n_1 P_1 + n_2 P_2} = n_i P_i$$

be the weight of the portfolio invested in asset $i$. This says that for weighting $w_i$, you have to buy (or sell)

$$n_i = w_i \frac{1}{P_i}$$

shares in asset $i$ at the price $P_i$ for each dollar of capital invested. If you invest a total of \$$W$, then the implied number of shares $Wn_i$ may not be an integer (although the rounding error here may be small if $W$ is large and/or $P_i$ is small). Nowadays, it is possible for retail traders to purchase fractional (but not real value) amounts of shares, albeit with high transaction costs.

The value of the portfolio at some future time period, denoted +, is given by

$$\begin{aligned} V_+ &= n_1 P_{1,+} + n_2 P_{2,+} \\ &= \frac{w_1}{P_1} P_{1,+} + \frac{w_2}{P_2} P_{2,+} \\ &= \frac{w_1}{P_1} P_1 (1 + R_1) + \frac{w_2}{P_2} P_2 (1 + R_2) \\ &= w_1 (1 + R_1) + w_2 (1 + R_2) \\ &= 1 + w_1 R_1 + w_2 R_2, \end{aligned}$$

where $P_{j,+}$ denotes the price of asset $j$ at the time period +, and $R_j$ are the net returns on asset $j$ over the holding period. It follows that the net return on the portfolio is precisely $w_1 R_1 + w_2 R_2$.

A key issue in practice is the rebalancing horizon (when you buy additional assets or sell assets and so change the weighting $w_i$) : daily, monthly, yearly, endogenous. This depends a lot on transaction costs, which increase with the number of transactions undertaken.

Some obvious starting points might be based on the way stock indexes are constructed, so value weighted, equal weighted, and price weighted.

**Example 70** *The equal weighted portfolio has* $w_i = 1/n$ *for* $n$ *assets, which means that an equal fraction of one's capital is allocated to each stock, which is achieved by purchasing* $1/nP_i$ *shares of each company. To maintain this equal weighting, one has to constantly rebalance as the relative prices of the stocks change.*

**Example 71** *An alternative is the price weighting. In this case, imagine buying one share in each company, so the initial investment is* $\sum_{j=1}^{n} P_j$ *and next period your capital will grow to* $\sum_{j=1}^{n} P_{j,+}$. *We write*

$$\frac{\sum_{j=1}^{n} P_{j,+}}{\sum_{j=1}^{n} P_j} = \frac{\sum_{j=1}^{n} P_j (1 + R_j)}{\sum_{j=1}^{n} P_j} = \sum_{j=1}^{n} w_j (1 + R_j),$$

*where*

$$w_j = \frac{P_j}{\sum_{j=1}^{n} P_j}, \quad j = 1, \ldots, n.$$

*This portfolio does not require rebalancing since one just holds onto the shares for the duration of the investment period, but the implied portfolio weighting changes over time due to the change in relative prices. One issue with this arises when stocks have wildly different price levels in which case the high-priced stocks will have the biggest share of the capital.*

**Example 72** *Finally, we may consider market value weighting like the S&P500. In this case,*

$$w_j = \frac{V_j}{\sum_{j=1}^{n} V_j} = \frac{n_j P_j}{\sum_{j=1}^{n} n_j P_j},$$

*where* $V_j = n_j P_j$ *is the value of company* $j$ *calculated as the number* $n_j$ *of shares outstanding times the price per share* $P_j$. *This also requires regular rebalancing as the relative prices and the number of shares change.*

Is the S&P500 portfolio well diversified? As of August 2024, the top 4 companies in the index were: Apple with 6.90%, Nvidia Corp with 6.68%, Microsoft Corp with 6.66% and Amazon.com Inc with 3.49%, together they represent nearly 25% of the index.

In practice, the past is not necessarily a good guide to the future!

## 6.2 Performance Measurement

How do we evaluate the performance of our portfolio strategy? In practice, we use time series data $\{1, \ldots, T\}$ to estimate the parameters like the mean vector and covariance matrix of asset returns. We calculate the portfolio weights using these estimated parameters. This introduces noise or random variability into the calculation, which can lead to poor performance. It is important to evaluate the performance of any portfolio using new data, data that has not been used in the parameter estimation. We next outline one way to do this.

Suppose that we construct our portfolio at time $T$ (i.e., buy and sell the specified assets in the specified proportion) based on estimates computed from the data at times $\{1, \ldots, T\}$, and hold for one period (day, week, month, year) and record the results at time $T+1$. The results may be the return on the investment or the total new value of the portfolio. We then repeat using the data at times $\{1, \ldots, T+1\}$ and record the results at time $T+2$ based either on the return on investment or the compounded value. We carry on like this for the whole evaluation period $T+1, \ldots, T+E$.

$$\overbrace{\text{- - - - - - - - - - - - - - -}}^{\textit{Estimation} \text{ or } \textit{Training Period}} | \quad \overbrace{\text{- - - - - - - - - - -}}^{\textit{Testing} \text{ or } \textit{Evaluation Period}}$$

We compare the results in terms of the average return over the evaluation period $T+1, \ldots, T+E$ or the compounded return, i.e., the ending value of the portfolio at $T+E$. This gives an average performance measure of a one period portfolio strategy based on $E$ evaluations of that strategy. This does not take account of the costs of trading, so it overestimates the likely realistic return.

## 6.3 Key Points

1. Mean-variance utility is a popular and useful framework for quantifying one's personal preferences between risk and return. It is a mathematical framework that allows one to find portfolios that are optimal according to this criterion.
2. Diversification reduces risk, provided assets are not perfectly correlated.
3. The efficient frontier is the place where any risk-averse investor would like to be. It is calculated by optimizing the mean-variance utility subject to constraints.

4. The capital asset pricing model predicts the risk-return trade-off that should operate in equilibrium where all investors are optimally choosing their portfolios.

## 6.4 Exercises

1. For the Fama-French daily data, calculate the sample mean and sample variance of the market return and compute the optimal

$$w_{opt} = \frac{1}{\gamma}\frac{\mu - r_f}{\sigma^2}$$

for $\gamma = 1, 5, 10$. Now do the same for each decade separately.

2. The S&P500 (with $N = 503$ assets currently) has $\sum_{i=1}^{N} w_i^2 = 0.0192$; Apple has 7.12% of the weight in the index. Is this well-diversified?

3. For $n = 5$ we have

$$\mu_{\mathcal{P}} = \sum_{j=1}^{5} w_j \mu_j = \mu_5 + \sum_{j=1}^{4} w_j(\mu_j - \mu_5),$$

$$\sigma_{\mathcal{P}}^2 = \sum_{j=1}^{5}\sum_{k=1}^{5} w_j w_k \sigma_{jk}$$

$$U = \sum_{j=1}^{5} w_j \mu_j - \gamma\left(\sum_{j=1}^{5}\sum_{k=1}^{5} w_j w_k \sigma_{jk}\right), \quad \sum_{j=1}^{5} w_j = 1$$

This is complicated to solve in general, have to solve four linear equations in four unknowns.

The global minimum variance portfolio in the case with zero correlation has weights (stocks with bigger variance have lower weight)

$$w_j = \frac{\sigma_j^{-2}}{\sum_{j=1}^{5} \sigma_j^{-2}}$$

and the corresponding variance is

$$\sigma_{GMV}^2 = \frac{1}{\sum_{j=1}^{5} \sigma_j^{-2}}$$

For the Fab5, these weights are estimated to be: 0.11980441, 0.25300446, 0.18150539, 0.20145736, 0.24422838; The mean and the standard deviation of the GMV portfolio with these weights is

$$\mu_{GMV} = 0.0011430025, \quad \sigma_{GMV} = 0.013989794.$$

# 7

# *Efficient Markets Hypothesis*

## Outline

This chapter delves into the Efficient Markets Hypothesis (EMH) and explores various perspectives on market efficiency. It addresses key concepts related to market behavior, the predictability of stock prices, and the implications of different forms of market efficiency. The chapter introduces the random walk hypothesis, various trading strategies, and the debate between active and passive portfolio management. By examining both traditional and behavioral views, the chapter provides a comprehensive understanding of market dynamics.

After reading this chapter, you will be able to:

- Understand the concept of the Efficient Markets Hypothesis and its significance in finance.
- Distinguish between the different forms of market efficiency: weak, semi-strong, and strong forms.
- Evaluate the Random Walk Hypothesis and its implications for stock price predictability.
- Analyze the effectiveness of technical analysis and momentum trading strategies in light of market efficiency.
- Examine the principles and practices of fundamental analysis and its alignment with the semi-strong form of EMH.
- Compare active and passive portfolio management, including their respective advantages and drawbacks.
- Apply the concept of EMH to real-world scenarios and trading strategies, assessing their validity and potential for abnormal profits.
- Critically assess the empirical evidence supporting or refuting the EMH through event studies and market anomalies.

DOI: 10.1201/9781003543121-7

## 7.1 Alternative Views of the Stock Market

One point of view is that markets are efficient (or approximately so) Fama (1970). Participants are rational and unbiased, and they value future expected cash flows accurately. They would buy if a stock was undervalued and sell if it was overvalued. Market forces respond to news quickly and make **prices the best available estimates of fundamental values**, i.e., values justified by likely future cash flows and preferences of investors/consumers. This is good for economic welfare because capital is flowing to its most productive uses.

The alternative point of view is that markets are inefficient because participants are irrational and have "cognitive and behavioral biases". For example: **Anchoring** (we rely heavily on the first piece of information introduced when making decisions) and **Framing** (we draw different conclusions based on the same evidence depending on how it is presented); **Confirmation Bias** (we tend to find and remember information that confirms our prior beliefs); Sunk Cost Fallacy (we invest more in things that have cost us something already even when there are better uses of that additional sum); Clustering Illusion (we find patterns and "clusters" in random data); Over optimistic and Over confidence. Most people (more about men) think they are above average; Loss Aversion and Disposition Effect. Investors are so fearful of losses that they focus on trying to avoid a loss more so than on making gains. It relates to the tendency of investors to sell assets that have increased in value, while keeping assets that have dropped in value. See Kahneman and Tversky (1979). One major argument that this point of view advances is that the stock market has excess volatility, an argument put forward by Shiller (1987). Bubbles and crashes, which are episodes where prices rise and fall rapidly, occur frequently, apparently unjustified by movements in fundamentals. Shiller argued that even in normal times, prices move unrelatedly to fundamentals. Sometimes the stock market overreacts to new information, and sometimes it underreacts to new information.

### 7.1.1 Efficient Markets Hypothesis

**Definition 14** *Fama (1970): A market in which prices always fully reflect available information is called efficient (EMH)*

If prices did not reflect all available information, then they would be predictable, which would imply opportunities for superior returns (a free lunch). This will be competed away immediately by a lot of hungry traders, and so prices must be unpredictable. If a security is believed to be underpriced, buying pressure leads prices to jump up to a level where they are no longer thought a bargain. If a security is believed to be overpriced, selling pressure leads prices to jump down to a level where they are no longer thought too expensive. The idea is that market forces respond to news quickly and make prices the best available estimates of fundamental values, i.e., the values justified by likely future cash flows and preferences of investors/consumers.

We distinguish among three forms of market efficiency depending on the information set (meaning the information that is available) with respect to which efficiency is defined

1. **Weak form.** (1) Information from historical prices are fully reflected in the current price; (2) One can't earn **abnormal profits** from trading strategies based on past prices alone.
2. **Semi strong form.** (1) All public information (past prices, annual reports, quality of management, earnings forecasts, macroeconomic news, etc.) is fully reflected in current prices; (2) One can't earn abnormal profits from trading strategies based on public information.
3. **Strong form.** (1) All private and public information is fully reflected in current prices; (2) One can't earn abnormal profits from trading strategies based on all information, including public and private.

We have the following ordering of the three hypotheses with strong form being the strongest and the weak form being the weakest:

$$Strong \Longrightarrow Semi\ strong \Longrightarrow Weak,$$

i.e., if the strong form holds, then the semi-strong form must hold, and the weak form must hold. The contrapositive is that if the weak form is false, then for sure the semi-strong form is false. The strong form hypothesis is not considered credible, since we might expect that private information relevant for stock valuation, only known to one person, should allow them to make a superior profit. For example, it is hard to believe that insider trading could not lead to abnormal profits. So we focus on weak form and semi-strong form.

There are two further points to make about the EMH. First, we have to say what is meant by normal profits and hence what is abnormal profits. Second, the distinction between price information and public information and between public and private information is perhaps not so easy as it may appear nowadays. For example, within a trading day, large trading firms pay exchanges to receive datafeeds that give them upto the microsecond information about prices, so price information is not freely available at this highest frequency, although it is free at the daily frequency. Finally, we should note that the amount of available information or data is expanding rapidly. As of 2024, the global datasphere is estimated to be 149 zettabytes, and is projected to reach 181 zettabytes by 2025. This is too much to download to your phone, although Large Language Models are able to access large parts of this. Complexity needs to be taken account of.

### 7.1.2 The Random Walk Hypothesis

The traditional model for stock prices, compatible with the EMH, says that stock prices evolve randomly.

**Definition 15** *The random walk (drunkard's walk)*

$$X_t = \mu + X_{t-1} + \varepsilon_t,$$

*where $X_t$ is prices or log of prices. The shock $\varepsilon_t$ is a random variable with mean zero, and is independently and identically distributed over time (like the outcome of a game of chance).*

This says that the current value is equal to last period's value plus a constant gain $\mu$ plus a random disturbance that could be positive or negative but is mean zero on average. Nowadays, the random walk model is usually expressed for log prices, which says that (logarithmic) returns are random with mean $\mu$, i.e.,

$$r_t = \log(P_t) - \log(P_{t-1}) = \mu + \varepsilon_t, \tag{7.1}$$

where $\varepsilon_t$ are i.i.d. with mean zero and variance $\sigma^2$. One may further assume that $\varepsilon_t$ are distributed as $N(0, \sigma^2)$, in which case the logarithmic returns $r_t$ are distributed as $N(\mu, \sigma^2)$. Note that under the specification (7.1), we can also show that returns themselves satisfy

$$R_t = \mu^* + \varepsilon_t^*,$$

where $\varepsilon_t^*$ is i.i.d. with mean zero and variance $\sigma^{*2}$; Exercise ? asks you to show this. We have already used this model to calculate $\mu, \sigma^2$ and make inference about these quantities (i.e., to test whether $\mu = 0$). The mean $\mu$ can be interpreted as a risk premium needed to compensate for the risk $\sigma^2$. The key assumption is that there is no predictability in $\varepsilon_t$, i.e., this is like the outcome of a coin toss and cannot be predicted based on past information. In which case, the best prediction of $\log(P_t)$ based on past information is just $\log(P_{t-1}) + \mu$. You can't do better than that.

There are many people who have tried to beat the market by different methods, which would be in violation of the EMH. We next discuss some trading strategies that are widely used.

### 7.1.3 Technical Analysts and Momentum Traders

So-called Chartists or technical analysts try to identify certain patterns in stock prices, hoping to exploit them and profit. They believe certain patterns are repeated in prices and give them names. For example, **Head and Shoulders** and **Double bottom**. Lo, Mamaysky, and Wang (2000) tried to make this into a rigorous discipline by describing the patterns mathematically.

Another quite widespread approach is to focus on simple definitions of trends or directions. **Momentum traders** believe that prices continue in the same direction, i.e., winner stocks will be winners next time, and losers will be losers next time. Another way of saying this is that stock returns are positively correlated with past returns (we discuss the concept of autocorrelation more in the next chapter). This belief suggests the trading strategy of going long (buy) winners and going short (sell) losers, or simply buying the stock market when the stock market has done well recently. **Contrarian traders** (also called reversal) believe exactly the opposite, namely that winner stocks will be losers next time, and losers will be winners next time. Another way of saying this is that stock returns are negatively correlated with past returns. This belief suggests the trading strategy of going short on winners and going long on losers. A famous example of this trade is called the **Dogs of the Dow** strategy, which buys the Dow Jones Industrial stocks that are relatively low in price compared to their 52-week high, but which still pay relatively high dividends. Some argue that momentum is the short-term tendency, whereas reversal is the longer-term feature.

All these trading strategies make use only of price information, and therefore the weak form EMH hypothesis says that they should not make abnormal profit.

### 7.1.4 Fundamental Analysis

Fundamental analysts estimate future cash flows from securities and their riskiness, based on their analysis of company-relevant data such as balance sheets as well as the economic environment in which it operates, to determine the proper value of securities. So-called value trading is described in detail in the textbook Graham and Dodd (1934). This often involves working with specific financial ratios. The **Return on Equity** is defined as

$$ROE = \frac{\text{Net Income}}{\text{Shareholders' Equity}}, \tag{7.2}$$

which is calculated usually on an annual basis. This financial ratio quantifies how much net income a company earns per dollar of invested capital. It says how efficiently a firm uses its money to generate profit. It can be calculated for both listed companies and unlisted companies that have to release annual reports. One can compare companies' ROEs against the industry average to determine its value. We can express ROE as the product of three other ratios as follows:

$$ROE = \frac{\text{Net Income}}{\text{Sales}} \times \frac{\text{Sales}}{\text{Total Assets}} \times \frac{\text{Total Assets}}{\text{Shareholders' Equity}}.$$

The first ratio is net profit margin (net income divided by sales). A company can improve its profit margin by making more money on each unit it sells. The second ratio is asset turnover (sales divided by total assets). A company can improve its asset turnover by increasing sales while keeping its total assets constant. The third ratio is financial leverage (total assets divided by shareholder equity). A company can improve its ROE by borrowing money and earning more on that money than it costs. Likewise, the Return on Assets (ROA) measures how efficiently a company is in generating profit from their total assets on their balance sheet. Tobin's Q can be defined for an individual company as

$$\boxed{Q = \frac{\text{Equity Market Value}}{\text{Book Market Value}}}. \tag{7.3}$$

A low Q ratio (less than 1) implies that the cost to replace a firm's assets is greater than the value of its stock. This implies that the stock is undervalued. Conversely, a high Q (greater than 1) implies that a firm's stock is more expensive than the replacement cost of its assets, which implies that the stock is overvalued. Tobin's Q is often calculated for the market as a whole and is used in macroeconomics. The usual judgement is that ROR and ROA are backward-looking and computed from the balance sheet, whereas the EMH is forward-looking.

Another financial ratio is the Price Earnings ratio (P/E)

$$\boxed{P/E = \frac{\text{Price per share}}{\text{Earnings per share}}}.$$

The price in the ratio is the current price, earnings are taken from company reports and are usually trailing 12 months (TTM). The P/E of an index is usually calculated as the (weighted, either equally or by market cap) harmonic mean of the P/E ratios of the individual companies. Some recent P/E's are given below for some prominent stock market indexes, including Dow Jones:

| | 2/03/21† | YEAR AGO† | ESTIMATE^ |
|---|---|---|---|
| DJIA | 30.36 | 22.81 | 20.05 |
| DJIAT | n.a. | 18.65 | 36.60 |
| DJIAU | 23.51 | 27.19 | 23.16 |

| | 2/03/21† | YEAR AGO† | ESTIMATE^ |
|---|---|---|---|
| Russell 2000 | n.a. | 37.93 | 68.69 |
| NASDAQ 100 | 38.75 | 27.96 | 29.89 |
| S&P 500 | 40.93 | 25.77 | 22.15 |

These numbers are widely reported and focused on, but their ability to forecast future earnings or future stock returns has been shown to be limited even in the short term. One issue is that company income statements and company accounts are often opaque and misleading. They are often constructed to present the best picture from the point of view of the company hiding weak spots. There are substantial differences in P/E ratios across industries so that tech stocks may have very high P/E ratios, especially in early stages, whereas utility companies usually have quite modest P/E ratios.

Trading strategies based on balance sheet ratios are incompatible with the semi-strong form efficient market hypothesis in the sense that EMH predicts they can only make the normal return, and so why go through all the effort of studying company accounts.

### 7.1.5 Active Versus Passive Portfolio Management

The Investment/Wealth/Asset management is a huge industry. Why does it exist? There are two general types of investment management:

**Active portfolio management.** Attempts to achieve superior returns (better than the $R_f + \beta(\mu_m - R_f)$ predicted by the CAPM) through security selection and market timing. **Security selection** amounts to picking misspriced individual securities, trying to buy low and sell high. **Market timing** consists of trying to enter the stock market at troughs and leave at peaks (switch to fixed income) to avoid negative stock market returns. This sector generally charges high fees. Returns to investors have to be calculated net of fees.

**Passive portfolio management.** This involves tracking a predefined index of securities with no security analysis whatsoever. Exchange Traded Funds (ETF's) were introduced by State Street Global Advisors in 1993. The most popular ETFs in the U.S. replicate the S&P 500 Index (SPDR) or the NASDAQ-100 (QQQ). ETF's can be bought or sold by individual investors with a much smaller cost than investing in "one unit" of the index itself, which would require the purchase of a certain number of shares of all the component stocks in the right proportion. The SPDR comes with an 0.09% expense ratio, meaning that an investor who buys \$1000 worth of the SPDR has to pay \$0.90 as management fees. There are also leveraged ETF's (that promise some multiple payoff) and negative ETF's (that promise minus the payoff of the "index"). There is no attempt to beat the market, in line with EMH (which says this is not possible) and the return on the strategy is just as predicted by the CAPM, i.e., $R_f + \beta(\mu_m - R_f)$. Passive investing is much cheaper than active management since no costs of information acquisition and analysis, lower transaction costs (less frequent trading), also generally greater risk diversification. This is a big growth sector, with more than \$10 trillion invested in passive funds now.

The 20 leading asset management companies (by AUM (assets under management)) as of 2022 are: BlackRock, Charles Schwab, Vanguard Group, UBS, Fidelity Investments, State Street Global Advisors, Morgan Stanley, JPMorgan Chase, Allianz, Capital Group, Goldman Sachs, BNY Mellon, Amundi, PIMCO, Legal & General, Prudential Financial, Deutsche Bank, Bank of America, Invesco, and T. Rowe Price. BlackRock in particular has over \$10 trillion dollars of AUM; it was founded in 1988. They offer both active and passive investment strategies for their clients. Blackrock is itself a public listed company, whereas Vanguard has a mutual structure whereby it is essentially owned by its customers. Hedge Funds are a pooled investment fund that trade in relatively liquid assets make extensive use of more complex trading, portfolio-construction, and risk management techniques in an attempt to improve performance, such as short selling, leverage, and derivatives. Financial regulators generally restrict hedge fund marketing to institutional investors, high net worth individuals, and accredited investors. The leading hedge funds include: Bridgewater Associates, Man Group, Renaissance Technologies, Millennium Mgmt, TCI Fund Mgmt., D.E. Shaw Group, Two Sigma Investments/Advisers, Farallon Capital Mgmt, and Citadel. Bridgwater Associates have over $100 billion AUM. They are typically managing wealthy individuals money and pursuing active investment strategies that include: global macro, directional, event-driven, and relative value (arbitrage).

Are active managers worth their fees? Maybe not. What can go wrong?

1. Need to consider both risk and return. Is any past superior performance due to taking higher risk in which case future performance could be very bad. CAPM says that expected return should be $R_f + \beta(\mu_m - R_f)$, and if the $\beta$ is high, on average, the return will be high.
2. Fees could eat up any performance benefits.
3. Are we sure of the performance gain? Hedge fund reporting can be very lacking in transparency. Bernie Madoff springs to mind.
4. It could just be luck, as we next explain.

**Example 73** *Role of luck—Imagine 10,000 managers whose strategy is to park all assets in an index fund, but at the end of every year, use a quarter of it to make (independently) a single bet on red or black in a casino. After 10 years, many of them no longer keep their jobs but several survivors have been very successful*

Suppose they all start with $1,000,000. At end of first year, they bet $250,000. If they win they get $500,000, if they lose, they get $0. At end of first year any given manager has $1,250,000 with probability 1/2 and $750,000 with probability 1/2 (ignore the 1/37 house advantage) plus the gain on the index fund over the year. If they win 10 times in a row, they have $1.25^{10}$ i.e., $9,300,000, investor of the decade. If they lost 10 times in a row, they are down to $56,000. Fired.

The chance that any given manager makes 10 wins in a row is very low, and specifically is

$$\Pr(\text{manager i has 10 wins}) = \frac{1}{2^{10}} \sim 0.001.$$

However, with 10,000 managers, it is very likely that at least one of them will have 10 wins, since

$$\begin{aligned}\Pr(\text{at least one manager has 10 wins}) &= 1 - \Pr(\text{none has 10 wins}) \\ &= 1 - \left(1 - \frac{1}{2^{10}}\right)^{10000} \\ &= 0.99994.\end{aligned}$$

This is sometimes called the **infinite monkey theorem** (when the number of managers goes to infinity): enough monkeys randomly typing will produce the complete works of Shakespeare for example.

Active management is a zero-sum game (not everybody can be above average) and many funds must lose so that others can win. Picking the right manager may be just as difficult as picking the right stocks. On the other hand, there are some well-known stock market legends! Warren Buffett's Berkshire Hathaway, over its 55 years of trading in the stock market, has returned an average of 20.5% a year, over double the return of the S&P 500 over the same time frame, which is the market average most people look at when speaking of the market in general. He's not the only one.

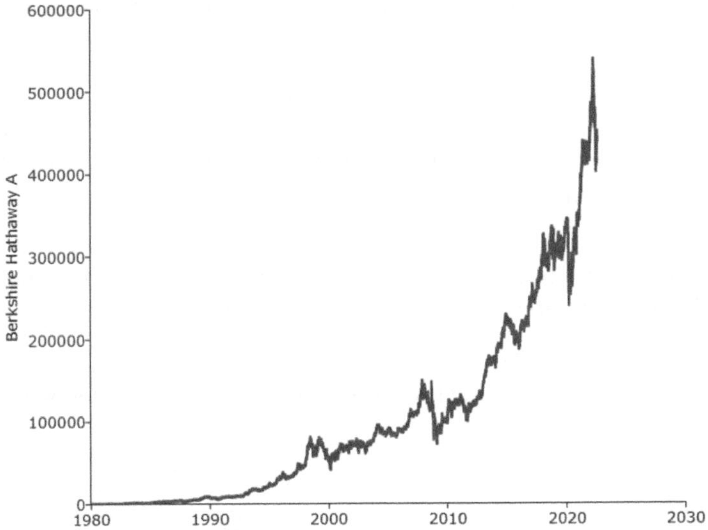


**FIGURE 7.1**
Berkshire Hathaway A stock price

## 7.2 Key Points

1. The Efficient Market Hypothesis (EMH) says that prices fully reflect all relevant information about the value of an asset.
2. The EMH says that many widely observed investment strategies should not make abnormal profits and therefore are not worth pursuing.
3. The EMH also predicts that stock prices should follow a random walk.

## 7.3 Exercises

1. Suppose that
$$\log(P_t) = \mu + \log(P_{t-1}) + \varepsilon_t,$$
where $\varepsilon_t$ is i.i.d. with mean zero and variance $\sigma^2$. Show that returns $R_t = (P_t - P_{t-1})/P_{t-1}$ satisfy
$$R_t = \mu^* + \varepsilon_t^*,$$
where $\varepsilon_t^*$ is i.i.d. with mean zero and variance $\sigma^{*2}$, and find $\mu^*, \sigma^{*2}$.
2. Suppose that
$$\log(P_t) = \mu + \log(P_{t-1}) + \varepsilon_t,$$
where $\varepsilon_t$ is i.i.d. with mean zero and variance $\sigma^2$. Compare two following different cases for the shock distribution
   (a) $\varepsilon_t \sim N(0, \sigma^2)$
   (b) $\varepsilon_t \sim \text{Cauchy}(0, \sigma^2)$, meaning the density of $\varepsilon_t$, denoted $f$, satisfies
$$f(x) = \frac{1}{\pi\sigma}\frac{1}{1+(x/\sigma)^2}, \qquad x \in \mathbb{R}.$$
3. Warren Buffett promoted a macro version of a contrarian strategy: Buy the S&P500 index if the ratio of its price to GDP is low, and sell the index if it is high: (*Be greedy when others are fearful and be fearful when others are greedy).*

# 8

# *Testing of EMH Based on Autocorrelations*

## Outline

This chapter explores the empirical testing of the Efficient Markets Hypothesis (EMH) through autocorrelation analysis. It addresses the logical foundations of EMH, methods for testing stock return predictability, and the implications of observed autocorrelation patterns. The chapter discusses different statistical techniques and their applications in testing market efficiency, compares markets based on deviations from EMH, and examines trading strategies and market anomalies.

After reading this chapter, you will be able to:

- Understand the foundations and logical issues of the Efficient Markets Hypothesis (EMH).
- Apply statistical hypothesis tests to evaluate stock return predictability.
- Analyze autocorrelation functions and their implications for market efficiency.
- Compare different markets based on their adherence to or deviations from EMH.
- Evaluate simple trading strategies based on autocorrelation patterns.
- Assess the stability of predictability over time and across different markets.
- Identify and understand market anomalies and their challenges to EMH.
- Apply variance ratios to measure cumulative predictability.

The **Efficient Markets Hypothesis** says that prices accurately reflect available information (past prices (weak form) or past prices plus other public information currently available (semi-strong form)). The price you pay for a stock is the right price at the time, although it may change in 2 seconds time in response to new information. If you knew or could predict that the price would decline, you would demand to pay a lower price or not buy at all. This is a theory. It has logic, but is it scientifically meaningful, and is it true?

DOI: 10.1201/9781003543121-8

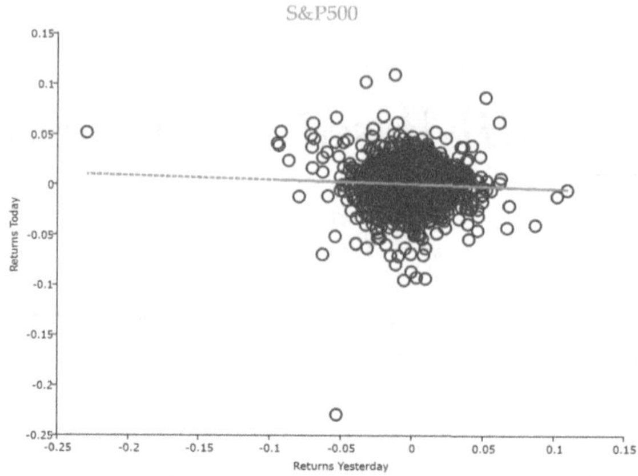


**FIGURE 8.1**
Scatterplot of Yesterdays' returns against Todays' returns, S&P500

We first point out a logical issue with the EMH raised by Grossman and Stiglitz (1980). They point out that if information collection and analysis are costly, which they generally are, there must be compensation for such activity in terms of extra risk-adjusted returns. Otherwise, rational investors would not incur such expenses and would not bring information into prices. Therefore, markets cannot be fully informationally efficient. Rather, one should see an "equilibrium degree of disequilibrium" reflecting the costs of information acquisition and the corresponding profits of traders who have so invested. At best, EMH is an approximation. To take this further, we may be more comfortable with weak form efficiency, since the costs of acquiring, say, daily price information is small, so we expect any deviation from EMH to be correspondingly small.

We want to test the implication of the weak form EMH that returns are unpredictable. We will approach this in two ways. First, we provide a statistical hypothesis test with EMH as the null hypothesis and assumed constant normal return. Second, we consider whether there are exploitable profit opportunities.

The methods we use are based on correlation analysis for stock returns in a time series context to measure predictability. First, we ask whether **we can predict tomorrow's stock returns from today's returns?** We let $X = yesterdayreturns$ $(R_{t-1})$ and $Y = todaysreturns$ $(R_t)$. Are these variables related? If there is a relationship, then we can use that to predict future stock returns in violation of the weak form EMH. We show the daily returns for the S&P500 from 1991-2019. We show the scatterplots of these variables along with the regression line in Figure 8.1. There appears to be a weak negative relationship with a correlation of $-0.04$, which is an order of magnitude smaller than was found by Galton in his classic study of height inheritance. For the

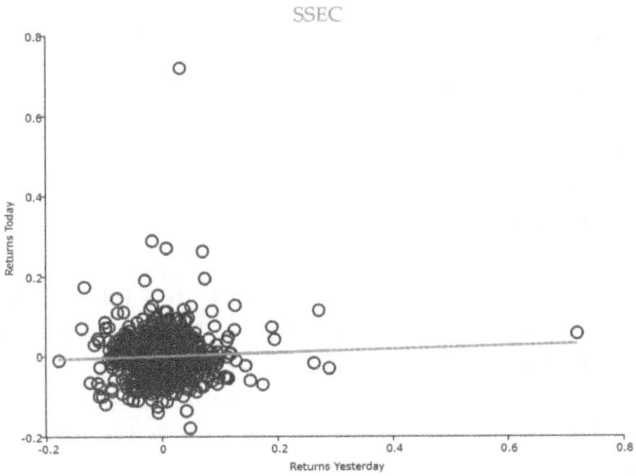


**FIGURE 8.2**
Scatterplot of Yesterdays' returns against Todays' returns, SSEC

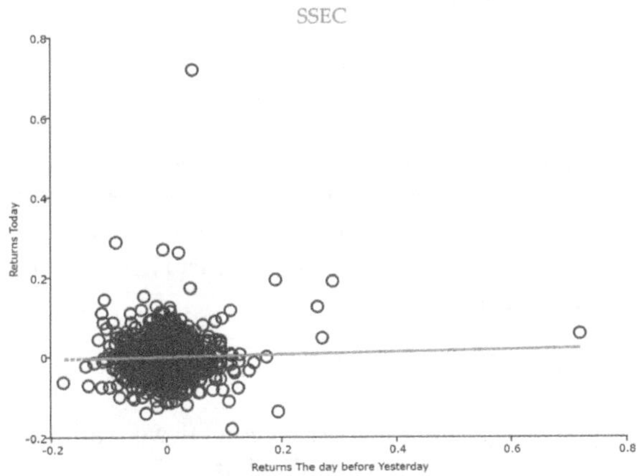


**FIGURE 8.3**
Scatterplot of Day before Yesterdays' returns against Todays' returns, S&P500

SSEC in Figure 8.2 we also have a weak relationship, but in this case, it is positive in slope.

What about earlier returns do they help? In Figure 8.3 we show the scatterplot of returns today against returns from the day before yesterday for the SSEC. It appears equally uninformative.

## 8.1 Testing of EMH

To predict stock returns $R_t$ we may use all past price or return information. We showed the scatterplot for $R_t$ against $R_{t-1}$ and $R_t$ against $R_{t-2}$. What about using all the past information $R_{t-1}, R_{t-2}, \ldots,$ how can we evaluate their contributions. We calculate the correlations between $R_t$ and any other past $R_{t-k}$ for $k = 1, 2, \ldots,$ and check to see if any past returns can help to predict returns. The key tool is called the Autocorrelation function (ACF), which combines all the possible horizons into one picture.

**Definition 16** *The population autocovariance and autocorrelation functions of a stationary series $Y_t$ are defined as follows:*

$$\gamma_k = \text{cov}(Y_t, Y_{t-k}) = E\left[(Y_t - E(Y_t))\,(Y_{t-k} - E(Y_{t-k}))\right]$$

$$\rho_k = \frac{\text{cov}(Y_t, Y_{t-k})}{\sqrt{\text{var}(Y_t)\text{var}(Y_{t-k})}} = \frac{\gamma_k}{\gamma_0}, \quad -1 \leq \rho_k \leq 1$$

*for $k = 0, 1, 2, \ldots$ Note that $\rho_k = E(\widetilde{Y}_t\widetilde{Y}_{t-k})$, where $\widetilde{Y}_t = (Y_t - E(Y_t))/\text{stdev}(Y_t)$.*

The quantity $\rho_1$ is the correlation between today and tomorrow, $\rho_5$ is the correlation between today and next week, $\rho_{22}$ is the correlation between today and next month, $\rho_{250}$ is the correlation between today and next year. In this case because $Y_t$ is stationary (i.e., $\text{var}(Y_t) = \text{var}(Y_{t-k})$, see equation 3.9), we can write the regression model

$$Y_t = E(Y_t) + \rho_k\,(Y_{t-k} - E(Y_{t-k})) + \varepsilon_t, \tag{8.1}$$

where the slope is exactly the autocorrelation. If we want to predict $Y_t$ from $Y_{t-k}$, the coefficient $\rho_k$ tells us how to do that.

We suppose that $Y_t$ is stock returns and that we have a sample of data $\{Y_1, \ldots, Y_T\}$.

**Algorithm 10** *We can estimate the population quantities by the sample equivalents as follows:*

$$\widehat{\gamma}_k = \frac{1}{T}\sum_{t=k+1}^{T}(Y_t - \overline{Y})(Y_{t-k} - \overline{Y}), \quad \overline{Y} = \frac{1}{T}\sum_{t=1}^{T} Y_t \tag{8.2}$$

$$\widehat{\rho}_k = \frac{\widehat{\gamma}_k}{\widehat{\gamma}_0}. \tag{8.3}$$

Note that by construction $-1 \leq \widehat{\rho}_k \leq 1$. We can predict $Y_{t+k}$ by $Y_{t+k|t} = \overline{Y} + \widehat{\rho}_k\left(Y_t - \overline{Y}\right)$.

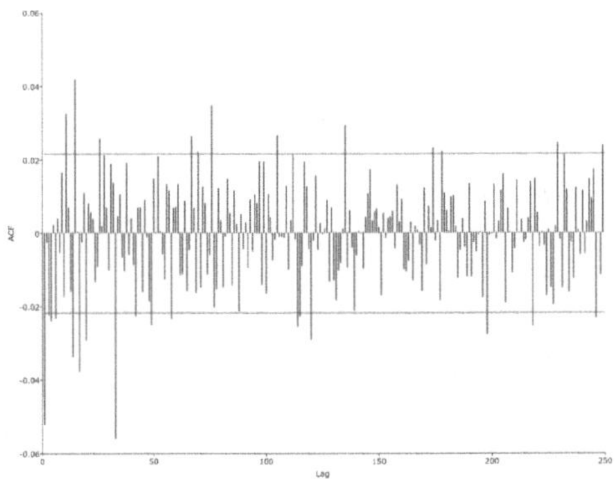

**FIGURE 8.4**
Sample autocorrelation function of daily S&P500 returns for lags 1-255, 1991-2019

These estimators are random variables subject to random variation across hypothetical samples. It can be shown, using the Law of Large Numbers (LLN), that under the EMH, $\widehat{\rho}_k$ converges to zero as $T \to \infty$ (i.e., if the sample size is very large) for all $k \neq 0$. We use the Central Limit Theorem (CLT), to say how much of the autocorrelation is real and how much is due to "sampling variability". In particular, $\sqrt{T}\widehat{\rho}_k$ is approximately standard normal for any $k \neq 0$ under the null hypothesis. It follows that the standard error of $\widehat{\rho}_k$ is

$$\boxed{\text{stderr}(\widehat{\rho}_k) = \frac{1}{\sqrt{T}}},$$

which does not depend on any unknown quantities. Therefore, you can test the null hypothesis by comparing $\widehat{\rho}_k$ with the so-called **Bartlett intervals**

$$[-z_{\alpha/2}/\sqrt{T}, z_{\alpha/2}/\sqrt{T}], \tag{8.4}$$

where $z_{\alpha/2}$ are normal critical values (1.96 for 95% level). Values of $\widehat{\rho}_k$ lying outside this interval are inconsistent with the null hypothesis. Equivalently, one can compare the Z-score $\sqrt{T}\widehat{\rho}_k$ with the critical values $\pm z_{\alpha/2}$. Literally, this is testing the hypothesis that $\rho_k = 0$ versus $\rho_k \neq 0$ for a given $k$. Figure 8.4 shows the ACF for the S&P500 daily stock return series, whereas Figure 8.5 shows the ACF for the SSEC daily stock return series. The S&P500 series shows some statistically significant negative autocorrelation over this time period in the first few lags ($k = 1, 4, 5$). However, longer horizon autocorrelations are often positive and/or statistically insignificant. Furthermore, the magnitude of the autocorrelation at all lags is small. The SSEC series shows some statistically significant positive autocorrelation over this time period in the first few lags. However, longer horizon autocorrelations are often

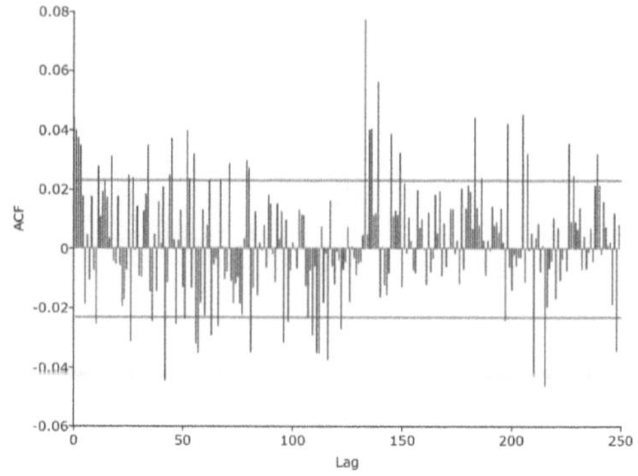


**FIGURE 8.5**
Sample autocorrelation function of daily SSEC returns for lags 1-255, 1991-2019

negative and/or statistically insignificant. Furthermore, the magnitude of the autocorrelation at all lags is small.

What about individual stocks? Are they autocorrelated in the same way as indices? The Dow Jones Industrial Average, as of January 2013, was composed of the following stocks. In the Appendix, we show the composition of the Dow Jones, as of 2021, and there have been big changes. In 2013, Exxon was the largest company in the index by market capitalization, but it has been surpassed by all the big tech stocks, and in particular, Apple is now the largest company in the Dow Jones.

| Name | Cap $b | Name | Cap $b |
|---|---|---|---|
| Alcoa Inc. | 9.88 | JP Morgan | 172.43 |
| AmEx | 66.71 | Coke | 168.91 |
| Boeing | 58.58 | McD | 90.21 |
| Bank of America | 130.52 | MMM | 65.99 |
| Caterpillar | 62.07 | Merck | 127.59 |
| Cisco Systems | 108.74 | MSFT | 225.06 |
| Chevron | 216.27 | Pfizer | 191.03 |
| du Pont | 42.64 | Proctor & Gamble | 188.91 |
| Walt Disney | 92.49 | AT&T | 200.11 |
| General Electric | 222.31 | Travelers | 28.25 |
| Home Depot | 94.47 | United Health | 53.21 |
| HP | 29.49 | United Tech | 77.89 |
| IBM | 219.20 | Verizon | 126.43 |
| Intel | 105.20 | Wall Mart | 231.02 |
| Johnson[2] | 198.28 | Exxon Mobil | 405.60 |

Individual stocks have different means and variances, which are taken account of in the computation of the autocorrelation. Figure 8.6 shows the value

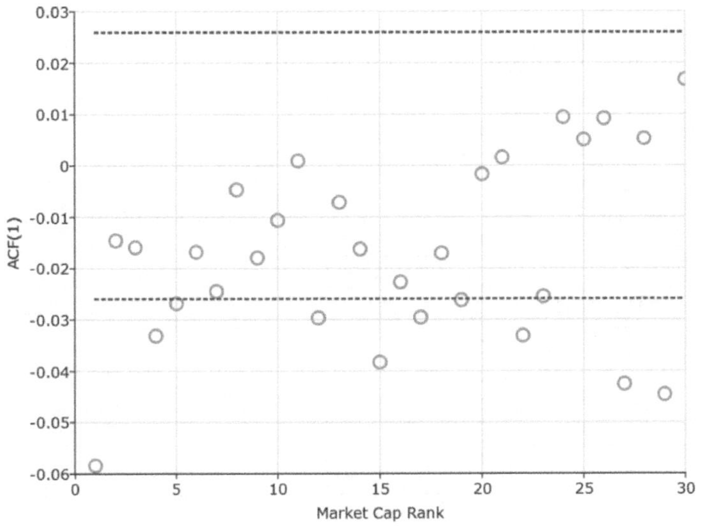


**FIGURE 8.6**
ACF(1) of daily Dow stock returns against market capitalization

of $\widehat{\rho}_1$ for all 30 Dow stocks along with the 95% confidence bands and organized by the size of the firm, market capitalization. Most of the autocorrelations are negative, and ten of them are statistically significant. Figure 8.7 shows the average autocorrelations across the thirty stocks for each lag $k$.

To conclude, we have some evidence of predictability in stock returns, which violates the EMH. Negative autocorrelation on the Dow Jones Stocks; Negative autocorrelation on the S&P500 index from 1991-2019 for the first few lags; Positive autocorrelation on the SSEC from 1991-2019 for the first few lags.

## 8.2 How to Compare Markets According to Their Deviations from This Theory?

How efficient is the Chinese stock market compared with the US market? Is the direction or type of predictability the same or different? The individual autocorrelations, some are positive and some are negative. How do we determine the balance of the direction, positive or negative? By summing them up basically. We need one more tool to do this.

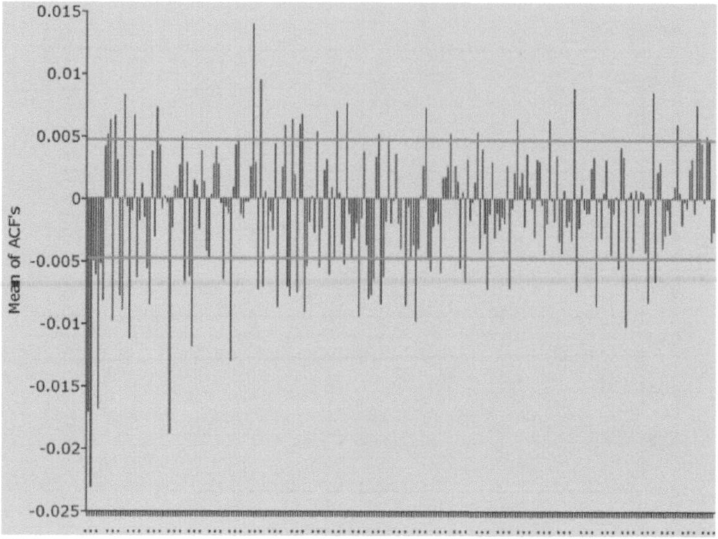


**FIGURE 8.7**
Average ACF of Dow stocks' daily returns against lags $j = 1, \ldots, 255$

The **variance ratio** measures cumulative predictability. It is defined as

$$\boxed{VR_K = \frac{\text{variance(k-period returns)}}{K \times \text{variance(1-period returns)}}}.$$

This is easy to compute, all you need is a sample of low frequency (k-period returns) and a sample of high frequency (1-period) returns. For example, weekly returns ($K = 5$) compared with daily returns ($K = 1$) gives us the $\text{VR}_5$.

One can show that in general, provided returns are stationary but not necessarily EMH compliant

$$VR_K = 1 + 2\sum_{j=1}^{K-1}\left(1 - \frac{j}{K}\right)\rho_j.$$

This is a weighted average of the autocorrelations. Under EMH, we should have all the $\rho_K = 0$ for $K \neq 0$ and so $VR_K = 1$. On the other hand, if $VR_K > 1$, this corresponds to what is called **momentum**, i.e., on balance positive autocorrelations. If $VR_K < 1$, this corresponds to **contrarian/reversal behavior** or negative feedback, i.e., on balance negative autocorrelations.

**Algorithm 11** *For any K:*

$$\widehat{VR}_K = 1 + 2\sum_{j=1}^{K-1}\left(1 - \frac{j}{K}\right)\widehat{\rho}_j.$$

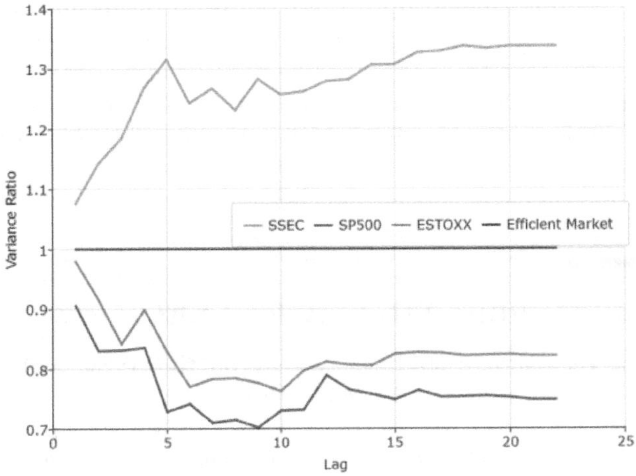


**FIGURE 8.8**
Variance ratios 1991-2019

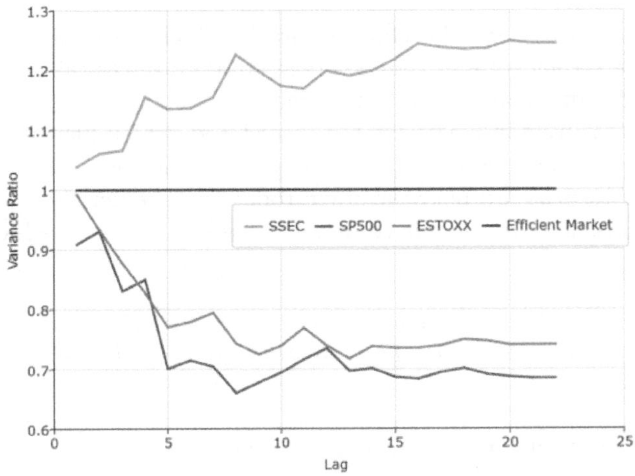


**FIGURE 8.9**
Variance ratios 2010-2019

We calculate the Variance Ratios for some stock markets in Figures 8.8 and 8.9.

There is some evidence of predictability based on past prices alone. The S&P500 and EStoxx have short-term contrarian behavior. Surprisingly, EStoxx seems to have less "inefficiency" than S&P500. The SSEC has short-term and longer-term momentum. The magnitude is quite small at short horizons but grows to be quite large around 2 months, then declines to 6 months, and then goes back up again. Since 2010, the momentum effect on SSEC has declined, while the contrarian effect on the S&P500 and EStoxx has increased.

We will next consider the economic significance of these findings, i.e., whether this autocorrelation can be made into profitable opportunities.

## 8.3 Simple Trading Strategy for SSEC

We develop a very simple trading strategy on the SSEC and calculate its profitability. It is based on the following observation.

**Example 74** *Suppose we take a family from Galton's data, and I bet you on whether the son is taller than average or shorter than average, with an equal payoff. In the absence of any information, this is a fair game, equal payoffs. But suppose I know that the father is taller than average, then it is more likely than not that the son is taller than average.*

We can test this with the Galton data in which case one finds that 65% of sons whose father is taller than average are themselves taller than average. This gives you an advantage in that game.

The SSEC is weakly positively autocorrelated, which likewise means that: If returns are above average today, we predict they will be above average tomorrow; If returns are below average today, we predict they will be below average tomorrow. We use this to define a trading strategy, which is defined next.

**Definition 17** *If $R_t > \overline{R}$ (mean value), then buy at the close. If $R_t < \overline{R}$ (mean value), then sell at the close. Rebalance (sell or buy back) every day at the close.*

The realized profit of this strategy at time $t+1$ is

$$\pi_{t+1} = \begin{cases} R_{t+1} & \text{if buy at } t \\ -R_{t+1} & \text{if sell at } t \end{cases}$$

We calculate the cumulative profit $\sum_{t=1}^{s} \pi_{t+1}$ $(s = 1, 2, \ldots, T-1)$, shown in Figure 8.10, and the average profit per day $\sum_{t}^{T-1} \pi_{t+1}/(T-1)$. For SSEC, the average profit per day (over 1991-2019) is 0.000884 (annualized value is 22.5%) to be compared with the mean return per day of 0.000469 (annualized value 11.9%) (what you get if you buy every day). The standard deviation of the daily profit is around 0.0224. In the more recent period, since 2010, profits declined, see Figure 8.11. However, this coincides with the market itself not performing well, and in fact, our strategy beats the market over this period.

**FIGURE 8.10**
Cumulative gain (not compounded) of trading strategy on SSEC from 1991 to 2019

**FIGURE 8.11**
Cumulative gain starting from 2010

Can we do better? Clearly, shorting the index whenever$R_t < \overline{R}$ seems a bit wasteful because we could still have $R_t > 0$ and still predict positive returns $R_{t+1} > 0$. We regress SSEC returns on SSEC yesterdays returns and obtain

$$R_{t+1} = \underset{(0.000265)}{0.000469} + \underset{(0.011780)}{0.042391}(R_t - 0.000469) + e_{t+1}, \quad R^2 = 0.002. \quad (8.5)$$

This is a very noisy regression, but still there is some predictability (which violates the EMH), because the standard error on the slope is small compared to the estimate. Our prediction for future returns based on this regression is

$$R_{t+1|t} = 0.000469 + 0.042391(R_t - 0.000469).$$

Clearly, we have $R_{t+1|t} > 0$ even for some range of values $R_t < \overline{R}$. We might consider the following trading strategy

**Definition 18** *If $R_{t+1|t} > 0$ (mean value), then buy at the close. If $R_{t+1|t} <0$ (mean value), then sell at the close. Rebalance (sell or buy back) every day at the close. Does this work better?*

Also, we have the option of earning the risk free rate $R_f$ (or zero) by not being in the market. Therefore, consider the portfolio

$$\mathcal{P} = \omega R + (1 - \omega)R_f,$$

where $\omega$ is the fraction invested in risky assets and $1-\omega$ is the fraction invested in riskless assets at time $t$ (notation suppressed). This includes our previous strategy, where we considered only $\omega \in \{-1, 1\}$, but now we allow $\omega \in \mathbb{R}$. Suppose our utility is mean variance $U = E(\mathcal{P}) - \gamma \text{var}(\mathcal{P})$, where $\gamma > 0$ is risk aversion then the optimal $\omega \in \mathbb{R}$ satisfies

$$\omega_{opt} = \frac{E(R) - R_f}{2\gamma \text{var}(R)}. \quad (8.6)$$

We can replace $E(R)$ by $R_{t+1|t}$ and var$(R)$ by the sample variance in this formula, in which case the weights will vary every day according to the prediction we make. Nowadays, a lot of sophisticated technology like machine learning, etc., goes into making predictions $R_{t+1|t}$ and $\text{var}_t(R_{t+1})$ and this can be easily incorporated into this framework. This implies we would change the weighting $\omega_{opt}$ every day as our predictions $R_{t+1|t}$ and $\text{var}_t(R_{t+1})$ change.

We seem to have found some profitable trading strategies. In practice, we need to consider several things. Transaction costs. When you buy and sell stocks, there is a fee to be paid to the market makers, essentially, each time. Lots of trading, lots of fees. The fees can eat up the profit. The analysis we gave does not consider the scale of investment. Furthermore, if you buy \$1,000,000,000 worth of stock, you will not only pay a fee. You will move the price yourself and so eliminate your profit opportunity. To conclude, don't try this at home.

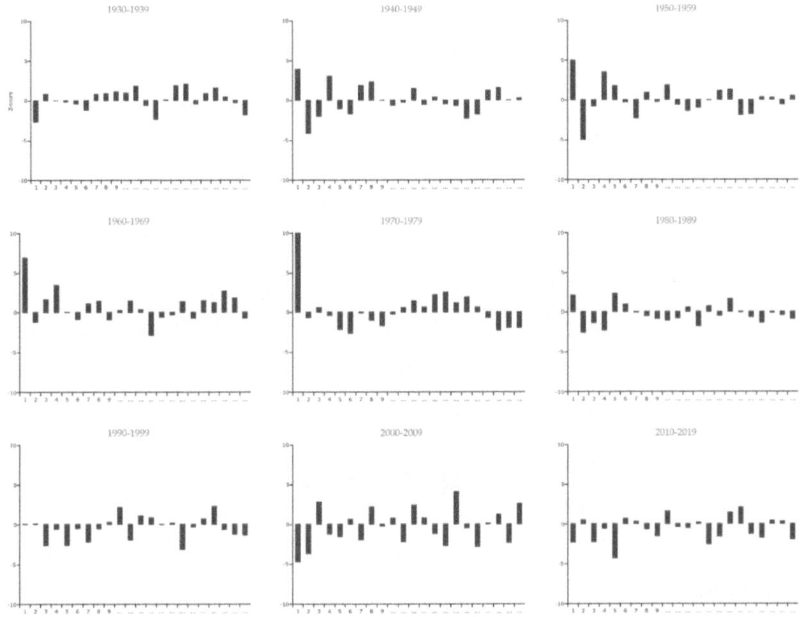


**FIGURE 8.12**
Autocorrelations on the S&P500 by decade

## 8.4 Is Predictability Stable Over Time?

**Are these autocorrelation patterns stable over time?** Not really. We show the S&P500 daily data Z-score of ACF by decade below. It seems that until 2000 the US market had momentum like the SSEC, i.e. positive autocorrelation at the first lag was the norm, whereas after 2000 this pattern has shifted to negative autocorrelation.

We also show the FF market return ACF by decade below, which tells a similar story. The 20th century was mostly about momentum, whereas the 21st century has switched to a reversal logic at the first lag, as far as the US is concerned.

## 8.5 Market Anomalies

An anomaly is something that is in disagreement with a theoretical prediction, in this case that of the EMH. There are many anomalies that have been documented in the literature. Below, we give some of the main ones.

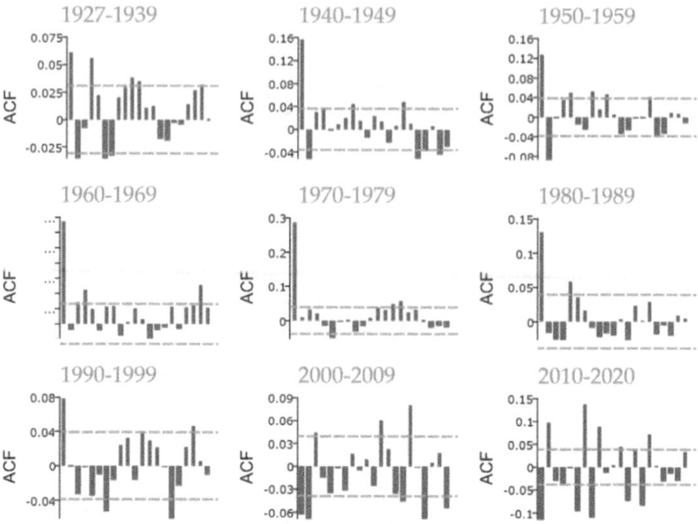


**FIGURE 8.13**
Autocorrelations on the FF market return by decade

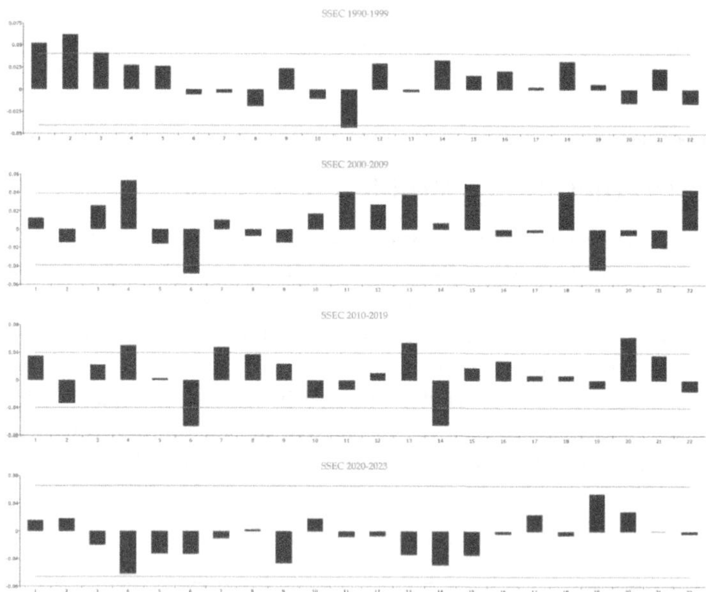


**FIGURE 8.14**
Autocorrelations on the SSEC daily return by decade from 1990

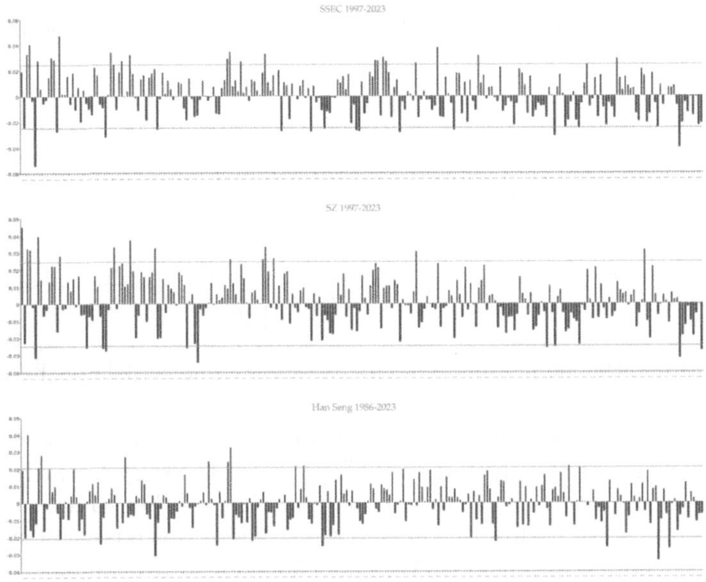


**FIGURE 8.15**
Comparison of SSEC, SZ index, and Han Seng daily index return autocorrelations

1. The small stock premium, Banz (1981): the returns of small stocks are higher after adjusting for risk than are the returns of large stocks.
2. Momentum and contrarian anomalies, Jegadeesh and Titman (1993) and de Bondt and Thaler (1985).
   (a) Over the short to medium term, winners tend to be winners and losers tend to be losers
   (b) Over the medium to long term, winners tend to be losers and losers tend to be winners
3. The January effect, returns are higher in January than in other months of the year.
4. The Monday effect, returns are lower on Mondays than other days of the week.

### 8.5.1 Econometrics of Calendar Effects

We focus on the calendar anomalies and how one might go about evidencing or disproving them. We suppose that the EMH is true, so that

$$R_t = \mu + \varepsilon_t,$$

where $\varepsilon_t$ is unpredictable. We embed this in the more general model

$$R_t = \mu + \sum_{j=1}^{K} \beta_j D_{jt} + \varepsilon_t, \tag{8.7}$$

where $D_{jt}$ are a full set of seasonal **dummy variables**: in the case of day of the week, $K = 5$, and:

$$D_{1t} = \begin{cases} 1 & \text{if day } t \text{ is Monday} \\ 0 & \end{cases}, \quad D_{2t} = \begin{cases} 1 & \text{if day } t \text{ is Tuesday} \\ 0 & \end{cases}, \ldots$$

In the case of the month of the year, $K = 12$. The null hypothesis is that $\beta_j = 0$, $j = 1, \ldots, K$.

It is not possible to estimate the regression (8.7) uniquely because of **multicollinearity**, specifically we have $\sum_{j=1}^{K} D_{jt} = 1$ for every $t$, which is exactly the same as the intercept column. Usual practice is either to drop one of the dummy variables or to drop the intercept, neither of which is satisfactory from an interpretation point of view. We prefer to work in two steps.

**Algorithm 12** *First, we estimate $\mu$ by the sample mean return*

$$\overline{R} = \frac{1}{T} \sum_{t=1}^{T} R_t$$

*and then subtract off from observed returns to obtain $\widetilde{R}_t = R_t - \overline{R}$. Second, we estimate the no intercept multiple regression of demeaned returns on seasonal dummies, i.e.,*

$$\widetilde{R}_t = \sum_{j=1}^{K} \beta_j D_{jt} + \varepsilon_t. \tag{8.8}$$

*This second stage regression is feasible because it does not contain an intercept, note.*

In this approach, we can estimate all $K$ dummy coefficients and present t-statistics for them (however, note that the joint distribution is singular, so the F statistic that usually accompanies regression output has to be interpreted with care). Below, we report the t-statistics for the day of the week effect and for the month of the year effect. We find strong evidence of a Monday effect in daily stock returns (significantly negative returns accrue on Monday only) up until around 1990; thereafter, this effect seems to have disappeared since the t-statistics are not significant, and even the relative returns on Monday are in some cases positive.

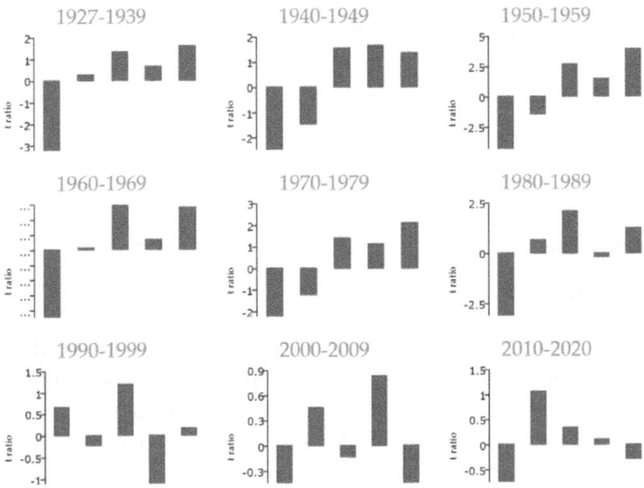


**FIGURE 8.16**
Day of the week effect on S&P500

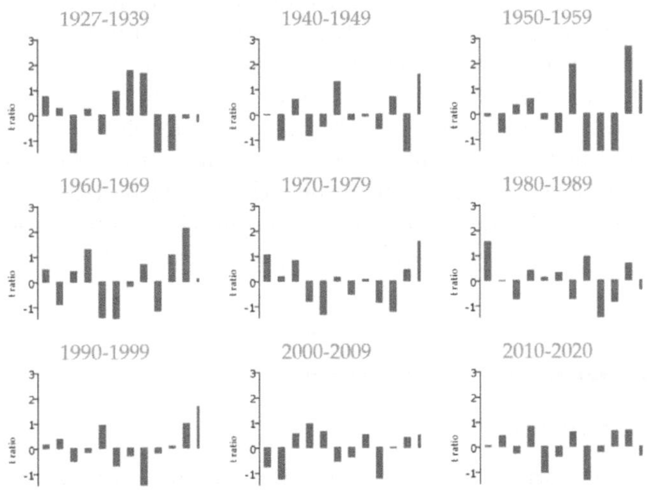


**FIGURE 8.17**
Month of the year effect FF market return

For interpretation purposes, one may prefer to do the regression with annualized returns (multiply daily returns by 255), in which case, the coefficients have the interpretation of how much they affect annual returns. Alternatively, one may wish to standardize returns in a statistical way (subtract mean and divide by stdev), in which case, the coefficients have interpretation in terms of standard deviations. Whichever way the regression is done (in daily returns, in annual returns, or in standardized returns) does not affect the statistical inference question, but it does affect the economic interpretation of the results and their comparability across securities.

## 8.6 Conclusion

We found some statistical evidence against the EMH. There does appear to be a small amount of predictability in daily stock prices. The direction of predictability appears to vary over time. It also varies across assets and across markets. Trading strategies can make money in theory, but in practice, we have to account for trading costs and other issues.

Market Anomalies such as the small stock premium, the January effect, and the Monday effect are known to have reduced or disappeared in later years. Ross called this the Heisenberg Principle of Finance: observing an anomaly brings about its own extinction because of trading. In addition, there is the **data mining** issue (related to the **infinite monkey theorem**). By trawling through many strategies, one will end up with a best one that appears to be very good. However, the size of the trawling ocean will introduce a (survivorship) bias in the perceived benefits of a trading strategy based on the best case predictability found. If $n$ is the total number of predictors, then there are a total of $2^n - 1$ different linear regression models with two predictors that one could fit to the sample data. For example, if $n = 30$, there are over a billion different linear regression models that could be tried; if one just reports the best one of these, then one is biasing the results. A solution is to use out-of-sample testing to validate any proposed model.

## 8.7 Key Points

1. The Autocorrelation function is a key tool for testing the weak form efficient markets hypothesis.
2. The sample values of the autocorrelation of daily stock returns are generally quite small and can be either positive or negative. This is true for both stock indexes and individual stocks from different countries.
3. There is some evidence that the EMH is violated, but it is statistically weak and its nature varies over time.

## 8.8 Exercises

1. Obtain daily price data from a market of your choice. The (equal weighted) moving average filter of a series $X_t$ is defined as

$$SMA_t^k = \frac{X_t + X_{t-1} + \ldots + X_{t+1-k}}{k},$$

where $k$ is the number of lags to include, sometimes called a bandwidth parameter. For daily stock prices, common values include 5, 10, 20, 50, 100, and 200. Compute the SMA for the time series. These smoothed values are often used in trading strategies of the contrarian type, that is: buy when $X_t < SMA_t^k$ and sell when $X_t > SMA_t^k$, or moment type trading strategies, that is, buy when $X_t > SMA_t^k$ and sell when $X_t < SMA_t^k$. The exponential weighted average is defined as

$$EWMA_t = \alpha X_t + (1-\alpha)EWMA_{t-1},$$

where $EWMA_1 = X_1$ and $\alpha \in (0,1)$. Can relate $\alpha = 2/(k+1)$, where $k$ is the number of time periods. Comment on the efficacy of these trading strategies for your dataset.

2. Forecasting Bitcoin using rolling windows. For the dataset BTC-USD calculate the daily returns $r_t$ from 2014-2024. Compare the rolling window versus the recursive window forecast as follows. For the dataset $\{r_{t-m}, \ldots, r_t\}$ calculate $\overline{r}_{t-m:t}, \widehat{\phi}_{t-m:t}$ (the first order autocorrelation of the data). Forecast $r_{t+1}$ by $\overline{r}_{t-m:t}$ or by

$$\widehat{r}_{t+1:t} = \overline{r}_{t-m:t} + \widehat{\phi}_{t-m:t}(y_t - \overline{r}_{t-m:t}).$$

Calculate the forecast errors $\widehat{\varepsilon}_{t+1}$. Then for rolling window calculate again with the data $\{r_{t-m+1}, \ldots, r_{t+1}\}$ and for the recursive forecast work with the data $\{r_{t-m}, \ldots, r_{t+1}\}$. and compute the Mean Squared Forecast Errors

$$\sum \widehat{\varepsilon}_{t+1}^2$$

3. Pairs trading. A common trading strategy involves working with stocks whose prices are believed to be linked and do not deviate too much. Let $P_t, Q_t$ be the closing prices of two stocks $A$ and $B$, and let $p_t = \log P_t$ and $q_t = \log Q_t$. One approach is to calculate the ratio of stock prices

$$\tau_t = \frac{P_t}{Q_t}$$

and the mean and variance $\overline{\tau}$, $s_\tau^2$ of a sample period of this ratio. Then we set the confidence band

$$\overline{\tau} \pm 1.96 s_\tau$$

and apply this to determine a trading strategy for a new period of data. One approach is: If $\tau_t \geq \overline{\tau} + 1.96 s_\tau$, then buy stock $B$ with price $Q_t$ and sell stock $A$ with price $P_t$. Hold until $\tau_t \leq \overline{\tau}$ and then close the trade (sell stock $B$ and but stock $A$. Investigate this trading strategy for pairs of stocks of your own choice.

4. Tracking error of ETF. The SPDR ETF is tracking the returns on the S&P500 index. In Figure 8.18, we show the daily tracking error, which is the difference in returns. Calculate the daily mean and standard deviation of the tracking error and its annualized version. Calculate the autocorrelation function and comment on the performance.

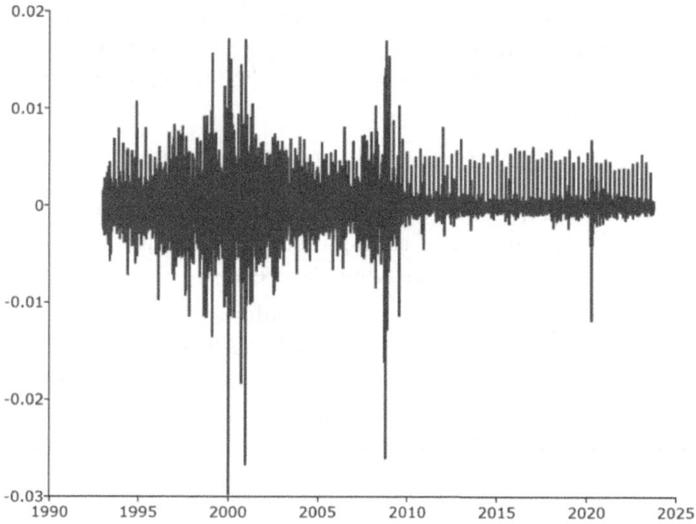


**FIGURE 8.18**
The daily tracking error of the SPDR ETF relative to the S&P500 index

# 9

# *Event Studies*

## Outline

This chapter examines the methodology and applications of event studies in financial economics. It focuses on assessing the impact of specific events on stock prices and other financial outcomes. The chapter covers the steps involved in conducting an event study, the definition and measurement of abnormal returns, and the analysis of various types of events, including firm-specific and market-wide events. By providing a structured approach to evaluating the effects of events, the chapter helps in understanding market reactions and testing the Efficient Markets Hypothesis (EMH).

After reading this chapter, you will be able to:

- Understand the purpose and methodology of event studies in financial research.
- Define events, selection criteria, and event windows for an event study.
- Measure normal and abnormal returns using statistical models.
- Apply the event study to real-world scenarios.
- Analyze the impact of firm-specific events like stock splits, earnings announcements, and mergers.
- Evaluate market-wide events and their effects on stock indices and specific industries.
- Use extensions of the event study methodology for special cases such as IPOs and exchange rate changes.
- Critically assess the results of event studies and their implications for market efficiency.

In this chapter, we discuss methodology for estimating the effect of an event on an outcome variable, which is a very central activity in empirical work. We start with an example.

The Challenger space shuttle exploded shortly after takeoff at 11:39 a.m. Eastern Standard Time on January 28, 1986. It killed all the astronauts and

DOI: 10.1201/9781003543121-9

was a major disaster for the US space project (especially after the huge success of the Apollo moon landing in 1969). Six months later, the US government report was released based on millions of pages of evidence by engineers and by the genius of the Nobel physicist Richard Feynman; it indicated that the fault was due to an O-ring (a seal) that had cracked due to recent cold weather in Florida, Rogers Commission (1986).

What was the effect of the disaster on the stock market as a whole? What was the effect of the disaster on the stock prices of the companies that made components of the space shuttle: Morton Thiokol; Lockheed; Martin Marietta; Rockwell International? By the market close of Jan 28th, we had

| Morton Thiokol | Lockheed | Martin Marietta | Rockwell Int'l |
|---|---|---|---|
| −11.86% | −2.14% | −3.25% | −2.48% |

The O-rings were made by Morton Thiokol! But perhaps the whole market went down, and Morton Thiokol is a very volatile stock—if it goes up, it goes up a lot, and if it goes down, it goes down a lot. No. The market was not widely affected by the crash, with the closing price on the day being 207.4 compared with the opening price of 207.42. So in this case, it is pretty clear that the effect on Morton Thiokol was due to the disaster.

We now turn to the general event study problem. In general, we have to care about what else happened at the same time as the event and try to control for it, and so we next discuss how to go about this. We want to measure the impact of an event on an outcome variable $Y$ to compare with the theoretical prediction. To address this, we may compare the before and after outcomes, i.e., compute $Y_{after} - Y_{before}$, but this may be biased because there may be many things happening at the same time as the event.

We propose to use a control group against which to measure the change in outcomes. Thus, we divide into treated and control units and compute the "diff in diffs"

$$\left(Y_{after}^{treated} - Y_{before}^{treated}\right) - \left(Y_{after}^{control} - Y_{before}^{control}\right) \tag{9.1}$$

This is a general principle applied in many fields, from Labor economics to medicine, etc. The questions that need to be addressed are: how to measure outcome $Y$, what are the treatment and control group, and what is before and after. Before we discuss these questions in detail, we present some types of applications we have in mind.

## 9.1 Financial Applications

We may classify events into either firm-specific or market-wide. *Firm-specific events* include: stock splits, reverse splits, share repurchase, mergers and acquisitions, earnings announcements, seasoned equity offering, inclusion in stock index, insider trading, Initial Public Offerings, short selling restrictions, and single stock circuit breakers. *Market wide events* include: Macroeconomic announcements, Regulatory changes such as Dodd-Frank, and the Covid-19 pandemic. We mostly concentrate on firm-specific events.

The main target outcome we consider is the effect of the event on the valuation of the firm or firms, i.e., whether the event increased or decreased the market value of the firm(s).

**Dividend Payments**. Many stocks pay dividends, often quarterly. For example, Apple is currently paying 0.23c per share dividends per quarter on a stock price of $146. What happens to the stock price at the ex-dividend date (i.e., when the dividend is paid)? If the market is efficient, then on average the stock price should fall by the amount of the dividend. Otherwise one has an opportunity for economic profit, one could buy the stock just before the dividend is paid and then sell it just after at the same price taking the dividend for free. One might conjecture that the stock price will not react fully; the stock price falls on average by less than the dividend. This is an empirical question.

**Stock Splits.** A firm splits its stock 2:1 means that it doubles the number of shares (allocating them pro rata to original owners) and halfs the price level. According to present value calculations this should have no effect on the valuation of the firm and on the return (which is the percentage change in price) on holding the stock. There are various other theories as to why stock splits may be beneficial to owners, managers, or brokers, which we discuss further below.

**Earning announcements.** Every quarter, listed companies in the US have to publicly announce various financial results over the previous quarter, including their earnings. Under strong-form efficiency, earnings announcement have no effect on the firm's stock price, because insiders already know this information perfectly. In fact, prior to the announcement, there is quite a lot of information widely known (publicly available) about the likely magnitude of a company's earnings, although this is not perfectly accurate. Therefore, under semi-strong form efficiency, the anticipated (by market participants) part of earnings should have no effect, but the unanticipated part should have an immediate and "permanent" effect on prices. That is, we should decompose the announced earnings into two components

$$\text{earnings} = \text{anticipated earnings} + \overbrace{\text{unanticipated earnings}}^{\text{surprise}}.$$

How to define/estimate anticipated earnings? Many analysts forecast company earnings, providing daily updates to their forecasts for the next quarter (and beyond) earnings. For a company like Apple this is a major industry in itself. The Institutional Brokers' Estimate System (IBES) is a database of analyst estimates and company guidance for 22,000 public companies. The database aggregates all of the available financial data on companies to aid investors in decision-making. Historical data is available from 1976, when IBES was introduced; it is now owned by Thomson Reuters.

$$\begin{aligned}\text{Earnings surprise} = {} & \text{announced earnings} \\ & - \text{the previous day's I/B/E/S mean forecast.}\end{aligned}$$

Perhaps allow a margin $\pm 2.5\%$.

Do these forecasts work well? Perhaps. We show how the forecasting of Amazon Earnings per Share worked during the first part of the Covid-19 pandemic. We show the "Estimates" and the actual announcements in 2020 (units are earnings per share in $)

| Date | Actual | Estimate |
|---|---|---|
| Q1 2020 | 5.01 | 6.25 |
| Q2 2020 | 10.30 | 1.46 |
| Q3 2020 | 12.37 | 7.41 |
| Q4 2020 | 14.09 | 7.23 |
| Q1 2021 | 15.79 | 9.54 |

Clearly, there was an underestimate of Amazon's earnings in Q2, which seemed to persist throughout 2020. This was at the beginning of the pandemic and the economy as a whole was badly affected and the analysts had not appreciated the big switch to online shopping that benefitted the company.

**Mergers and Acquisitions.** Company A announces a takeover bid for Company b on day x. What is the effect of the announcement: on the value of company A?; on the value of company b? After a successful bid, there is only company A+b and one would like also to know what is the effect on the value of the combined company. Is it higher than the combined value before the merger? After an unsuccessful bid, one would like also to know what is the effect on the values of the two companies. Famous successful acquisitions include Microsoft acquisition of Activision in 2023.

**Example 75** *In 2014, Pfizer made three offers to purchase Astra Zeneca. These are shown in Figure 9.1 as green triangles compared to the normalized prices of the two companies on the first trading day of 2014: the first offer being around 30% higher per share than the prevailing market price and the final offer being more than 50% higher than the prevailing market price on January 1st. Ultimately, their acquisition did not succeed. Overall, there was a positive effect on the share price of Astra Zeneca during the year, but a negative effect on the share price of Pfizer.*

**FIGURE 9.1**
Pfizer takeover offers to Astra Zeneca during 2014

## 9.2 Seven Steps in an Event Study

The traditional approach to event studies has seven steps, which are outlined below.

1. Event Definition
2. Selection Criteria
3. Normal and Abnormal Returns
4. Estimation Procedure
5. Testing Procedure

6. Empirical Results
7. Interpretation and Conclusion

### 9.2.1 Event Definition and Selection Criteria

One must first define the event of interest and the period of study. In particular, one should determine the event window, the frequency of data, and which stock or stocks to include in the study. We discuss below the choice of event window, as it can have a big effect on the presentation of results.

### 9.2.2 Null and Alternative Hypothesis

The Efficient Market Hypothesis says that there should be an immediate and permanent effect (including no effect if such is warranted). This, of course, ignores physics. The speed of light imposes a constraint on the speed of any adjustment. Therefore, in practice, "immediate" and "permanent" must be defined with some "flexibility"—it requires a judgement call as to whether a specific reaction is consistent with EMH predictions or not.

There are different types of alternative responses to events in the case of inefficient markets. Specifically, we may have underreaction: a gradual adjustment to a new level; or we may have overreaction: an adjustment that overshoots the new "correct" level and then returns to it. Figure 9.2 shows some different idealized types of reactions to an event. One purpose of the event study is to try to identify the type of adjustment as to whether it is broadly consistent with the EMH or whether it is more consistent with an overreaction, etc.

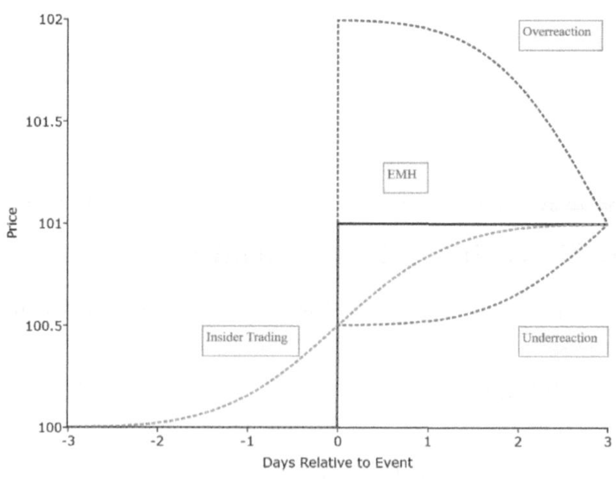


**FIGURE 9.2**
Shows examples of price trajectories around the event at time 0

We discuss briefly two possible examples of market overreaction. The FTSE250 stock price around the 2016 Brexit referendum shown in Figure 9.3, and the Zoom conferencing stock price during the Covid-19 pandemic shown in Figure 9.4. Maybe these are good topics for discussion.

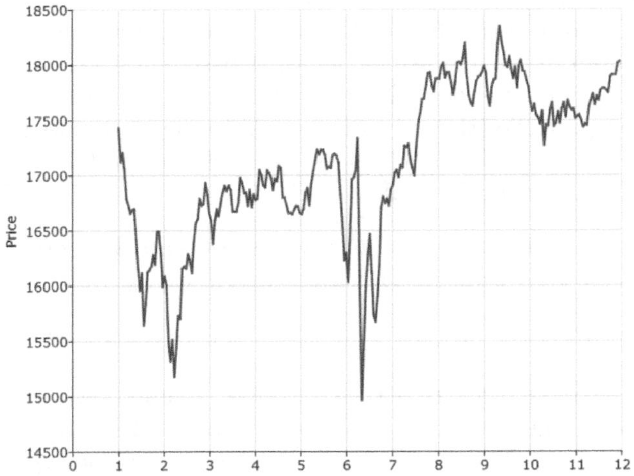


**FIGURE 9.3**
FTSE250 index level around Brexit referendum in 2016 (by months of 2016)

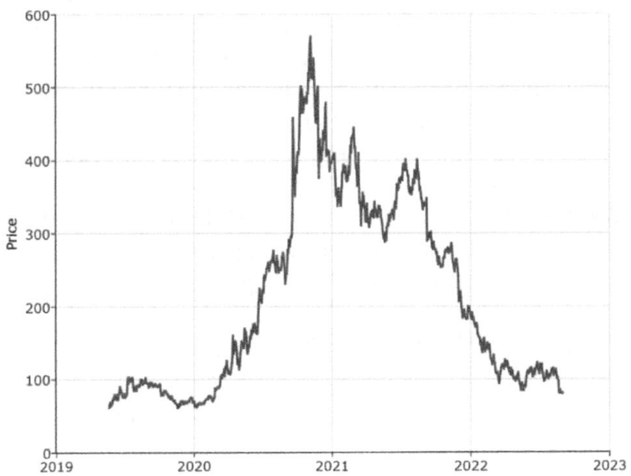


**FIGURE 9.4**
Zoom conferencing stock price from IPO to 2022

### 9.2.3 Normal Return Definition

How do we know what the stock price (return) would have been in the absence of the event (or in the absence of any effect due to the event)? We note that the correlation between *contemporaneous* stock returns is much higher than the correlation between current and future returns. This doesn't help in forecasting future returns, but it does help to estimate what the stock price would have been in the absence of the event based on what happens to other stocks that did not experience the event. The market return $R_{mt}$ is the return on the market portfolio (that is, all the stocks in the market weighted by value (in practice S&P500 index)). This has a special place in finance and features in the so-called **Market Model.**

**Definition 19** *(Market Model) Individual stock returns $R_t$ are related to contemporaneous market returns via linear regression*

$$R_t = \alpha + \beta R_{mt} + \varepsilon_t, \quad E(\varepsilon_t) = 0, \ \text{var}(\varepsilon_t) = \sigma^2.$$

The market model says that the stock goes up and down with the market according to the value of $\beta$ and has separate so so-called idiosyncratic movements due to $\alpha + \varepsilon_t$. The parameter $\beta$ (beta) measures the systematic risk of stock, the higher the value of $\beta$, the more risky is the stock because its own returns are amplified returns on the market. If the market is up 10% and if $\beta = 1.5$, then this says that the stock's return goes up on average by 15%. If the market is up 10% and if $\beta = 0.5$, then this says that the stocks return goes up on average by 5%. The parameter $\alpha$ (alpha) measures the idiosyncratic mean return of the stock. If $\alpha > 0$ we say that the stock earns excess risk adjusted return (defined as $R_t - \beta R_{mt}$). Usually, $\alpha$ is quite small. The parameter $\sigma$ (sigma) measures the variability of the idiosyncratic shock. If $\sigma^2 = 0$, the stock moves perfectly in lock step with the market. We have, by the properties of variance, that $\text{var}(R_t) = \beta^2\text{var}(R_{mt}) + \text{var}(\varepsilon_t)$, i.e., the total variance of stock return can be decomposed into the common part $\beta^2\text{var}(R_{mt})$ and the idiosyncratic part $\text{var}(\varepsilon_t)$.

We use Ken French data on industry portfolio returns and market returns daily from 1927 to 2020. For the agriculture sector, we show the data in Figure 9.5 along with the regression line, which is given below

$$R_{agric} = \underset{(0.0079)}{0.0186} + \underset{(0.0074)}{0.788}\, R_{market}, \quad R^2 = 0.316,$$

This sector has low risk ($\beta < 1$) and a small and positive and statistically significant $\alpha$. For the aero sector shown in Figure 9.6 we have the following

$$R_{aero} = \underset{(0.0076)}{0.0233} + \underset{(0.0071)}{1.245}\, R_{market}, \quad R^2 = 0.557$$

This sector has high risk ($\beta > 1$) and a small and positive and statistically significant $\alpha$.

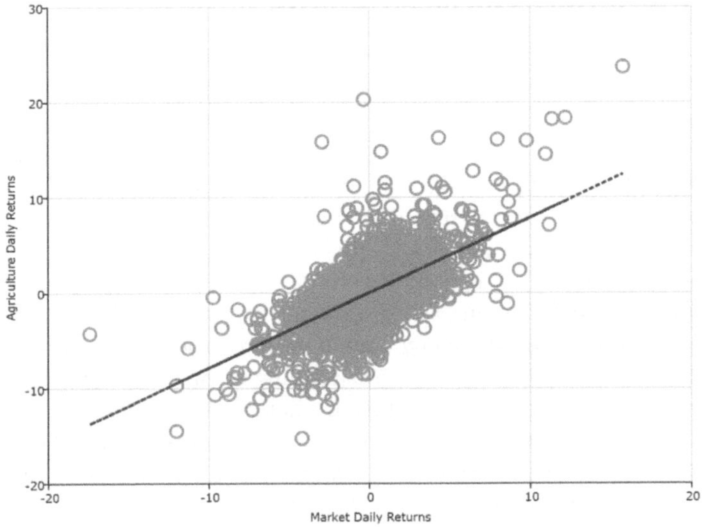


**FIGURE 9.5**
Agriculture sector daily returns against market returns. Scatter plot with regression line

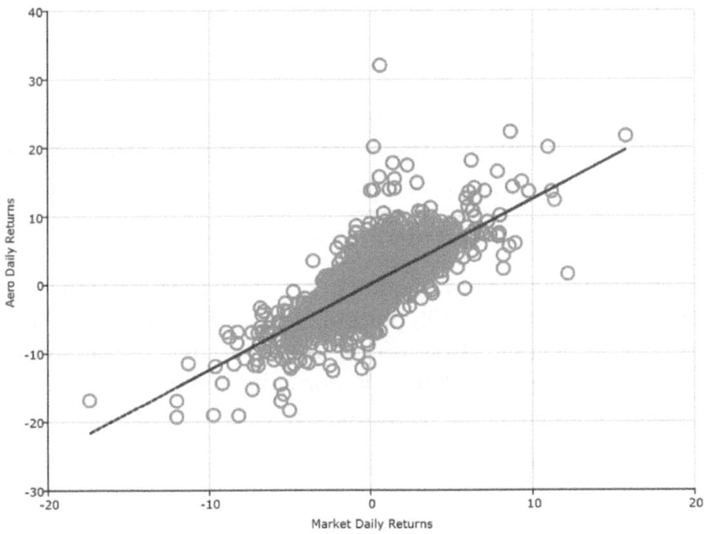


**FIGURE 9.6**
Aero sector daily returns against market returns. Scatter plot with regression line

### 9.2.4 Measuring Abnormal Return

The event window consists of observed returns at times $t = 1, \ldots, E$. The length and location of the event window depend on the purpose of the study. For example, one might choose $E = 3$ days (labelled as $-1$,0,+1 days relative to the calendar date of the event), or $E = 61$ months (labelled as $-30, \ldots, 0, \ldots, 30$ relative) as in the Fama et al study discussed below. It is good practice to experiment a bit with the event window to explore the robustness of results with respect to this choice.

The estimation window is used to estimate the unknown parameters $\alpha, \beta, \sigma$ of the market model. Again, there is some variation in best practice here depending on the data frequency and how long the event window is. The window should be long enough so that sampling error in the estimator is not of concern, and yet not too long that the parameters might change. Some authors advocate adding a "quarantine" period of length $k$ to separate the estimation window from the event window. For example, the estimation window might be $-270, \ldots, -21$ days relative to the calendar date of the event.

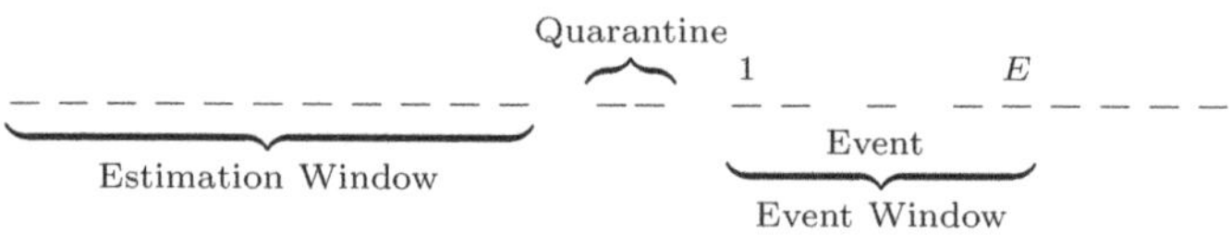


We predict the returns that should occur during the event window using the market model, i.e., normal returns are

$$NR_t = \alpha + \beta R_{mt}, \quad t = 1, \ldots, E,$$

and then compare with the actual returns that happened $R_t$. We define the so-called Abnormal Returns as the actual returns minus the normal returns

$$AR_t = \overbrace{R_t}^{treated} - \overbrace{(\alpha + \beta R_{mt})}^{control}, \quad t = 1, \ldots, E. \tag{9.2}$$

In practice we estimate the parameters $\alpha, \beta$ using the estimation window data.

On average, under the null hypothesis of no effect the Abnormal Returns should be zero on average. How do we know whether the abnormal returns are large or small? Suppose that $\varepsilon_t$ is normally distributed. Then under the null hypothesis of no effect the Abnormal Return should satisfy

$$AR_t = \varepsilon_t \sim N(0, \sigma^2), \quad t = 1, \ldots, E.$$

The standard error associated with $AR_t$ is just $\sigma$ (or rather its estimate). Therefore, we compare the $AR_t$ with $\pm z_{\alpha/2}\sigma$ for a two sided $\alpha$-level test. In practice, many authors work with the Cumulated Abnormal Return, which is defined for each $t$ in the event window as

$$CAR(\tau) = \sum_{t=1}^{\tau} AR_t, \quad \tau = 1, \ldots, E. \tag{9.3}$$

That is, $CAR(1) = AR(1)$, $CAR(2) = AR(1) + AR(2)$, $CAR(3) = AR(1) + AR(2) + AR(3), \ldots$ Then under the null hypothesis of no effect the Cumulative Abnormal Return should satisfy

$$CAR(\tau) = \sum_{t=1}^{\tau} \varepsilon_t \sim N(0, \tau\sigma^2).$$

The standard error associated with $CAR_t$ is just $\sigma\sqrt{\tau}$ (or rather its estimate $\widehat{\sigma}\sqrt{\tau}$).

**Algorithm 13** *Given the estimation window data* $\{R_1, R_{m1}, \ldots, R_T, R_{mT}\}$ *we estimate* $\widehat{\alpha}, \widehat{\beta}$ *and*

$$\widehat{\sigma}^2 = \frac{1}{T} \sum_{t=1}^{T} \left(R_t - \widehat{\alpha} - \widehat{\beta} R_{mt}\right)^2.$$

*Given the event window data* $\{R_1, R_{m1}, \ldots, R_\tau, R_{m\tau}\}$ *(note we are reusing the subscripts, but the event window data are different from the estimation window data) we compute* $\widehat{AR}_t = R_t - \widehat{\alpha} - \widehat{\beta} R_{mt}$ *for every period in the event window,* $t = 1, \ldots, E$ *and* $\widehat{CAR}(\tau) = \sum_{t=1}^{\tau} \widehat{AR}_t$ *for every period in the event window,* $\tau = 1, \ldots, E$*. We compare* $\widehat{AR}_t$ *with the confidence bands* $\pm z_{\alpha/2}\widehat{\sigma}$*; we compare* $\widehat{CAR}(\tau)$ *with the confidence bands* $\pm z_{\alpha/2}\widehat{\sigma}\sqrt{\tau}$*.*

Under the null hypothesis, $\widehat{AR}_t$ and $\widehat{CAR}(\tau)$ should lie inside their confidence bands. Under the alternative, they should exceed the bands somewhere with probability tending to one.

Provided the estimation window is large, replacing $\alpha, \beta, \sigma^2$ by estimates is approximately valid, meaning it has no effect on the confidence band. We note that common practice is to report the AR and the CAR along with the confidence bands and allow the reader to implicitly test the hypothesis. This implicitly obscures a multiple testing problem that our null hypothesis is really that there is no crossing throughout the whole event window, and to do this test properly, we would have to adjust the critical values to reflect the worst case scenario. We will not go there.

### 9.2.5 Volkswagen Emissions Scandal

On 20150918, the US Environmental Protection Agency issued a Notice of Violation accusing Volkswagen of installing so-called defeat devices in their diesel cars to reduce emissions only during the testing cycle. There had been an ongoing investigation by the EPA into their conduct since 2014. This scandal eventually led to large penalties in the US and other countries. We look at the effect of this event. The announcement itself had a massive negative effect on the stock price of VW.

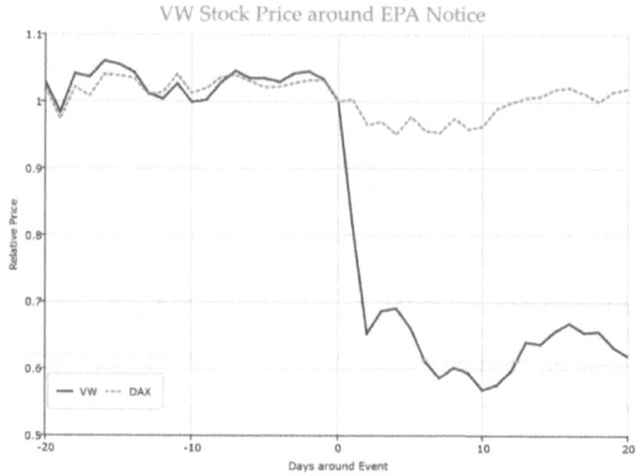


**FIGURE 9.7**
VW price around EPA notice

We calculated the market model for VW using daily data and the DAX as the market index. The results are shown below

$$R_{VW} = 0.00031 + 0.8813 R_{DAX}, \quad \sigma = 0.021455.$$

According to this, VW has a beta close to one. In Figure 9.8 we show the AR over an event window of ±20 days along with the 95% confidence band. We note that there was no evidence that the information content of the announcement was leaked before it took place, and then, when it did take place, it had a very strong and statistically significant negative effect on the value of VW, controlling for the market change. There were two days of negative effect, followed by two days of positive effect, followed by another three smaller but significant negative days.

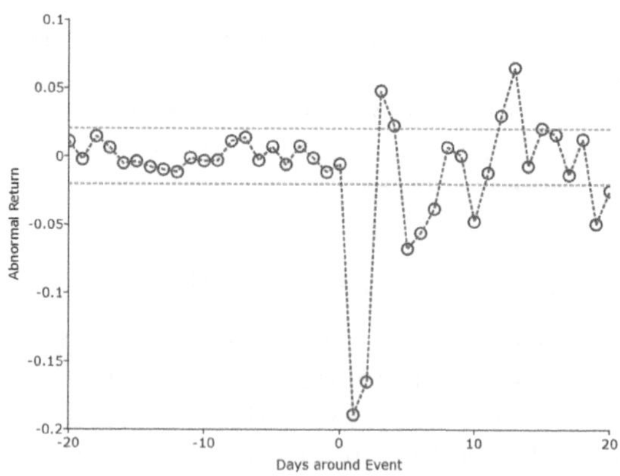


**FIGURE 9.8**
Abnormal return on VW around EPA notice, ±20 day event window

We next show in Figure 9.9 the CAR for the ±20 days event window around the EPA announcement. Clearly, the significant return movement happened only at the announcement date and not before. The announcement set in motion a negative trend to VW value that persisted until beyond the end of our window.

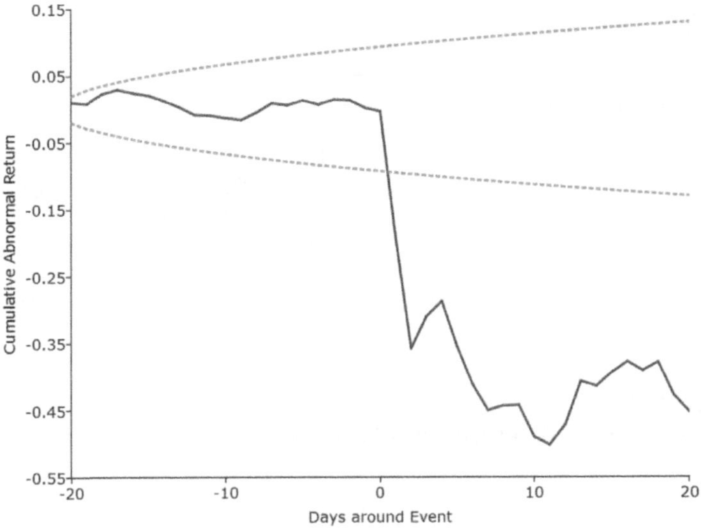


**FIGURE 9.9**
Cumulative abnormal return on VW around EPA notice, ±20 day event window

We next look at a longer window ±600 days to see if there was any movement in the CAR prior to the public notice by the EPA. In fact, the initial findings against Volkswagen were made in early 2014 by researchers from the University of West Virginia who carried out road testing of the emissions and found upto ten times the legal amount (i.e., the amount found in lab tests). This became public knowledge shortly after as they wrote a paper on it. By considering the longer window, we can test whether those findings themselves had an effect on the stock price. There appears to be somewhat of a dip in the VW share price after 2014, but it was not so substantial and it was not statistically significant, whereas 2015 had a large economic and statistically significant effect, even when the event window originated such a long time before. It seems like only when the government agency got serious did the market consider this to be an actual disaster for the company.

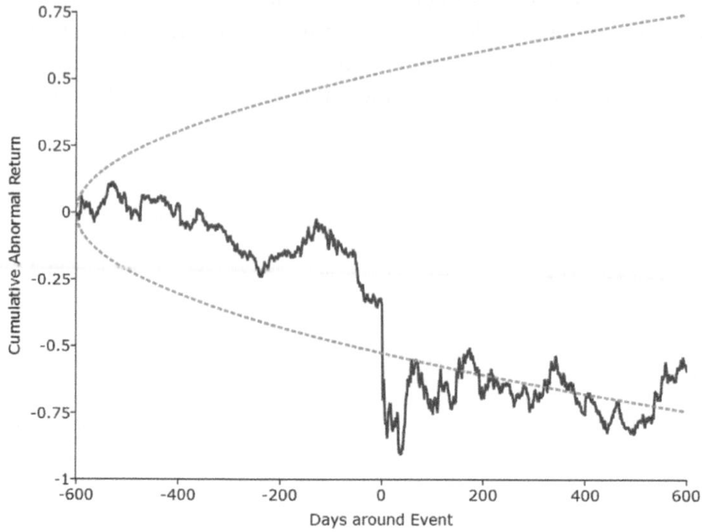


**FIGURE 9.10**
Cumulative abnormal return on VW around EPA notice, ±600 day event window

### 9.2.6 Aggregating Abnormal Returns for Statistical Power and Absence of Normality

In some cases, we may be studying a general phenomenon, such as a stock split that is experienced by many firms, albeit at different calendar times. In this case, we assume that the abnormal returns are all comparable in the event time. In this case, we may average the AR or CAR over all firms, that is, let

$$AAR_t = \frac{1}{n}\sum_{i=1}^{n} AR_{it}, \quad ACAR(\tau) = \frac{1}{n}\sum_{i=1}^{n} CAR_i(\tau). \tag{9.4}$$

Under the null hypothesis of no effect

$$\begin{aligned} AAR_t &= \frac{1}{n}\sum_{i=1}^{n} \varepsilon_{it} \sim N\left(0, \frac{1}{n^2}\sum_{i=1}^{n} \sigma_i^2\right), \\ ACAR(\tau) &= \frac{1}{n}\sum_{i=1}^{n}\sum_{t=1}^{\tau} \varepsilon_{it} \sim N\left(0, \frac{1}{n^2}\sum_{i=1}^{n} \tau\sigma_i^2\right), \end{aligned}$$

where $\tau$ is the number of days since the beginning of the event window. This averaged CAR is more precisely estimated than the firm specific one.

**Algorithm 14** *In practice we compute for* $t, \tau = 1, \ldots, E$ *in the event window*

$$\widehat{AAR}_t = \frac{1}{n}\sum_{i=1}^{n}(R_{it} - \widehat{\alpha}_i - \widehat{\beta}_i R_{mt}), \quad \widehat{ACAR}(\tau) = \frac{1}{n}\sum_{i=1}^{n}\sum_{t=1}^{\tau}(R_{it} - \widehat{\alpha}_i - \widehat{\beta}_i R_{mt}).$$

*We compare with the intervals:*

$$\pm z_{\alpha/2} \times \frac{1}{\sqrt{n}} \times \widehat{\overline{\sigma}} \quad or \ \pm z_{\alpha/2} \times \frac{1}{\sqrt{n}} \times \widehat{\overline{\sigma}} \times \sqrt{\tau}, \tag{9.5}$$

$$\widehat{\overline{\sigma}} = \sqrt{\frac{1}{n}\sum_{i=1}^{n}\widehat{\sigma}_i^2}, \tag{9.6}$$

*where* $\widehat{\sigma}_i^2 = T^{-1}\sum_{t=1}^{T}(R_{it} - \widehat{\alpha}_i - \widehat{\beta}_i R_{mt})^2$ *are computed from the estimation window data.*

When there are a large number of firms, aggregation improves the precision of the estimation and the power of the test a lot. In fact, if there are a large number of firms, the above confidence interval is valid even in the case where $\varepsilon_t$ is not normally distributed. This can be an important consideration when the data are daily returns, where normality seems to be a poor assumption.

## 9.3 Stock Splits: Why Do Firms Split Their Stocks?

Why do firms split their stocks if it should not affect the company's valuation? There are several explanations.

1. Achieving an optimal trading range. When the price level is too high, it is harder for retail investors to participate. Some evidence for this in terms of the average price level of US stocks: according to Weld, Michaely, Thaler, and Benartzi (2009), it has kept pretty much in the range \$30-40 since the 1930's despite a massive increase in the level of stock indexes.[1] This says that stock splits should improve liquidity.
2. Achieving an optimal effective tick size. The bid-ask spread is bounded from below by the tick size, but what really matters for traders is the relative tick size (and hence the relative bid-ask spread), which is determined largely by the price level. Too small a tick size discourages liquidity provision, too large a tick size is costly for retail investors especially.

[1]The original average price of the DJIA (12) in 1896 was \$41. At the time of writing the average price of the 30 stocks contained in the Dow Jones Industrial Average was \$166, so the \$30-40 seems a bit low, but nevertheless, there is a strong tendency for US stocks to split themselves to achieve lower prices.

3. Brokers promote stocks with lower prices more than stocks with higher prices because their relative commissions are or were higher (now there is zero commission trading platforms like Robinhood).
4. Signaling. A split signals that managers expect future sustainable improvements in earnings and dividends.

On 20200730, Apple announced a 4 for 1 split to take place on 20200828. Price was then around \$500→\$125. The stock split will have zero impact on Apple's fundamentals or market value but will help the stock "appeal to a broader base of investors," Apple said. Compare with Amazon etc. Closing prices on 31/04/2021: Amazon \$3467.42; Apple \$131.46; MSFT \$252.18; FB \$324.90; Google \$2410.12; Tesla \$709.44. Prices on 02/08/2022. Alphabet \$114.86, Amazon \$135.39, Apple \$161.51, Meta \$159.93, MSFT \$278.01. Recently, the five tech stocks have all carried out stock splits and are trading in a similar price range.

Others have a different view. Berkshire Hathaway (Warren Buffett's company) stock prices soars above \$200,000 (Financial times, 15/08/14). He wrote

> Shareholder eugenics might appear to be a hopeless undertaking. However, were we to split the stock or take other actions focusing on stock price rather than business value, we would attract an entering class of buyers inferior to the existing class of sellers (WB, Letter to shareholders 1983)

A hard to trade stock encourages investors to take a long-term view and locks out those more likely to trade on emotion or short-term financial need.

Some institutional investors are prohibited from investing in stocks whose price is too low, thereby prohibiting oversplitting or indeed encouraging reverse splits such as the Citibank reverse split of 2011.

### 9.3.1 Some Facts

The Announcement day (when the split is announced) is, according to Weld et al. (2009), on average 52 days prior to the Ex-date (when the split is made, which is during non-trading hours). The EMH says that neither the announcement nor the actual split should have any effect. Therefore, the event window typically may start with the announcement day and end after the split day. Or one may present two separate event studies, one for the announcement and one for the split itself.

Most splits are 2:1, but sometimes the splits can be 10 or even 20 to one. We might imagine that the effect of the split could vary with the size of the split, and this hypothesis could be investigated. Empirically, stock splits are procyclical—many stock splits at the end of a bull market, and hardly any splits occurred during the Global Financial Crisis.

### 9.3.2 Literature

Dolley (1933) studies stock splits between 1921-1931 and drew several conclusions about the motives underlying the corporate decision. He looked only at the (adjusted) price change between the first trading of the "new shares" and the last trading of the "old shares," as he called them. He found on balance, around two-thirds of the splits were accompanied by small price increases through the transition. This was a simple before and after comparison and was applied in an era that was very different from today in terms of the frequency of trading and the nature of intermediation, etc.

Fama et al. (1969) argues that Dolley did not control for the price appreciation trend that may be established prior to the split, and therefore the analysis suffers from a sample selection issue. This paper introduced what is now the standard methodology for carrying out event studies. They use the simple market model applied to monthly stock returns on 622 stocks, including 940 splits over the period 1927-1959. The key point is that they used a large event window around the split date, $\pm 30$ months, and averaged over all stock splits. They find that the ACAR increased linearly up to split date and then stayed constant. That is, there were abnormal returns prior to the split date but not after. They argued that their results are consistent with the semi strong form of efficiency. Most of the effect occurs a long time before the actual split date. They argue that split announcement signals that dividends may increase in future. Provides some evidence on this by dividing into high dividend after ex group and low dividend after ex group. Found that the high group had positive ARs after the ex-date, while the low group has negative ARs upto a year after the ex-date.

### 9.3.3 Dow Splits

We consider a total of 167 splits of Dow stocks (for the samples we obtained from Yahoo, which in some cases go back to 1960). We show in Figure 9.11 when the Dow splits occurred, which evidences their strongly procyclical nature.

What is the typical size? We found the following distribution, most splits are 2 for 1 in our sample.

| Size | Number |
|---|---|
| <1.5 | 3 |
| 1.5 | 30 |
| 2 | 119 |
| 3 | 12 |
| 4 | 3 |

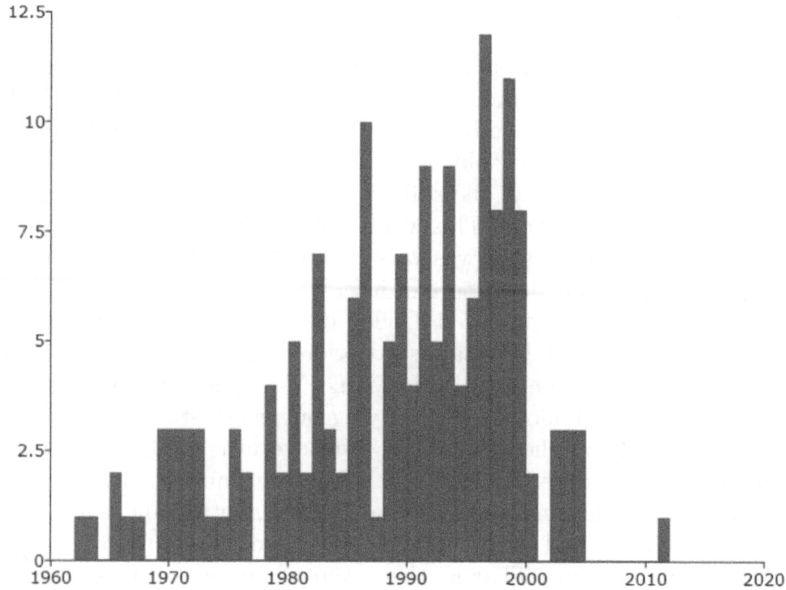


**FIGURE 9.11**
When did Dow stocks split?

### 9.3.4 Exxon Splits

We show some results Exxon, for whom there were 5 splits during the sample period. Figure 9.12 shows the ±52 day AR for each one along with confidence bands, while Figure 9.13 shows the ±52 day CAR for each one, along with the confidence bands. The responses seem quite varied, with some splits having apparent positive reactions and others having negative reactions.

We next consider the AAR and ACAR across these five splits in Figures 9.14 and 9.15. The ACAR shows a slight dip before and around the announcement, but from around 20 days before the split to 20 days after the ACAR increases and reaches statistical significance.

We next look at longer event windows in Figure 9.16 and the average over the five splits in Figure 9.17. The averaged CAR shows that there does seem to be a Fama surge prior to the announcement, but there is also a post-split surge of equal economic magnitude.

We next look at shorter windows in Figures 9.18 and 9.19. The ACAR shows consistently positive around the split with statistical significance on 10 out of 11 days.

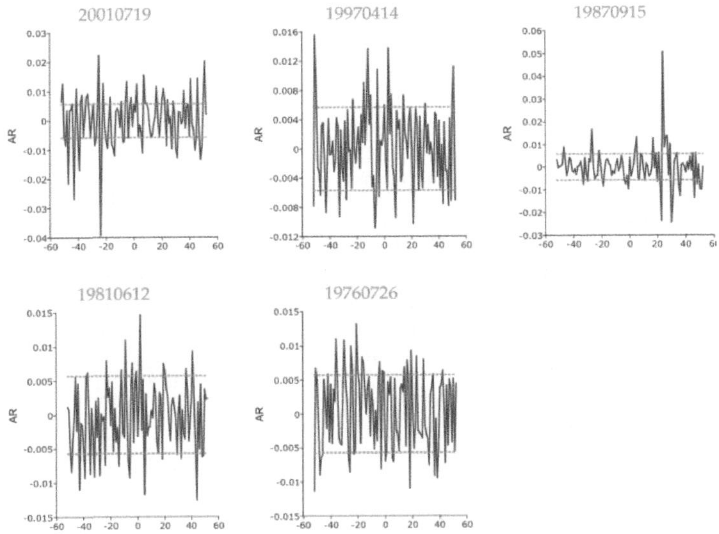


**FIGURE 9.12**
Abnormal returns over event window ±52 days

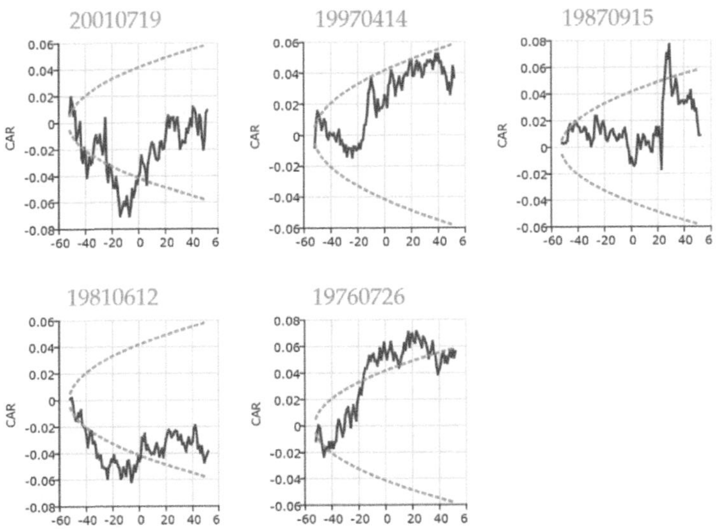


**FIGURE 9.13**
Cumulative abnormal return over event window ±52 days

## 9.4 Extensions to the Methodology

In some cases, there is no available pre-event window for estimation. For example, **Initial Public Offerings** (IPOs) of firms. When companies grow to a

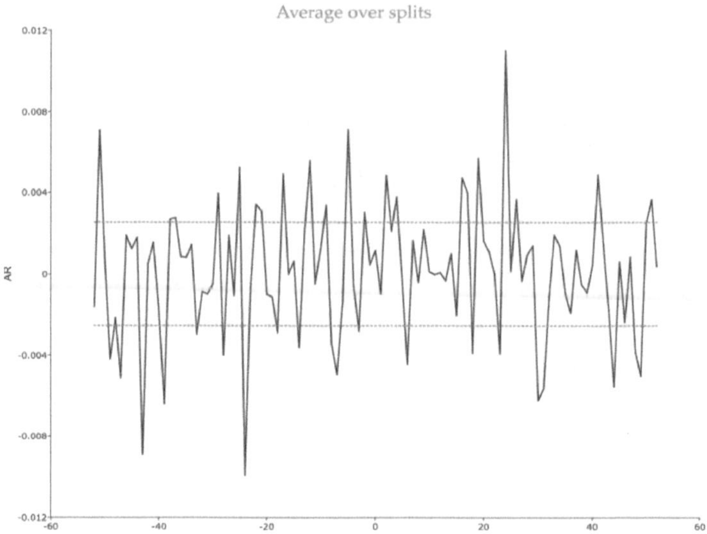


**FIGURE 9.14**
Averaged abnormal returns over event window ±52

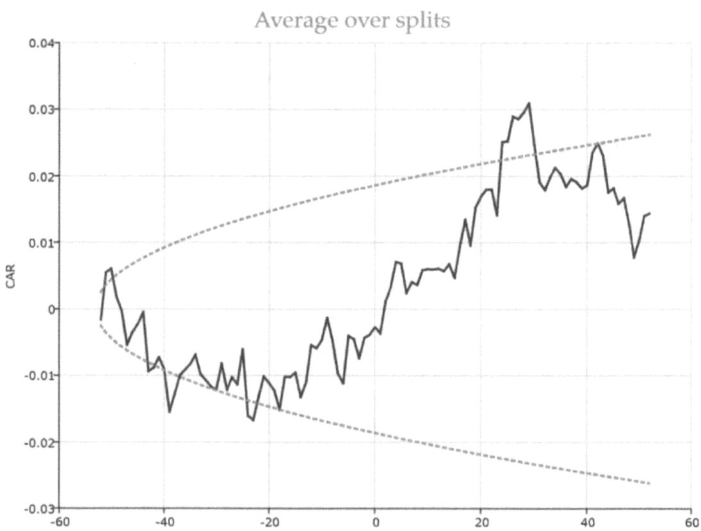


**FIGURE 9.15**
ACAR over event window ±52

certain size, often the owners want to "go public", in which they sell shares in the ownership of the company to the public and in return they receive money. The company then has a listing on a stock exchange, and its shares trade in

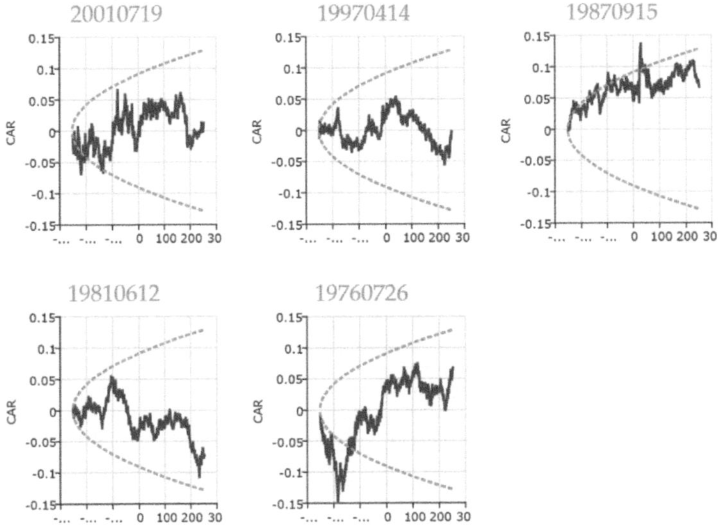


**FIGURE 9.16**
CAR over event window ±252 days

**FIGURE 9.17**
ACAR over event window ±252 days

the secondary market with publicly recorded prices. The process of IPO takes a number of forms, but the question is whether the IPO was correctly valued. The difficulty here is that prior to the IPO, no official prices are available. In this case, one can instead use the post event window for estimation of the market model and then proceed as before.

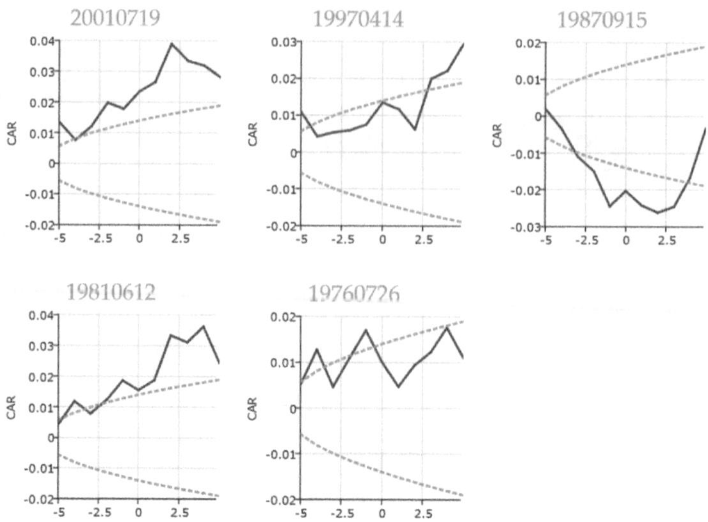


**FIGURE 9.18**
CAR over event window ±5 days

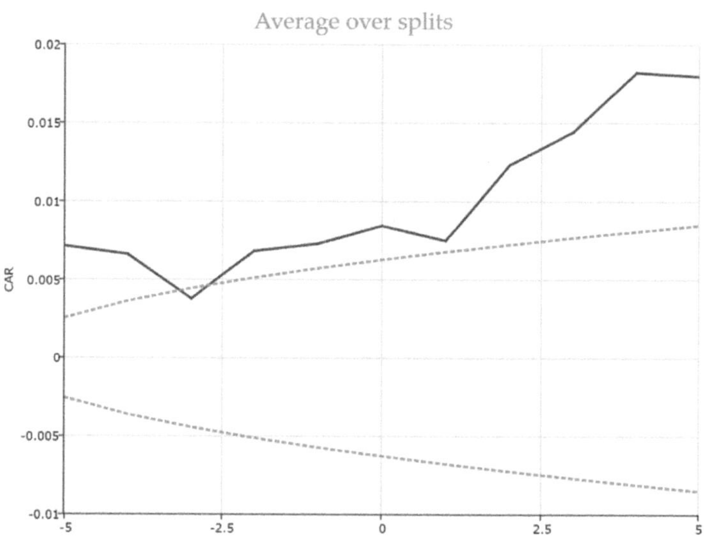


**FIGURE 9.19**
ACAR over event window ±5 days

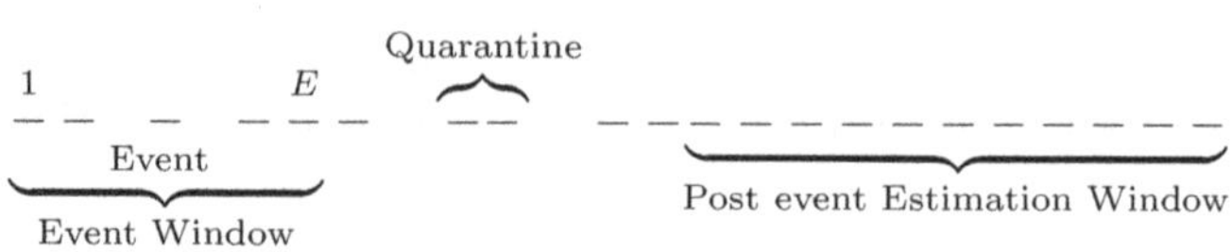

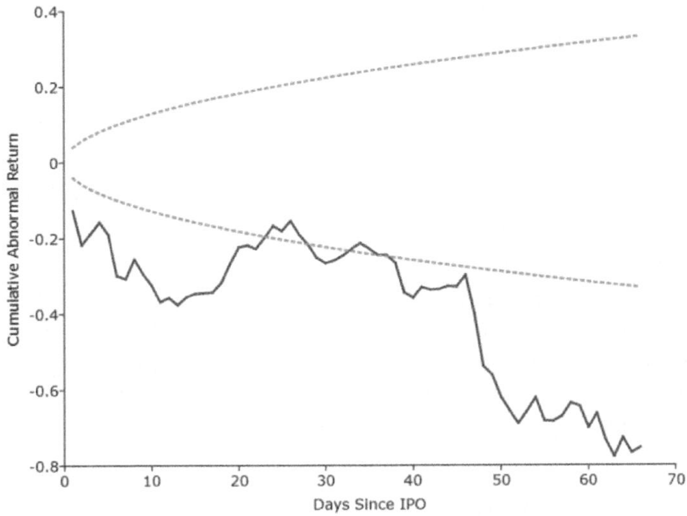


**FIGURE 9.20**
Shows the CAR following the Facebook IPO upto +66 days after the initial offering

**Example 76** *Facebook IPO, May 18th 2012 offered at $38 per share ($104 billion valuation). In this case, we take the estimation window to be 2013 and then calculated the CAR as above for the period following the IPO. The IPO was somewhat of a disaster, see the twitter handle #Faceplant. This is reflected in the negative CAR from day one and beyond shown in Figure 9.20.*

### 9.4.1 Matching Methodology

In some cases, the market model is not feasible or appropriate. For example, suppose we wanted to do "real time" analysis of an Initial Public Offering, so we can't use future as yet unavailable data. In this case, an alternative approach is to match each event firm $i$ with a matched firm (or listing) $m(i)$ based on observed characteristics like market capitalization and industry. The matched firm has pre-event trading data that can be used in lieu of the IPO firm. There are two approaches to calculating abnormal returns:

**Algorithm 15** *(1) Calculate*

$$AR_{it} = R_{it} - R_{m(i),t}, \quad t = 1, \ldots, E.$$

*(2) Calculate*

$$AR_{it} = R_{it} - \widehat{\alpha}_{m(i)} - \widehat{\beta}_{m(i)} R_{mt}, \quad t = 1, \ldots, E,$$

*where in the second equation $\widehat{\alpha}_{m(i)}, \widehat{\beta}_{m(i)}, \widehat{\sigma}^2_{m(i)}$ are estimated using the matching firm returns over the estimation window. Either way, let*

$$CAR_i(\tau) = \sum_{t=1}^{\tau} AR_{it}.$$

Under the null hypothesis, these abnormal returns should be mean zero. To calculate the standard errors one may assume that $AR_{it} \sim N(0, 2\sigma^2_{m(i)})$ and $CAR_i(\tau) \sim N(0, 2\tau\sigma^2_{m(i)})$.

For example, we match Google with Facebook to investigate the Facebook IPO $R_{FB} - R_G$. The issue here is about how to calculate the variance of the difference. We may assume that the event window returns are uncorrelated and have the same variance. In that case, we can estimate the variance of $R_{it} - R_{m(i),t}$ by $2s^2_{m(i)}$, where $s^2_{m(i)}$ is the variance of Google daily returns.

### 9.4.2 Buy and Hold

Some authors have argued that to identify a long-term effect, one should consider the so-called buy-and-hold returns, that is, calculate

$$\mathcal{R}_\tau = \frac{P_\tau}{P_1}, \quad \mathcal{R}_{m\tau} = \frac{P_{m\tau}}{P_{m1}}, \tag{9.7}$$

where $P_1$ is the price of the IPO firm at the IPO (first day of the event window) and $P_{m1}$ is the price of the matched firm on the same date, while $P_\tau, P_{m\tau}$ are the prices at times $\tau = 1, \ldots, E$. We may calculate the buy and hold ratio

$$BH_\tau = \frac{\mathcal{R}_\tau}{\mathcal{R}_{m\tau}}, \quad \tau = 1, \ldots, E$$

as our treatment effect. Under the null hypothesis (that there is no effect) we should have $T_\tau = \log(BH_\tau) \sim N(0, \mathrm{var}(\log(BH_\tau)))$. We may estimate $\mathrm{var}(\log(BH_\tau))$ using the estimation window data.

### 9.4.3 Market Wide Events

In some cases, we want to check the effect on the market of an event, such as the Wuhan lockdown of January 2020 and the Western lockdowns of March 2020. We suppose the constant mean model, i.e., that under the null hypothesis

$$R_{mt} = \mu_m + \varepsilon_{mt},$$

where $\varepsilon_{mt}$ has mean zero and variance $\sigma^2_m$.

**Algorithm 16** *We estimate the mean market return from the estimation window, and then, calculate the abnormal return and the CAR during the event* *window period, thus*

$$AR_t = R_{mt} - \widehat{\mu}_m, \quad CAR(\tau) = \sum_{t=1}^{\tau} AR_t, \quad \tau = 1, \ldots, E$$

$$\widehat{\mu}_m = \frac{1}{T}\sum_{t=1}^{T} R_{mt}, \quad \widehat{\sigma}_m^2 = \frac{1}{T}\sum_{t=1}^{T} (R_{mt} - \widehat{\mu}_m)^2.$$

*We then compare $CAR(\tau)$ with $\pm z_{\alpha/2}\widehat{\sigma}_m\sqrt{\tau}$ for a two sided $\alpha$-level test.*

This gives the global effect of the event on the stock market as a whole. Regarding the pandemic, we may also be interested in relative effects, i.e., whether particular companies or industries had an additional effect beyond the effect on the market as a whole. For example, the airline industry suffered more than Amazon. This can be studied by applying the standard market model event study approach to individual stocks or industries.

Suppose you wish to test whether the Chinese market suffered worse than the US market from the Covid-19 pandemic. In that case, you calculate $CAR^{US}(\tau)$ and $CAR^{China}(\tau)$ and examine the difference. Actually, we must first convert to a common currency to control for exchange rates' appreciation. That is, we should calculate returns in a common currency. We then define the difference

$$T(\tau) = CAR^{US}(\tau) - CAR^{China}(\tau).$$

Under the null hypothesis that they suffered equally, $T(\tau)$ should be zero and lie within the confidence bands $\pm z_{\alpha/2}\sqrt{(\widehat{\sigma}_m^{US})^2 + (\widehat{\sigma}_m^{China})^2}\sqrt{\tau}$.

### 9.4.4 Abnormal Trading Volume

The focus of most event studies is on market valuation effects, but it is also often of interest to look at other variables like trading volume. Suppose that volume $V$ is a random variable with a constant mean $\mu_V$ (the average daily volume) and variance $\sigma_V^2$, which can be estimated from the estimation window. Then, we can define abnormal volume as

$$AV_t = V_t - \mu_V.$$

We may compare Abnormal Trading Volume with the confidence band $\pm z_{\alpha/2}\sigma_V$. Alternative approaches include working with logarithms of volume (which is more closely approximated by normal distribution) and market model regressions in levels and logs. That is, we suppose that

$$\log(V_t) = \alpha + \beta \log(V_{mt}) + \varepsilon_t, \tag{9.8}$$

where $V_{mt}$ is the market wide trading volume. We can estimate the parameters $\alpha, \beta, \sigma^2$ using estimation window data and then calculate Abnormal Volume as the residual over the event window.

Figure 9.21 shows the abnormal volume for VW.

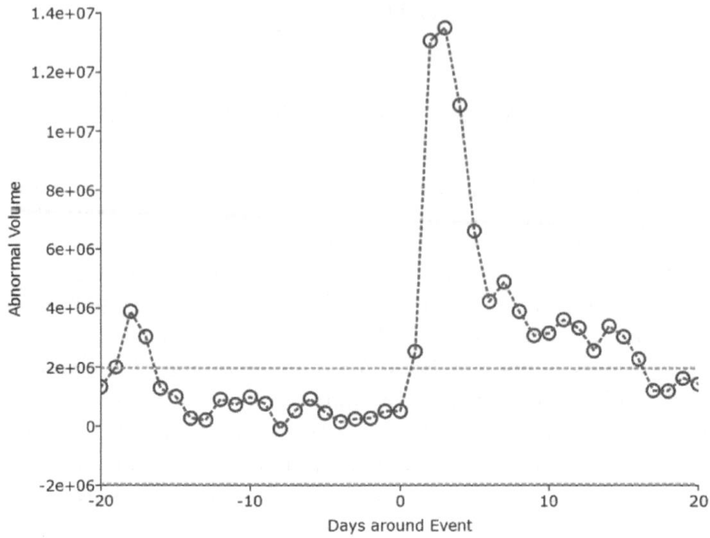


**FIGURE 9.21**
Abnormal trading volume of Volkswagen around EPA announcement

### 9.4.5 Exchange Rate Event Study

We may also be interested in the effect of big events on exchange rates. The net return per dollar on the carry trade is

$$R_t = \frac{E_t}{E_{t-1}}(1 + r_{ft}^A) - (1 + r_{ft}^H),$$

where $E_t$ is the exchange rate at time $t$, $r_{ft}^A$ is the foreign interest rate, and $r_{ft}^H$ is the domestic interest rate. The international Fisher effect says that the return on the carry trade should be zero in expectation.

$$E(AR_t) = E(R_t) = 0, \tag{9.9}$$

and so the return can be used as an abnormal return. In many cases, the interest rate differential is small (say Japan and USA for daily data), in which case the abnormal return can be approximated further as

$$AR_t = \frac{E_t}{E_{t-1}} - 1 \simeq \log(E_t) - \log(E_{t-1}).$$

We estimate $\text{var}(AR_t) = \sigma_E^2$ and then compare $AR_t$ with $\pm z_{\alpha/2}\sigma_E$ and $CAR(\tau)$ with $\pm z_{\alpha/2}\sigma_E\sqrt{\tau}$ for two sided $\alpha$-level tests. For example, did the COVID lockdowns (Wuhan lockdown Jan 23rd, 2020, US Federal lockdown March 24th, 2020) have a significant effect on dollar RMB exchange rate?

### 9.4.6 Regression Approach

An alternative way of thinking about event studies is by an augmented market model regression, that is, let

$$R_t = \alpha + \beta R_{mt} + \gamma_1 D_{1t} + \ldots + \gamma_E D_{Et} + \varepsilon_t,$$

where $D_{1t}$ is the dummy variable that is one if the calendar time $t$ is equal to the first day of the event window, $D_{2t}$ is the dummy variable that is one if the calendar time $t$ is equal to the second day of the event window, etc. One can estimate the parameters $\alpha, \beta, \gamma_1, \ldots, \gamma_E$ together using the full sample of data (deleting observations for a quarantine period if one likes). The abnormal returns are the estimated $\gamma's$, i.e., $AR_1 = \gamma_1, \ldots, AR_E = \gamma_E$, while $CAR(\tau) = \sum_{j=1}^{\tau} \gamma_j$. The standard errors for the abnormal return are just the usual regression standard errors and the standard errors for $CAR(\tau)$ are just $\sqrt{\tau}$ times those for the abnormal returns. This approach is flexible because one can extend the analysis to allow for multiple events with the same set of data. In fact common practice now is also to add additional so-called Fama-French factors to the regression as well, to better capture common movements. This involves fitting a multiple regression with betas for each included factor.

## 9.5 Conclusion

Event study methodology can be used to evaluate the effect of any event on stock prices. See Cram (1997) for a list of event studies. Nowadays, many event studies are done with high-frequency data and very short event windows. For example, the effects of announcements such as the Federal Reserve Board interest rate decision and Nonfarm payroll. Figure 9.22 shows the effect of such an announcement on the FTSE100 index, stock return, and trading volume using one-minute data from 2012. This particular event seemed to elicit a very rapid response in the price and return.

## 9.6 Key Points

1. Event study methodology is useful for studying the effect of events on stock prices controlling for other factors.
2. Abnormal return is defined through a market model regression and is used to provide a measure of the effect of the event on stock prices and the way in which that effect migrates over time.

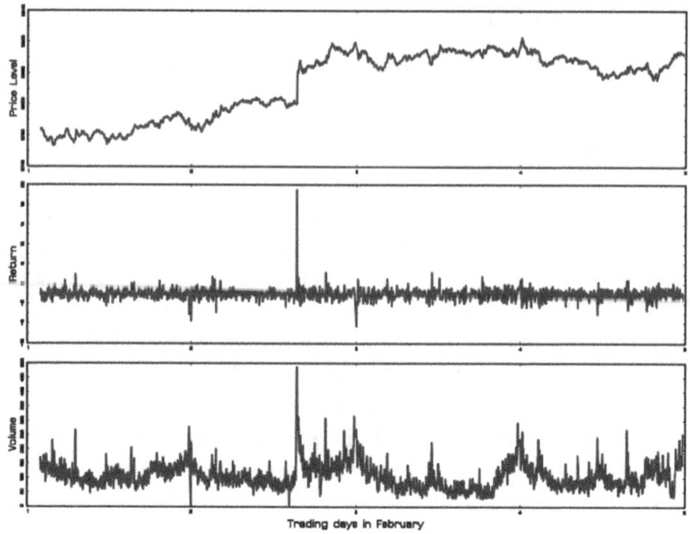


**FIGURE 9.22**
FTSE100 one minute data during nonfarm payroll announcement

3. We provide a formal test of statistical significance that constitutes an evidence bar around the magnitude of the effect.

# 10

# *Equity Premium*

## Outline

This chapter explores the concept of the equity premium, an essential yet elusive parameter in finance. The equity premium represents the excess return on stock market investments relative to risk-free government securities, offering insights into the risk-reward tradeoff in financial markets. The chapter investigates the definitions, measurements, and variations of the equity premium, as well as the factors contributing to the equity premium puzzle. It also examines the risk-free rate and its behavior over time, providing a comprehensive analysis of the equity premium's implications for investors and markets.

After reading this chapter, you will be able to:

- Understand the different definitions of equity premium, including Realized, Historical, and Expected Equity Premiums.
- Analyze the risk-free rate, its time series behavior, and its role in calculating the equity premium.
- Evaluate the historical performance of equity premiums and their variations across different countries and time periods.
- Assess explanations for the equity premium puzzle, including statistical illusions and alternative economic models.
- Examine the implications of the equity premium for long-term investments and market efficiency.
- Critically evaluate the variations in the equity premium across different markets and over time.

The equity premium (also called market risk premium, equity risk premium, market premium and risk premium) is essentially the excess return on stock market investment (the market index) relative to risk free government securities. This is one of the most important and discussed, but elusive parameters in finance. We expect it to be positive to reward people for taking on risk (assuming that they are risk averse). How big should it be? How is it determined? Does it vary across countries? Does it vary across time?

DOI: 10.1201/9781003543121-10 

Some confusion arises from the fact that the term equity premium is used to designate different concepts. The main definitions for us are:

1. Realized Equity Premium (REP): time series of historical excess returns of the stock market over treasuries.
2. Historical Equity Premium (HEP): historical average excess return of the stock market over treasuries.
3. Expected Equity Premium (EEP): expected excess return of the stock market over treasuries.

We define the (market) risk premium (EEP) as the expected return on the market minus the risk free rate

$$\pi_m = E(R_{mt} - r_{ft}) = E(R_{mt}) - r_{ft},$$

where $r_{ft}$ is the risk free rate that is known at time $t-1$ (i.e., the return that will accrue at time $t$ is known), whereas $R_{mt}$ is the stock market return between $t-1$ and $t$, which is defined as

$$R_{mt} = \frac{P_{mt} - P_{m,t-1} + D_{mt}}{P_{m,t-1}} = \overbrace{\frac{P_{mt} - P_{m,t-1}}{P_{m,t-1}}}^{\text{Capital gain}} + \overbrace{\frac{D_{mt}}{P_{m,t-1}}}^{\text{Dividend yield}},$$

where $D_{mt}$ is dividends paid in t-1,t. If dividends are paid at some point $t-s$ for $s \in (0,1)$, then one way to proceed is to reinvest the dividend in the stock paying the price $P_{t-s}$ per share. The stock return is a random variable whose future realization is unknown at time $t-1$. We suppose that $\pi_m$ does not vary over time (even though the risk free rate $r_{ft}$ manifestly does vary over time); this is the parameter of interest. The EEP is defined through these assumptions and is what economic logic refers to.

**Algorithm 17** *The Realized Equity premium for period t is $REP_t = R_{mt} - r_{ft}$, which can be positive or negative even for annual data. The sample average of the realized risk premium is the HEP*

$$HEP = \frac{1}{T}\sum_{t=1}^{T}(R_{mt} - r_{ft}).$$

*Define also the standard deviation of the risk premium.*

$$SEP = \sqrt{\frac{1}{T}\sum_{t=1}^{T}(REP_t - HEP)^2},$$

By the **Law of Large Numbers** we expect that $HEP \simeq \pi_m$ provided $T$ is large. This means that if $\pi_m > 0$, then we should find $HEP > 0$ with high probability if it is based on a long sample. Actually, the issue is that many authors have found the HEP to be what they consider to be implausibly large. Mehra and Prescott (1985) say

> "Historically, the average return on equity has far exceeded the average return on short-term virtually default-free debt. Over the ninety-year period 1889-1978, the average real annual yield on the Standard and Poor 500 Index was seven percent, while the average yield on short-term debt was less than one percent. The question addressed in this paper is whether this large differential in average yields can be accounted for by models that abstract from transactions costs, liquidity constraints, and other frictions absent in the Arrow-Debreu set-up. Our finding is that it cannot be, at least not for the class of economies considered. "

This became a whole literature by itself called **The Equity Premium Puzzle.** Empirically, the observed risk premium of equities is too high relative to the variation of aggregate consumption; this is hard to explain with standard economics models. We look in the exercises at how we might determine reasonable values for risk aversion.

We first look at the performance of the risk-free rate itself and then compare it with the performance of the stock market.

## 10.1 The Risk Free Rate

### 10.1.1 Long Horizon Return on Fixed Income Investments

We focus on the short-term risk-free rate (interest rate), the guaranteed amount payable on short-term government securities, e.g., the one-month Tbill rate. This is nominally riskless (the US Federal government has not defaulted ever, although many state governments have) and the future payoff is known at the time of purchase. We calculate the long-term return on this investment, i.e., by purchasing a new Tbill every month and reinvesting the proceeds. We obtain the Tbill rate from the Ken French website. In Figure 10.1 we show the cumulated gross return since 1927 (blue line) along with the Consumer Price Index (CPI) (red line) set to one in 1927. The nominal gross profit on Tbills is 21.03 at the end of 2020, while the CPI is 14.88 at the end of 2020. Therefore, the capital gain in real terms is 21.03/14.88, which for a nearly hundred-year period is almost negligible, and I think most people would agree!

### 10.1.2 Time Series Behavior of Daily Risk Free Rate

The behavior of the time series of the daily risk-free rate is quite different from the behavior of daily stock returns. The series has a low average level, but is always positive, see Figure 10.2. Most of the time it has low day-to-day variation, although it ranges over a relatively wide range, and occasionally has very abrupt changes, see Figure 10.3. It is a very persistent time series,

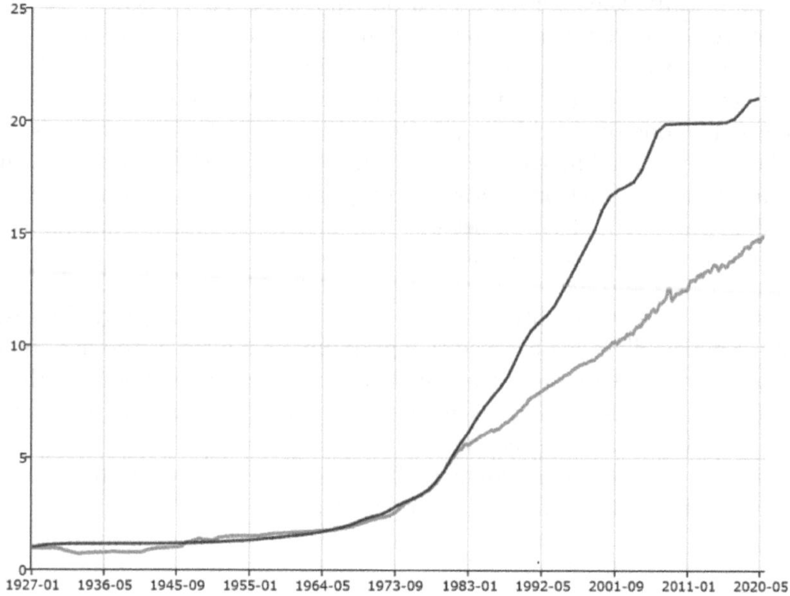


**FIGURE 10.1**
Long-term appreciation of the Tbill and CPI

meaning that it is highly predictable from day to day. It has a very strong positive autocorrelation, as shown in Figure 10.4.

The return on long-term government bonds behaves similarly

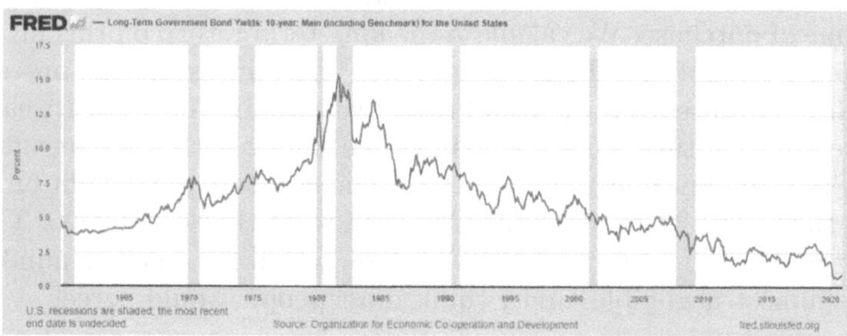


We now return to the equity premium.

**FIGURE 10.2**
The daily one month Tbill rate

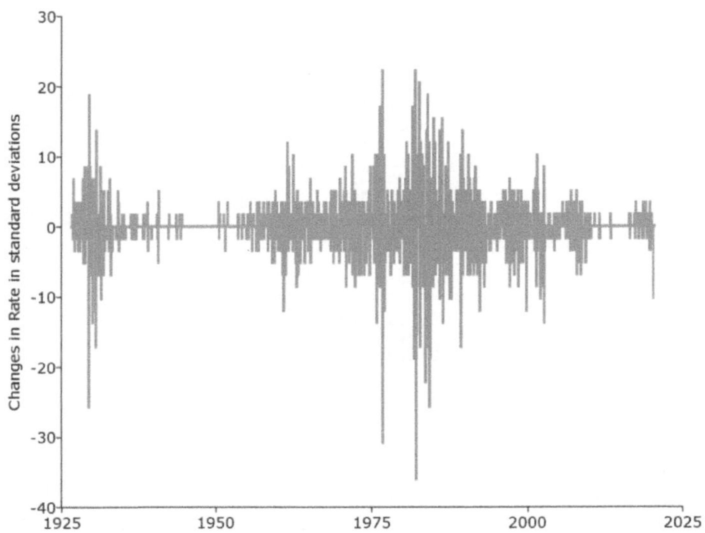


**FIGURE 10.3**
Changes in the Tbill rate normalized by standard deviation

## 10.2 Equity Premium

We show below in Figure 10.5 the FF market return data for the annual holding period, along with the risk-free rate and the corresponding realized equity premium over the period 1927-2023.

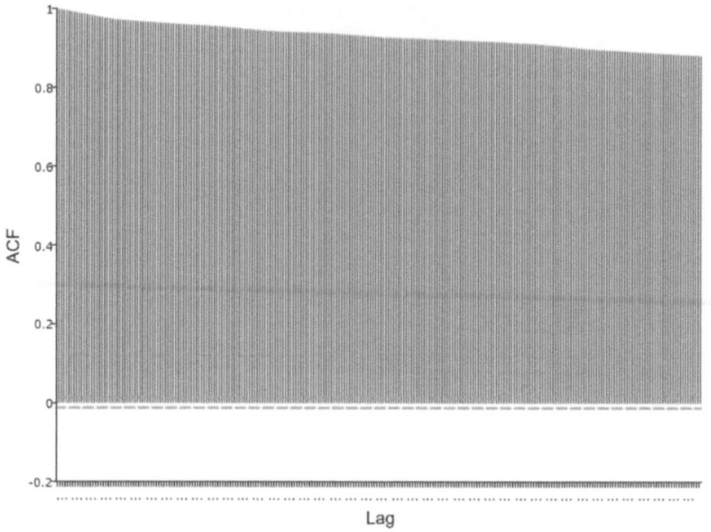


**FIGURE 10.4**
Autocorrelation function of the Tbill rate out to 255 lags

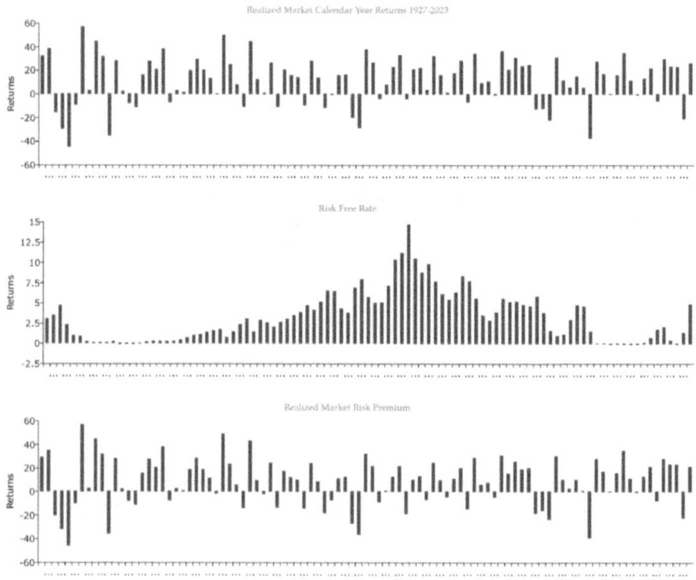


**FIGURE 10.5**
Annual return on FF market index and the Tbill rate along with the realized annual risk premium

For the FF data, with annual holding period, 1927-2023 ($n = 97$), we find that the mean of the risk-free rate is 3.302% with a standard deviation 3.081, while the stock market return had a mean of 11.836% with a standard deviation 20.062. In this sense, the variability of the stock market return is much greater than the variability of the risk-free rate. The HEP (estimated equity premium) is

$$HEP = 8.69\%, \quad SEP = 20.32\%, \quad \text{stderr} = 2.06\%.$$

The 95% confidence interval for $\pi_m$ is therefore,

$$[4.64, 12.73] \, .$$

This interval does not include zero, so we are 95% confident that the expected risk premium lies above zero, which is good news in the sense that this finding is consistent with the view that risk aversion is the dominant behavior of investors. However, there is quite a lot of uncertainty about the value of the risk premium reflecting the wide variation in the annual realized risk premium. If I told you that I was confident that your dining bill would be between 46 and 127 dollars. You might be dissatisfied with my answer.

The growth of the level of the stock market is substantial indeed over the long horizon, albeit with wide swings. Over the long horizon, other prices rise as well. The consumer price index (CPI) rose from 17.4 in 1927 to 259.101 in 2020 (annual averages), around a 13.89 fold increase, an annual average rate of 2.95%. This affects the value of your accumulated capital whether this arise from equities or fixed income returns. It seems reasonable that in comparing investments over the long horizon, one should work with real returns that normalize capital by the CPI.

Finally, what is the relationship between the stock market return and the risk-free rate, or the equity premium and the risk-free rate? The contemporaneous correlation is almost zero using the annual data over the whole period.

### 10.2.1 Explanations for the Equity Premium Puzzle

A large number of explanations for the puzzle have been proposed. There are many new **asset pricing models** that make modifications to the assumed preferences of investors, and include imperfections in the model of risk aversion and allow for credit constraints to be binding on consumers. These explanations are all plausible, but the models are really quite complicated, so we consider here the question of whether the risk premium is as large as people have argued it is.

### 10.2.2 Statistical Illusion

The most basic explanation is that there is no puzzle to explain: that the equity premium is not too high, or at least we don't know whether it is or

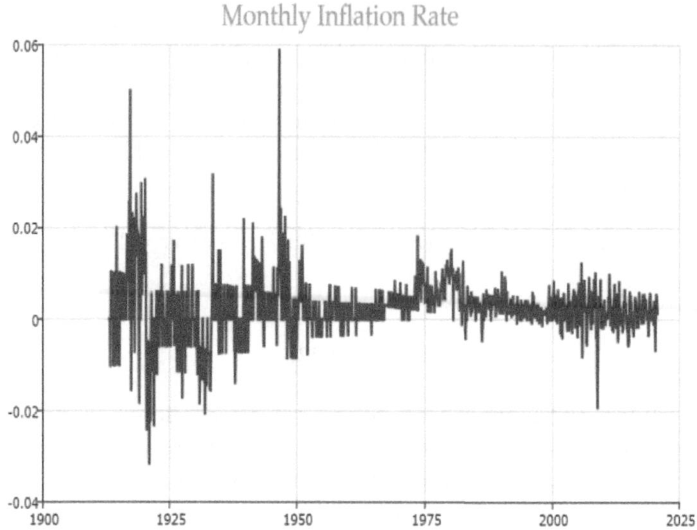


**FIGURE 10.6**
Monthly inflation rate

not. Essentially, it is claimed that we don't have enough statistical power to distinguish the equity premium from a small positive number that would be more reasonable from the point of view of risk aversion. This arises from considering a number of issues.

*Low number of data points*: the period 1900–2024 provides only 124 years, which is not a large number of years statistically, given the variability of returns. This manifests itself in wide confidence intervals, i.e., a lot of uncertainty about the true value.

*Sample period/data choice*: We can get quite different answers depending on which dataset we look at. The HEP varies greatly depending on which points are included. Using data starting from the top of the market in 1929 or starting from the bottom of the market in 1932 (leading to estimates of equity premium of 1% lower per year), or ending at the top in 2000 (vs. bottom in 2002) or top in 2007 (vs. bottom in 2009 or beyond) can substantially change the overall conclusion.

*Sample selection bias*: The US equity market is the most intensively studied in equity market research. Not coincidentally, it had the best equity market performance in the 20th century. Other stock markets (e.g. Russia, Germany, and China) produced a gross return of zero over this period due to bankruptcy events.

Dimson, Marsh, and Staunton (2014) compare risk premia across countries over 1900-2014 period across the whole world; this somewhat addresses the selection bias issue. They find that equities outperformed fixed income everywhere and equities beat inflation everywhere, except perhaps those countries with extinction events. Prospectively, the world equity premium was: versus 10-year bonds around 3%; versus short-term bills 4.3%. They do not give a confidence interval, but one can infer one from the variation across countries (from 2.9% to 6.5%), that the standard error of these numbers is around 0.25. These are much more modest numbers than those produced by Mehra and Prescott.

Fernandez (2010) reviews 150 textbooks on finance and valuation and found that the range of values reported in the 150 textbooks were from 3% to 10% with an average value of 6.7%. Surveys of professional economists and market professionals find an even wider range. In conclusion, the rumors of an outsized risk premium seem greatly exaggerated.

### 10.2.3 Does the US Risk Premium Vary Over Time?

Suppose that $X_1, \ldots, X_n$ and $Y_1, \ldots, Y_m$ are two sample of data. We want to test whether they have the same mean. For example, we want to test whether stock returns in the 1960's had the same mean as stock returns in the 1970's. For example, we want to test whether Chinese stock returns have the same mean as US stock returns. For example, suppose we want to test whether stock returns are the same during an election period as during a non-election period. In each case, we will choose different data, but the testing strategy is the same.

We look at the Annual Risk Premium on the US Market (FF data), which is given in the table below across two subperiods

| Period | Mean | Stdev |
|---|---|---|
| 1927-1972 | 9.67 | 22.42 |
| 1972-2019 | 7.45 | 18.29 |

In this case, the test statistic (3.5) is $T = 0.52226864$, which is not statistically significant. We cannot reject the hypothesis that the mean return is the same in the two subperiods at the 5% level. The sample size is small here, so it is hard to discriminate. Economically, there is a big difference in the equity premium in the earlier period from the later period, but statistically it is not significant at the usual level.

We may also test whether the level of risk is the same across the two subperiods. This is called the F-test for the equality of variances

**Algorithm 18** *We compute the ratio of the two variances,*

$$F = \frac{s_X^2}{s_Y^2} = \left(\frac{0.224}{0.183}\right)^2 = 1.498. \tag{10.1}$$

*We compare with the critical value* $F_{\alpha,46,45} = 1.638$.

We do not reject this null hypothesis either, although the difference in variance appears quite large it is not statistically significant.

We next compare the risk premium during presidential election years with non-election years. The results indicate that there is almost no difference in the risk premium during the 24 election years, 1928, 1932, in comparison with the 72 non-election years. One might obtain better results by focusing on the key parts of the election years to do the statistical test.

| Period | Mean | Stdev |
|---|---|---|
| election | 8.472 | 16.217 |
| nonelection | 8.577 | 21.699 |

In conclusion, it is not so clear that the equity risk premium is too large given how uncertain our estimates are. It appears to vary over time and across countries, although statistically those variations are not significant. It also depends on the holding period. In Figure 10.7 we show the variation in the equity risk premium for a ten-year holding period. This is calculated as

$$\prod_{t=1}^{10}(1 + R_{mt}) - \prod_{t=1}^{10}(1 + r_{ft}),$$

where $R_{mt}$ and $r_{ft}$ are the annual market return and annual risk-free rate within the decade. In that case, 2 out of 10 decades have negative risk premia.

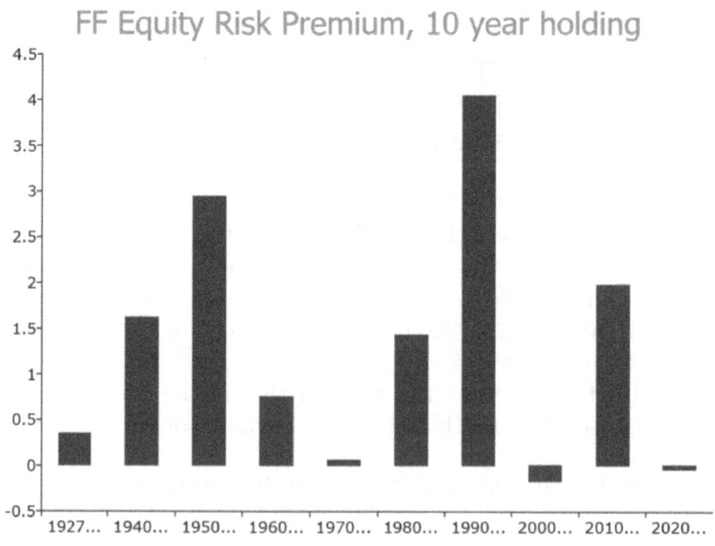


**FIGURE 10.7**
Ten-year horizon realized risk premia FF market index and Tbill

### 10.2.4 Conclusions

The risk-free rate is small, does not vary very much, and is very predictable. The risk premium is dominated by the behavior of the risky asset, the stock market return. This varies over time and country a lot but is hard to measure statistically. Over the long term, equities beat fixed income and inflation, at least during the one version of history we have experienced. Nevertheless, even over ten-year horizons, one does find negative risk premia. One cannot find 20-year periods where risk premia are negative.

## 10.3 Key Points

1. The equity premium is the difference between the return on the stock market and the risk-free interest rate. In the United States, this risk premium has generally been high, of the order of 4-10% per year.
2. The equity premium does seem to vary over time and country, and there is a huge degree of uncertainty about its value.

## 10.4 Exercises

1. Suppose that your attitudes to risk are defined by mean variance preferences, i.e.,

$$U = E(X) - \gamma \text{var}(X).$$

Consider the following choices

$$X_1 = \begin{cases} 100 & prob\ \frac{1}{2} \\ 200 & prob\ \frac{1}{2} \end{cases}, \quad X_2 = 140.$$

Calculate $U$ for each choice as a function of $\gamma$. For what value of $\gamma$ are you indifferent between $X_1, X_2$.

# 11

# *Fundamentals Versus Bubbles*

## Outline

This chapter explores the debate between fundamentals and bubbles in driving stock prices, questioning whether these prices are influenced by intrinsic values or irrational market behaviors. The chapter examines historical examples of bubbles, the theoretical frameworks explaining them, and the present value models used to assess stock price movements. It also delves into the implications of behavioral finance and the challenges of predicting long-term returns.

After reading this chapter, you will be able to:

- Understand the contrasting views on stock price determinants: fundamentals versus bubbles.
- Analyze historical financial bubbles and crashes, including their causes and consequences.
- Apply present value relations, including the Dividend Discount Model and the Gordon Growth Model, to evaluate stock prices.
- Evaluate the Shiller Variance Bounds Test and its implications for stock price volatility.
- Investigate the predictability of long-term stock returns using dividend-price ratios and other financial metrics.
- Assess the role of behavioral finance in explaining market anomalies and investor behavior.

There are two competing views of financial markets. (1) Stock prices are driven by fundamental values or rational expectations of what those fundamental values will be in the future. This is the view maintained in the efficient markets hypothesis, the CAPM, etc. (2) Stock prices are driven by animal spirits, fads, bubbles, and irrational exuberance. This is the view maintained by **Behavioral Finance**, see Thaler (2016). Perhaps both these views have something useful to say and sometimes one and sometimes the other prevails.

DOI: 10.1201/9781003543121-11

One typically thinks of bubbles as a pervasive market wide phenomenon with rapid increases in prices ultimately followed by a crash. There are many well-known examples of bubbles in financial history: tulips in Amsterdam (1634-37), the Mississippi bubble (1719-20), and the South sea bubble (1720). In the 20th century, the roaring 20s and the turn of the century tech bubble are well known. More recently, the words Bitcoin and bubble have become synonymous. Many academic studies have been devoted to explaining why these events were not well explained by fundamentals.

Scheinkman (2014) presents three stylized facts about bubbles: (1) Asset price bubbles coincide with increases in trading volume; (2) Asset price bubbles often coincide with financial or technological innovation; (3) Asset price implosions seem to coincide with increases in the assets' supply. He builds a model with agents having fluctuating heterogeneous beliefs (they have different opinions about the correct valuations) and different trading costs in going long or short, specifically, it costs them more to take on short positions than to take on long ones. This translates into optimists' beliefs being more fully expressed in the market. Because of the fluctuating beliefs the optimist can expect an even greater optimist to arrive to buy off him. Everyone is rational but bubbles arise and propagate and ultimately crash. Scheinkman proposes to limit leverage (prevent trading under margin) and to facilitate and even encourage short selling.

During a bubble, there does seem to be a disconnect between fundamentals and prices. There is a lot of empirical work questioning the connection between prices and fundamentals in normal times, i.e., when prices are not rising rapidly. We just mention here some well-known studies. Cutler, Poterba, and Summers (1989) and Fair (2002) investigated large price moves on the S&P500 (daily and intradaily in the latter case) and tried to match the movements up with news stories reported in the New York Times and Wall Street Journal the following day. They found that many large movements were associated with monetary policy, but there remained many significant movements that they could not find explanations for. Fundamentals for stock prices are difficult to measure and potentially include all macroeconomic news that can drive the market, so it is difficult to make strong conclusions. Roll (1984) is a famous study of the market for orange juice futures for which the fundamentals are pretty simple to measure—weather, in particular the number of frost days in Florida. He found some disconnect between the movements in orange juice futures and the weather. Online betting markets such as Betfair provide a closer connection between prices and fundamentals, since the payoff is purely determined by the result of a sports match or election. More recent examples include Bitcoin and the so-called meme stocks such as GameStop.

**What are fundamentals?** Regulation can affect the cash flow of all companies, the degree of competition in an industry will affect the competition, and the level of innovation in the industry. Macroeconomic news such as interest rates, inflation and unemployment affects all firms through their earnings and costs. In some sectors/countries, exchange rates are important. Weather

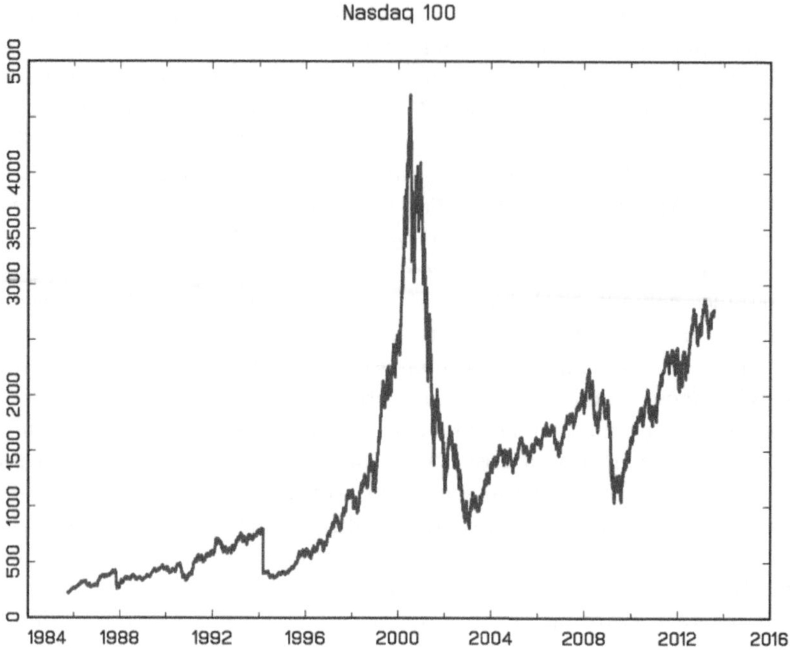


**FIGURE 11.1**
The NASDAQ stock market index level

can be important for retail and agriculture. For companies, we usually work with their Earnings and Dividends. Graham and Dodd (1934) have a long discussion about the relevance of the balance sheet, i.e., the net asset position of the company. But nowadays, a lot of companies don't hold many assets but lease them from others. Specifically,

> *In 2015, Uber, the world's largest taxi company, owns no vehicles; Facebook, the world's most popular media owner, creates no content; Alibaba, the most valuable retailer, has no inventory; and Airbnb, the world's largest accommodation provider, owns no real estate.*

We show some bubbly examples in Figures 11.1-11.5.

After the bubble comes the crash... Famous examples of stock market crashes in the US markets include: October 24th 1929, October 19th 1987, May 6th, 2010 Flash Crash (no prior bubble). Each of these market events has been the subject of a lot of research and newspaper coverage as well as government reports. Typically, these reports do not identify a single causal explanation but several factors that played a role. So even in these well-known extreme cases, it is hard to pin specific blame. Shin (2010) argues that a major factor in the 1987 crash was the **endogenous risk** induced by the dynamic

**FIGURE 11.2**
The NASDAQ stock market index continued

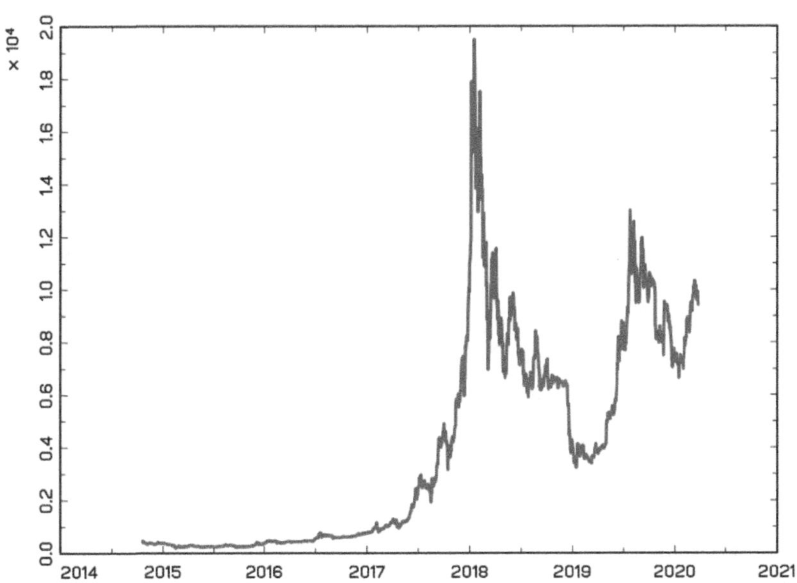


**FIGURE 11.3**
Bitcoin price level from 2014 to 2020

hedging strategies of portfolio insurance companies. The Flash Crash in the US stock market on May 6th, 2010. Partly blamed on High Frequency (Computer) Trading (HFT) and Algorithmic (Computer) Trading (AT). Figure 11.6 shows

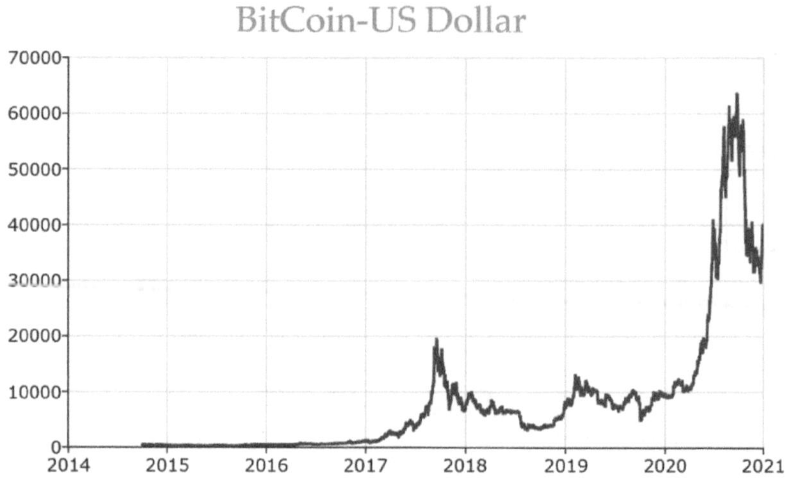


**FIGURE 11.4**
Bitcoin level continued

**FIGURE 11.5**
Gamestop price level

the Emini near term futures (a futures contract on the S&P500 index that is widely followed) price for every transaction during one hour of trading during the day, along with the change in price between consecutive transactions. The drama was concentrated in a matter of 5 minutes during which the price fell nearly 10% and then rebounded.

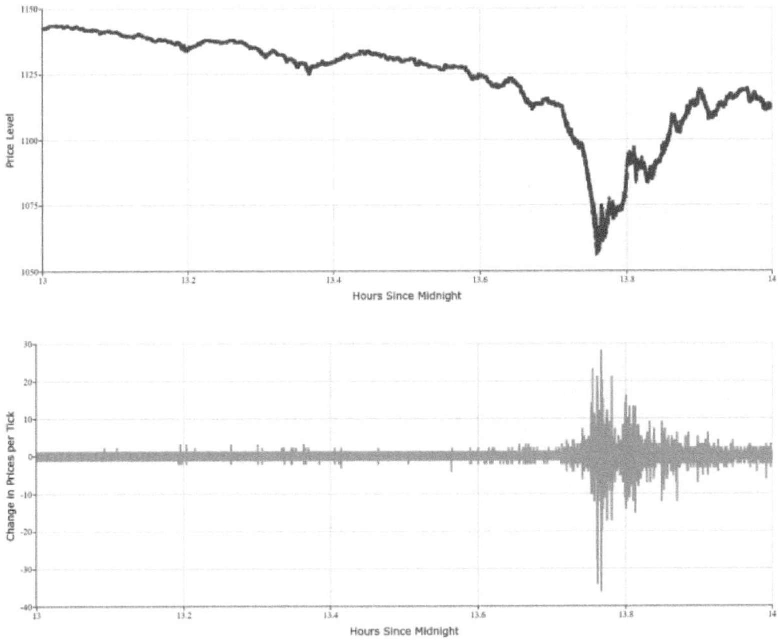


**FIGURE 11.6**
Flash Crash May 6th 2010, Emini level

On the other hand, there are authors who dispute the bubble explanations. Garber (1990) proposes market fundamental explanations for the three famous historical bubbles. Pástor and Veronesi (2006) argue that the turn of the 20th century tech bubble was at least partly explained by an increase in the uncertainty about average future profitability in the late 1990s, and the rational response of investors to that uncertainty.

## 11.1 Present Value Relations

We next present the **Dividend Discount model**, which says that stock prices depend on future cashflows and discount rates in a rational way. There is some debate about the relationship between dividends and earnings. Earnings arise from their customers and reflect the performance of the company. Typically, listed companies set dividends at some rate in response to their previous fortunes but they prefer not to make rapid adjustments in response to recent good news or bad news. Some tech companies do not pay dividends at all. We here will use the letter D to denote the cashflows.

The current price is denoted $P_t$ and future earnings or dividends are denoted $D_s$

$$\underset{today}{\underline{P}} - - \underset{year+1}{\underline{D_{t+1}}} - - \underset{year+2}{\underline{D_{t+2}}} - - \underset{year+3}{\underline{D_{t+3}}} - - \underset{year+4}{\underline{D_{t+4}}} - \cdots$$

We suppose that money today is worth more than the same amount of money next year. We saw how this worked for certain cashflows. In practice, future company cash flows are uncertain. In this case, we must forecast the future earnings. Denote this forecast by

$$E_t(D_{t+i}), \tag{11.1}$$

that is, the expected value of the uncertain random value $D_{t+i}$ taken at time $t$ using all the information available at time $t$. We will use the law of iterated expectation that $E_t E_{t+1} D_{t+2} = E_t D_{t+2}$, that is, the forecast of the forecast is the forecast.

Then we suppose that the present discounted value of the expected future cash flows is well defined

$$\boxed{PDV_t = \frac{E_t(D_{t+1})}{1+R} + \frac{E_t(D_{t+2})}{(1+R)^2} + \cdots = \sum_{i=1}^{\infty} \left(\frac{1}{1+R}\right)^i E_t(D_{t+i})},$$

where $R$ is the required rate or discount rate, e.g., $R = 0.05$. We assume that price equals PDV, i.e.,

$$P_t = PDV_t. \tag{11.2}$$

In practice, we may also want to include in the valuation, the net asset value of the company, but usually this is small relative to the implied value of future earnings. For example, the current price of AAPL is \$222 but its net asset value per share is around \$4.

This model has a number of simplifications. We suppose the infinite horizon for mathematical convenience. We also implicitly assumed risk neutrality here.

**Example 77** *Suppose that $R = 5\%$ and Amazon earnings per share are forecast to be*

| 2024 | 2025 | 2026 | 2027 | 2028 | 2029 | 2030 | 2031 |
|---|---|---|---|---|---|---|---|
| 10 | 11 | 12 | 15 | 18 | 20 | 22 | 25 |

*What is the correct price per share? We have*

$$\begin{aligned} P &= \frac{10}{1.05} + \frac{11}{1.05^2} + \frac{12}{1.05^3} + \frac{15}{1.05^4} + \frac{18}{1.05^5} \\ &\quad + \frac{20}{1.05^6} + \frac{22}{1.05^7} + \frac{25}{1.05^8} = 103.79 \end{aligned}$$

But, do we expect Amazon to stop trading in 2031? If not, how do we continue? One approach is to make a Terminal Value assumption, that is, let $TV_T$ be the terminal value at time $T$, i.e., what the company will be worth then. It follows that

$$PDV_t = \sum_{i=1}^{T-t} \left(\frac{1}{1+R}\right)^i E_t(D_{t+i}) + TV_T.$$

Specifically, suppose that

$$E_{2031}(D_{2032}) = 1.03 \times D_{2031}, \ldots, E_{2031}(D_{2031+i}) = 1.03^i \times D_{2031}.$$

Therefore, we have

$$\begin{aligned} P &= 103.79 + \frac{ED_{2032}}{1.05^9} + \ldots \\ &= 103.79 + \overbrace{\frac{25}{1.05^8}\left(\frac{1.03}{1.05} + \frac{1.03^2}{1.05^2} + \cdots\right)}^{TV_T} \\ &= 103.79 + 871.43 \\ &= 975.22. \end{aligned}$$

Ignoring the terminal value makes a big difference.

### 11.1.1 The Gordon Growth Model Special Case

Suppose that dividends are uncertain but on average grow at a constant rate $G$ forever, i.e.,

$$E_t(D_{t+1}) = (1+G)D_t \text{ or } E_t\left(\frac{D_{t+1}}{D_t}\right) = 1 + G.$$

It follows that for all $i = 1, 2, \ldots$

$$E_t(D_{t+i}) = (1+G)^i D_t.$$

Substituting this into the price formula, we get, provided that $G < R$,

$$P_t = \sum_{i=1}^{\infty} \left(\frac{1}{1+R}\right)^i (1+G)^i D_t = D_t \sum_{i=1}^{\infty} \left(\frac{1+G}{1+R}\right)^i = \frac{(1+G)}{R-G} D_t.$$

The current price $P_t$ is determined by current dividends $D_t$, and by the discount rate $R$ and by the assumed growth rate of fundamentals.

### 11.1.2 Comparative Statics of Gordon Growth Model

We repeat the formula for prices derived above

$$\boxed{P_t = \frac{(1+G)}{R-G} D_t}. \tag{11.3}$$

This says that prices depend on $G$ in a positive way and $R$ in a negative way, and also depend on current dividends in a positive way. If required returns $R$ increases, prices must fall. If dividends are anticipated to grow faster, the price will rise. If a company announces a dividend cut, we should expect to see prices fall.

We can also write this equation in terms of the price dividend ratio (the price/earnings ratio), which is predicted to be a constant and not to vary over time

$$\frac{P_t}{D_t} = \frac{1+G}{R-G}. \tag{11.4}$$

If we make assumptions about the right-hand side, we can derive predictions about the P/D ratio. For example, if $R = 7\%$ and $G = 3\%$, then $P/D = 25.75$. For example, if $R = 5\%$ and $G = 3\%$, then $P/D = 51.5$.

We can also rearrange the equation to put $R$ on the left-hand side so that

$$\boxed{R = \frac{D_t(1+G)}{P_t} + G = \frac{E_t(D_{t+1})}{P_t} + G}. \tag{11.5}$$

If we make assumptions about the right-hand side (dividend growth rate $G$, the current price $P_t$, and forecasted dividends $E_t D_{t+1}$), we can derive predictions about $R$ (labelled as the expected return or the cost of equity).

We also have

$$P_t = \frac{(1+G)}{R-G} D_t, \quad P_{t+1} = \frac{(1+G)}{R-G} D_{t+1},$$

from which it follows that

$$\boxed{\frac{P_{t+1}}{P_t} = \frac{D_{t+1}}{D_t}}, \tag{11.6}$$

because of the cancellation of the constant. This shows that growth in price level should match the growth in dividends or fundamentals more generally. This reflects the logic that prices should be related to fundamentals.

### 11.1.3 Shiller Variance Bounds Tests

Does this model work? Does it describe stock price movements? In the Gordon model, we have (11.6). It follows in particular that

$$\operatorname{var}\left(\frac{P_{t+1}}{P_t}\right) = \operatorname{var}\left(\frac{D_{t+1}}{D_t}\right).$$

In fact, dividends are very stable; they fluctuate very little about an upward trend. Consequently, stock prices should be stable. In fact, stock prices appear to fluctuate wildly.

Shiller (1981) shows how (more generally) the variability of the dividend process sets an upper bound to the variability of the stock price. Specifically, if you observed all future dividends, calculate

$$PDV_t = \sum_{i=1}^{\infty} \left(\frac{1}{1+R}\right)^i D_{t+i}$$

for some given $R$, and then compare $PDV_t$ with $P_t$. Shiller calculates an approximation

$$\boxed{PDV_t = \sum_{i=1}^{T-t} \left(\frac{1}{1+R}\right)^i D_{t+i} + TV_T},$$

where $TV_T$ is the approximate terminal value at time $T$. He assumed that after time $T$, dividends grow at the average rate of the sample. The discount rate $R$ is calculated as the average discount rate of his sample period. He showed that in the data, this bound is violated, stock returns are just too variable relative to dividends.

**Shiller's Data was downloaded from his website.** Figure 11.7 shows $P_{t+1}/P_t$ at the annual frequency for what he calls the S&P500 index. The average value is 1.057 with a standard deviation 17.8%. By comparison, the dividend growth series shown in Figure 11.8 has the mean value 1.0031 with a standard deviation 1.10%.

We next show in Figure 11.9 the stock price along with the PDV of future dividends.

### 11.1.4 Predictability of Long Horizon Returns

We next derive an additional consequence of the dividend discount model. When the stock pays dividends, the total return to equity is defined as

$$1 + R_{t+1} = \frac{P_{t+1} + D_{t+1}}{P_t},$$

which includes a capital gain part and an income part (the dividend). Then, we can write using the Gordon model assumptions and taking expectations

$$\begin{aligned} E_t(1 + R_{t+1}) &= E_t\left(\frac{P_{t+1} + D_{t+1}}{P_t}\right) \\ &= E_t\left(\frac{P_{t+1}}{P_t}\right) + E_t\left(\frac{D_{t+1}}{P_t}\right) \\ &= E_t\left(\frac{D_{t+1}}{D_t}\right) + E_t\left(\frac{D_{t+1}}{D_t}\right)\frac{D_t}{P_t}. \end{aligned}$$

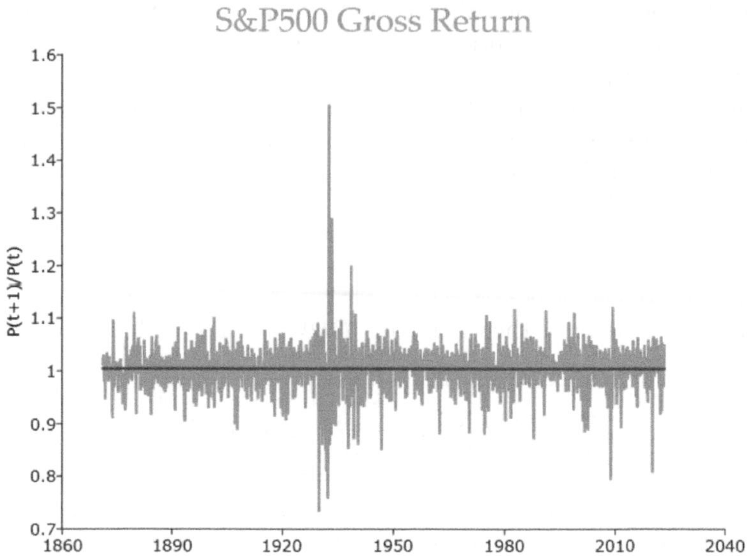


**FIGURE 11.7**
Monthly gross return on S&P500

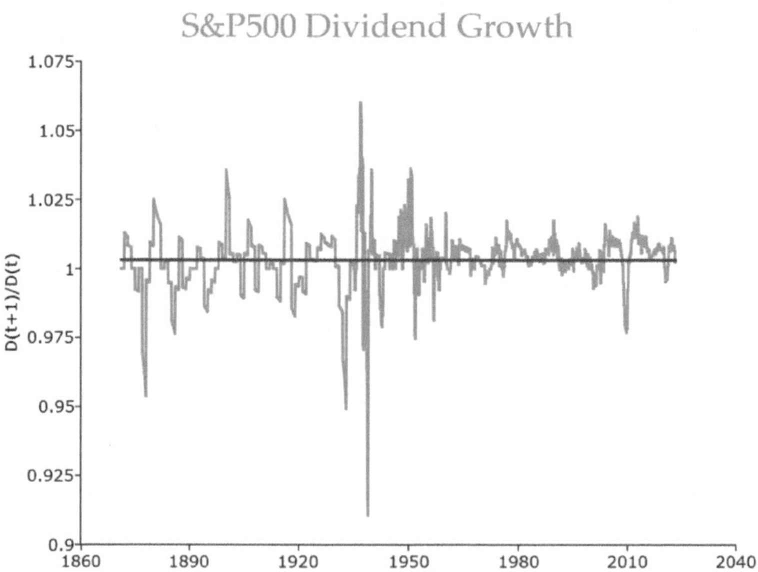


**FIGURE 11.8**
Monthly dividend growth on S&P500

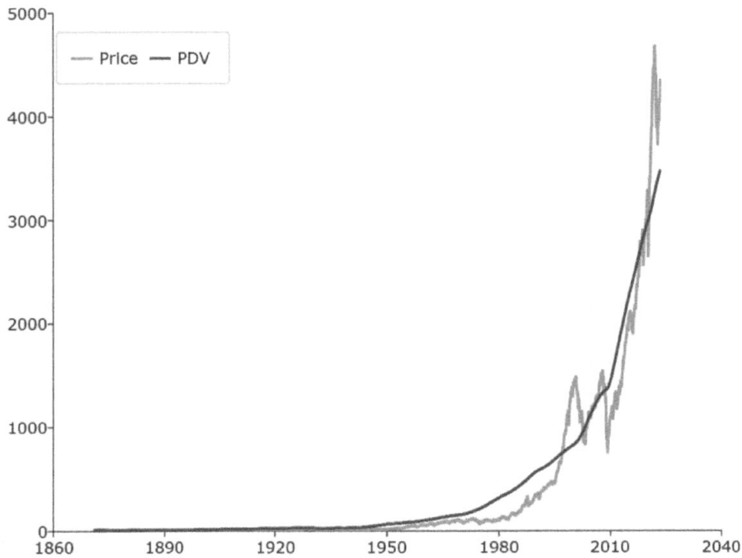


**FIGURE 11.9**
Price and PDV of monthly S&P500

If we assume dividend growth is constant, then the dividend price ratio should predict future stock returns, i.e., the regression below should hold

$$R_{t+1} = \alpha + \beta \frac{D_t}{P_t} + \varepsilon_{t+1} \tag{11.7}$$

with $\alpha = \beta$, where $\varepsilon_{t+1}$ is mean zero. Below we show the S&P 500 dividend yield (12-month price/dividend ratio). This is a persistent series compared with stock returns, meaning that it is very predictable and follows in the same direction with strong momentum.

Common practice in this literature is to regress long-horizon log stock returns on the log dividend price ratio. That is, with $r_{t:t+K} = \log(P_{t+K}) - \log(P_t)$ being the return from period $t$ to $t + K$, we consider the regression

$$\boxed{r_{t:t+K} = \alpha + \beta \log\left(\frac{D_t}{P_t}\right) + u_{t:t+K}}. \tag{11.8}$$

CLM report results for 1927-1994 and two subperiod 1927-1951 and 1951-1994 in their Table 7.1. They use real variables, i.e., stock prices adjusted for inflation. They find that long-horizon returns are very predictable

"At a horizon of 1-month, the regression results are rather unimpressive: The $R^2$ statistics never exceed 2%, and the t-statistics exceed 2 only

**FIGURE 11.10**
Price dividend ratio

> in the post-World War II subsample. The striking fact about the table is how much stronger the results become when one increases the horizon. At a 2-year horizon the $R^2$ statistic is 14% for the full sample...at a 4-year horizon the $R^2$ statistic is 26% for the full sample."

This is called long horizon predictability of stock returns. It could be about the time-varying risk premium that we expect investors to require. This predictability does not necessarily contradict our finding of little predictability of stock returns by their own history, since we are using additional information.

We recalculate using rolling forty-year windows. The first window is 1870.1 to 2010.1, the second window is 1870.2 to 2010.2, and so on until the last window is 1984:3 to 2024:3; each window is labelled by the midpoint. We also consider different horizons $K \in \{1, 3, 12, 24, 36, 48, 60\}$. Figures 11.11 and 11.12 show the results. We find that $R^2(i, 1) \leq \ldots \leq R^2(i, 60)$, i.e., predictability increases with horizon. However, we also find a lot of variability over $i$, the 40-year periods centered on 1970 and 1940 both have high $\mathrm{R}^2$ at long horizon, but the intermediate period and subsequent periods do not (until recently that is). Similarly, the slope coefficients of the regressions vary a lot, and there are even some periods where they go negative.

There is an active area of research to establish long-run predictability. Cochrane (1999, p.37) describes this as one of the three most important facts in Finance in his survey *New Facts in Finance*

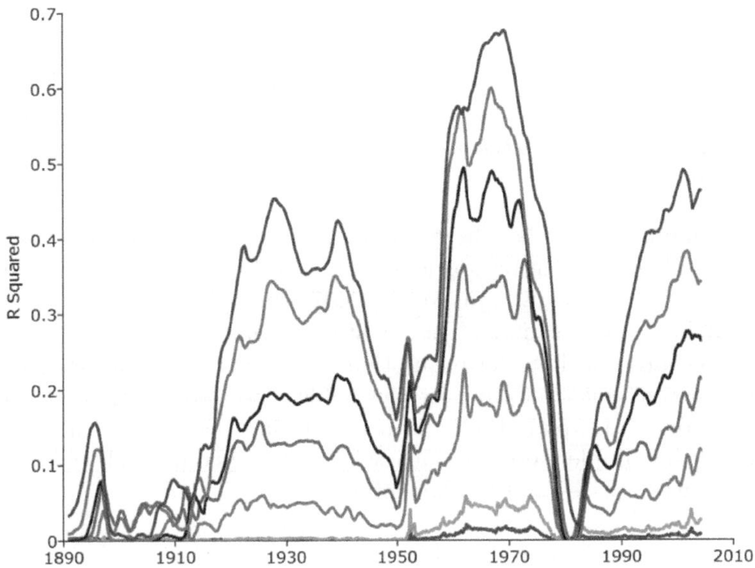


**FIGURE 11.11**
Rolling window (±20 years) $R^2$ of predictive regression

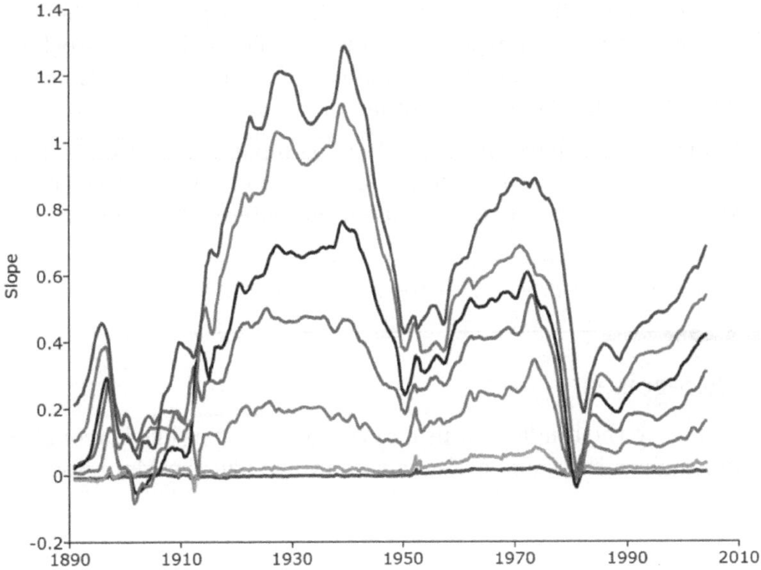


**FIGURE 11.12**
Rolling window (±20 years) slope coefficient of predictive regression

*Now, we know that . . .*

*[Fact] 2. Returns are predictable. In particular: Variables including the dividend/price (d/p) ratio and term premium can predict substantial amounts of stock return variation. This phenomenon occurs over business cycle and longer horizons. Daily, weekly, and monthly stock returns are still close to unpredictable. . .*

This claim is debatable. There is a lot of time variation in the predictability, and whether it is real or spuriously induced by aggregation has not been settled. In my view, Goyal and Welch (2007) showed that any in sample improvement fails out of sample. The debate goes on.

More recently, authors have questioned whether assuming that discount rates $R$ are constant over time is reasonable. By allowing time-varying discount rates one can explain the high variability in stock prices. Another generalization of this simple model is to allow for risk aversion, which again weakens the link between prices and fundamentals.

## 11.2 Key Points

1. The dividend discount model says that stock prices are the present discounted value of expected future cash flows. That is, stock prices are driven by fundamentals, or rather, market expectations about what those fundamentals will be.
2. Some authors have questioned the comparison between the large volatility associated with stock prices and the relatively small volatility associated with common measures of fundamentals.

## 11.3 Exercises

1. What are the fundamentals for crypto currencies like Bitcoin? What determines the value of famous paintings like the Mona Lisa?

# 12

# *Volatility and Risk*

## Outline

This chapter focuses on the concept of volatility and its crucial role in financial markets. Volatility, often synonymous with risk, is explored through various methods of measurement and its implications for asset pricing, risk management, and market quality. The chapter covers time-varying volatility, intra-period volatility, and advanced models like GARCH that help predict future risk. Additionally, it addresses alternative measures of risk, such as implied volatility from option prices and semivariance, providing a comprehensive understanding of how volatility impacts financial decision-making.

After reading this chapter, you will be able to:

- Define volatility and understand its significance as a measure of risk in financial markets.
- Explore the different methods of measuring volatility, including rolling window and intra-period volatility.
- Analyze volatility using high-frequency data and specific indicators like the Parkinson estimator.
- Derive the implied volatility from option prices and understand its role in market expectations.
- Apply GARCH models to forecast future volatility based on past returns and understand their use in risk management.
- Investigate alternative risk measures like semivariance and their relevance in assessing downside risk.
- Critically evaluate the statistical properties of volatility measures and their implications for market behavior.

DOI: 10.1201/9781003543121-12

## 12.1 What is Volatility?

Volatility is the term used to describe the variability or dispersion of returns. It is synonymous with big swings of prices in either direction, with unpredictability and uncertainty. Volatility is also synonymous with risk, the higher the volatility, the riskier the security. As we have argued investors care about both return and risk, and so their measurement and forecasting is a key issue. This chapter is about the measurement of volatility or risk. We have measured risk or volatility so far by the variance or standard deviation of the asset return calculated using all the available data, which yields a single number. We would like to measure volatility at high frequency since it seems clear that it varies from day to day.

We show again the time series of daily returns on the S&P500, which shows that there appear to be times when volatility is high and times when volatility is low. Let us try to be more precise about this.

We can think of returns as having a direction (up or down) and a magnitude, that is, we can write

$$\boxed{R_t = \overbrace{|R_t|}^{magnitude} \times \overbrace{\text{sign}(R_t)}^{direction}},$$

$$\text{sign}(x) = \begin{cases} 1 & \text{if } x > 0 \\ -1 & \text{if } x < 0. \end{cases}$$

The magnitude (absolute value) is what we think of as volatility. There seem to be periods where there are consistently large magnitude returns of both signs and other periods where the magnitudes seem typically small. We plot below the magnitude of daily returns, which looks like a city skyline with denser parts and less dense parts.

We may say that there are high-volatility periods and low-volatility periods. Goodbye Kansas, we no longer think that the i.i.d. assumption we made in earlier chapters is a good one.

We found that the return on assets is hard to predict. There is some predictability, but it is small and not stable over time. We next look at the autocorrelation of the magnitude of returns $|R_t|$ and the autocorrelation of the sign$(R_t)$ series. The absolute value series shows strong and statistically significant positive autocorrelation out to a horizon of one year, whereas the sign series shows a similar lack of autocorrelation to the raw return series.

This implies that there is a lot of predictability in the absolute value of returns. This does not violate the EMH: knowing the absolute value of returns is not directly of help in trading. We fundamentally need to know whether the market is going up or down, and the direction itself seems as hard to predict as the return series. So to conclude, there is evidence that volatility changes

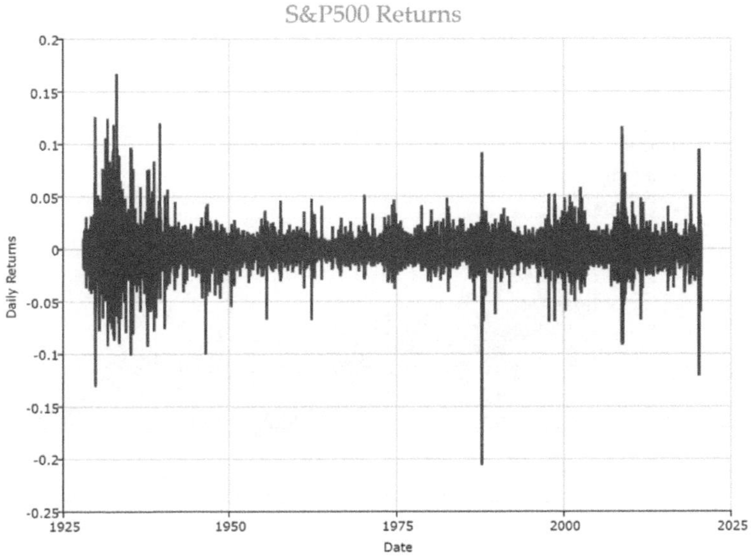


**FIGURE 12.1**
Daily S&P500 returns

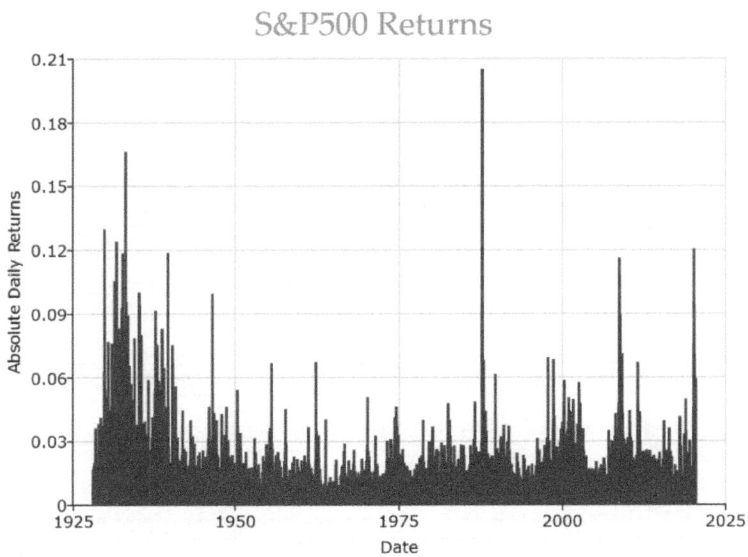


**FIGURE 12.2**
Absolute value of daily S&P500 returns

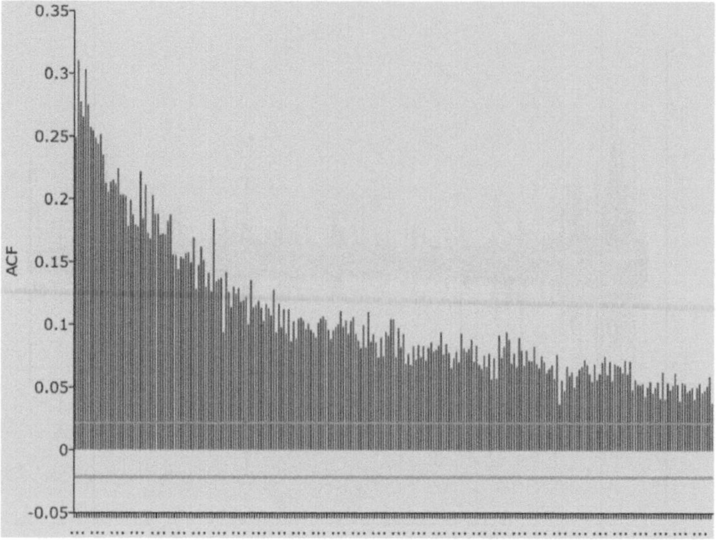


**FIGURE 12.3**
Autocorrelation of the absolute value of S&P500 daily returns out to 255 lags

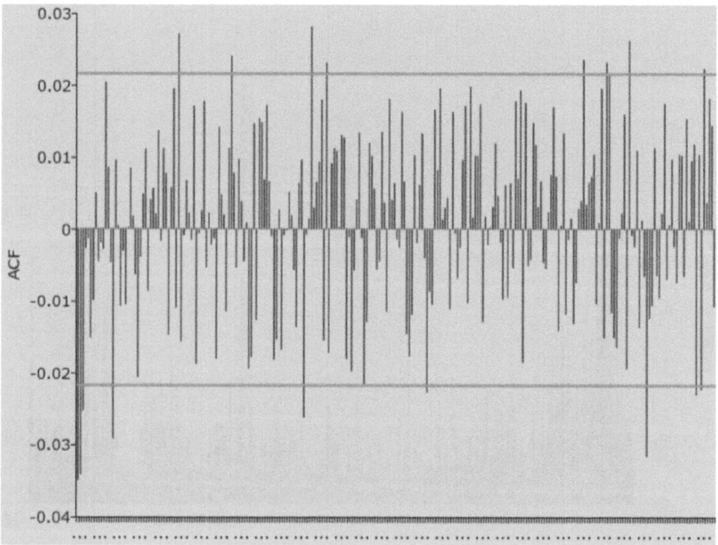


**FIGURE 12.4**
Autocorrelation of the sign of S&P500 daily returns out to 255 lags

over time, i.e., there are volatility clusters, and these changes appear to be predictable over time. We discuss different ways of measuring volatility: Intra-period or Realized Volatility; Implied Volatility; the GARCH Model and its variants.

## 12.2 Why Care About Volatility?

Risk (Volatility) measurement is central to finance. Volatility is an important concept for financial markets related to risk. The main applications include:

1. Asset pricing. The Conditional Capital Asset Pricing Model specifies the trade-off between time-varying risk and time-varying expected return in the stock market.
2. Risk Management/Value at Risk. The main input for many procedures is an estimate of volatility at a certain horizon.
3. Portfolio Allocation requires measurement of volatility matrix.
4. Measuring market quality. Highly volatile markets discourage retail participation, and regulators try to discourage high levels of volatility or introduce mechanisms such as circuit breakers that spread it out over time.

We next consider three different general approaches to measuring and modeling it.

## 12.3 Rolling Window or Intra-period Volatility

Let's suppose that we are interested in monthly returns $R_t$, but we also have higher frequency data, say daily data $R_t(j)$, $j = 1, ..., n$, where $n$ is the total number of observations inside each period (assumed constant for simplicity). For example, we measure returns on January 2nd, January 3rd,...,January 31st.

**Algorithm 19** *We estimate the volatility of the stock over the month* $[t, t+1]$*, denoted* $\widehat{\sigma}^2_{t+1}$*, as the sample variance of within-period returns*

$$\widehat{\sigma}^2_{t+1} = \frac{1}{n}\sum_{j=1}^{n}\left(R_t(j) - \overline{R}_t\right)^2, \quad \overline{R}_t = \frac{1}{n}\sum_{j=1}^{n} R_t(j).$$

This can be considered an ex-post measure of volatility, meaning it is a measure of the volatility that happened in the period $t, t+1$. Specifically, we have January volatility, February volatility, etc. We show in Figure 12.5 the S&P500 monthly standard deviation of daily returns as a monthly time series.

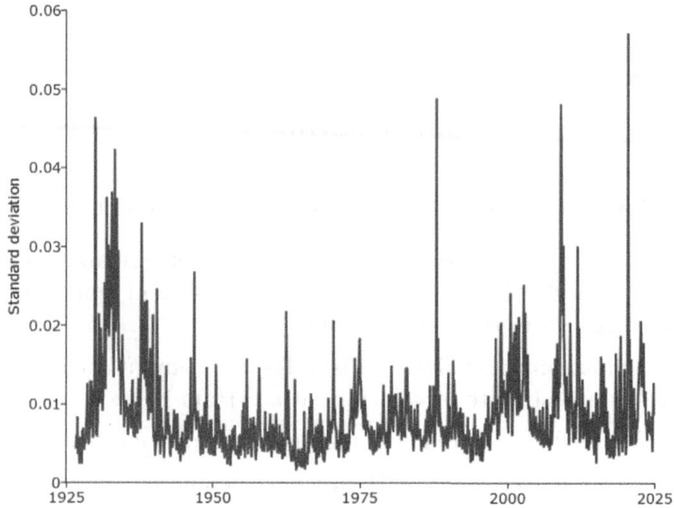


**FIGURE 12.5**
Shows monthly standard deviation of daily FF market return from 1926 to 2024

This scheme involves a non-overlapping series of "windows" as follows

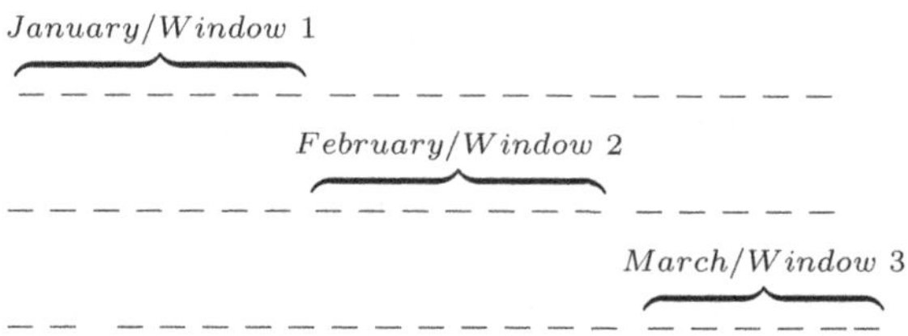


The windows are non-overlapping, because they have no days in common by the nature of the calendar. We obtain by this a monthly volatility measure. Of course, the choice of month as the unit is somewhat arbitrary. One could choose 5 days or 20 days, or whatever; note that calendar months are not equal in duration, and some Februaries may have only 19 trading days, whereas March may have 23 days.

We may instead consider overlapping (rolling) windows of some fixed size $n$, shown below

$$\overbrace{-\,-\,-\,-\,-\,-\,-\,-\,-\,-\,-}^{Window\ 1}\,-\,-\,-\,-\,-$$

$$-\,\overbrace{-\,-\,-\,-\,-\,-\,-\,-\,-\,-\,-}^{Window\ 2}\,-\,-\,-\,-$$

$$-\,-\,\overbrace{-\,-\,-\,-\,-\,-\,-\,-\,-\,-\,-}^{Window\ 3}\,-\,-\,-\,.$$

In this case, we may calculate a daily volatility measure by considering a rolling window that is centered on a given day and includes some days forward and some days backward. For example, to estimate the volatility on January 15th we may consider a window containing the returns on January 1st to January 31st, whereas to calculate the volatility on January 16th, we may consider a window containing the returns on January 2nd to February 1st, etc.

We show in Figure 12.6 the S&P500 rolling window (size 22) standard deviation of daily returns with confidence interval.

**Algorithm 20** *The confidence interval for this estimate can be computed as*

$$\widehat{\sigma} \pm 1.96 \times \sqrt{\frac{\widehat{\sigma}^2}{44}}, \tag{12.1}$$

*where $\widehat{\sigma}$ is the (global) standard deviation of the stock return series using all the sample data.*

Under the null hypothesis of no variation in volatility, $\widehat{\sigma}_{t+1}$ should lie within this interval. It does not. This can be considered evidence that volatility varies over time.

There were big spikes in volatility during: the 1929 crash and the great depression, the 1987 crash, the tech crash around 2000, the Global Financial Crisis around 2008, and the COVID-19 pandemic. The advantage of the rolling window measure is that it is widely available given just daily stock returns. The disadvantage is that it is ex-post and further that this estimator depends on stock returns from days around the day in question.

## 12.4 Volatility Measures Using Only Open, Close, High, and Low

We would like to calculate a daily measure of volatility that does not include data from other days, as the rolling window method does. One could calculate the intraday variance using data from within the day, the so-called realized volatility. In practice, this requires access to high-frequency data, which requires a lot of work to process. Instead, we consider measures that are computed from widely available data on the intraday high and low prices. Yahoo,

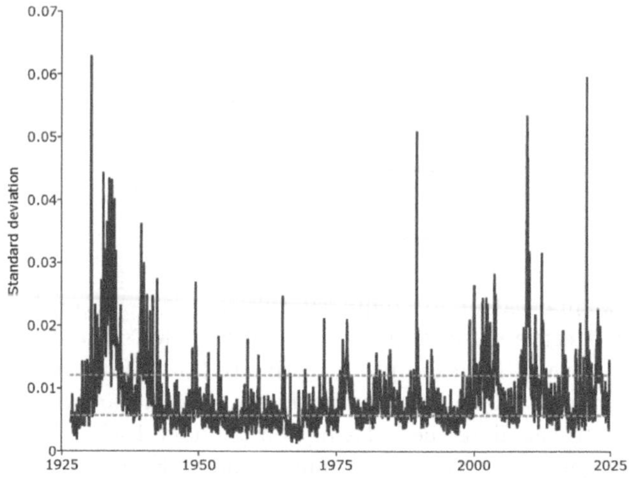


**FIGURE 12.6**
Shows rolling window (n = 22) standard deviation of daily FF market return

Bloomberg, etc., all report the daily opening price, closing price, the intraday high price, and the intraday low price, denoted: $P_O$, $P_C$, $P_H$, and $P_L$.

**Algorithm 21** *The realized range is defined as*

$$V^{HL} = \frac{P_H - P_L}{P_L}. \tag{12.2}$$

This can be interpreted as the maximum profit you could make in a single day trade if you bought at the intraday low and sold at the intraday high. This can also be interpreted as being proportional to the volatility parameter $\sigma$ (standard deviation per unit time) of a Brownian motion when the transaction price data (on which the high and low prices are reported) infill the day, meaning there are lots of intraday transactions.

**Algorithm 22** *The Parkinson (1980) estimator*

$$V^P = \frac{(\log P_H - \log P_L)^2}{4 \log 2}. \tag{12.3}$$

This also has an interpretation as a (consistent) estimator of the volatility parameter $\sigma^2$ (variance per unit time) of a Brownian motion when the transaction price data (on which the high and low prices are reported) infill the day.

The realized range on the S&P500 is reported below. It looks similar to other measures in terms of the peaks and troughs. It is very positively autocorrelated, which means it has strong momentum, and it has a positively skewed distribution, as one can see from the histogram.

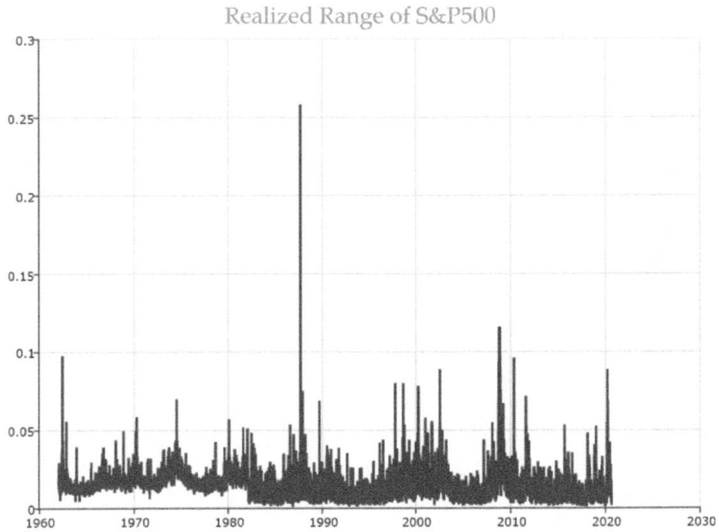


**FIGURE 12.7**
Realized range of S&P500 daily returns

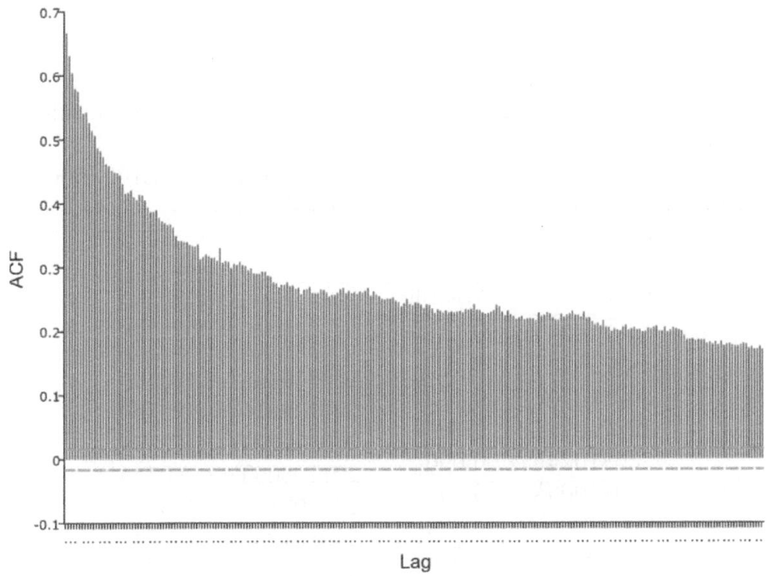


**FIGURE 12.8**
Autocorrelation of realized range out to 255 lags

The distribution is right-skewed: most of the time, the value is modest and occasionally there are very big values relative to the mean.

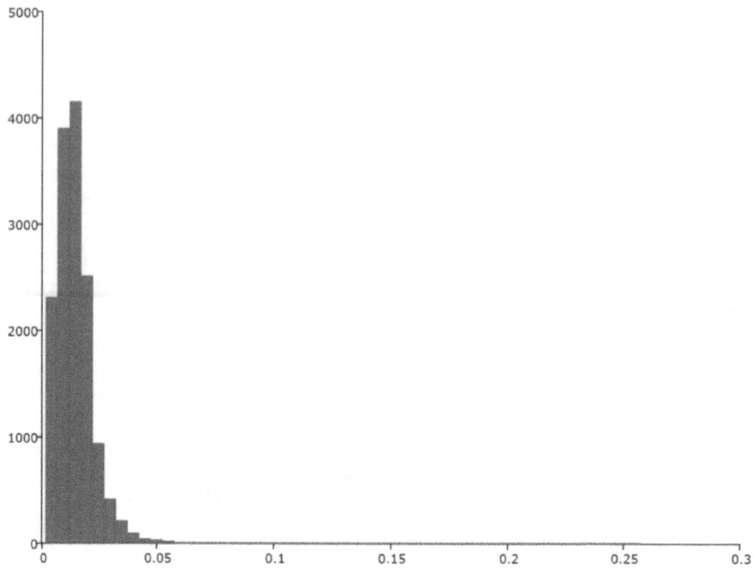


**FIGURE 12.9**
Histogram of realized range

This is an ex-post measure of volatility, and so this measurement by itself does not allow us to forecast future volatility. For that, we would need to construct a time series model.

We next show the top 20 most volatile days on the FTSE100 index over the period 1984-2017 (minus means market closed down, $P_C < P_O$, plus means market closed up, $P_C > P_O$).

| Date | Volatility |
|---|---|
| 19871020Tu | 0.131- |
| 19871022Th | 0.115- |
| 20081010F | 0.112- |
| 19971028Tu | 0.096- |
| 20081024F | 0.096- |
| 20081006M | 0.094- |
| 20081008W | 0.094- |
| 20080919F | 0.093+ |
| 20081124M | 0.090+ |
| 20081015W | 0.084- |
| 19871019M | 0.081- |
| 20020920F | 0.080+ |
| 20081013M | 0.076+ |
| 20010921F | 0.076+ |
| 20081029W | 0.075+ |
| 20110809Tu | 0.074+ |
| 20090114W | 0.074- |
| 20080122Tu | 0.074+ |
| 20020715M | 0.071- |
| 20081016Th | 0.070- |

There doesn't seem to be a favored day of the week for the UK market. We update this calculation to include data up to 2021, in which case we find that the following days entered the top twenty:20200312Th=0.122-, 20200309M=0.097-, 20200316M=0.095-, 20200324Tu=0.095-. The COVID-19 pandemic was a very volatile time for the UK stock market.

We next show the top 20 most volatile days on the S&P500 index since 1960-2017.

| Date | Volatility |
|---|---|
| 19871019M | 0.257- |
| 19871020T | 0.123+ |
| 20081010F | 0.107- |
| 20081009Th | 0.106- |
| 20081113Th | 0.104+ |
| 20081028T | 0.101+ |
| 20081015W | 0.100- |
| 20081120Th | 0.097- |
| 20081013M | 0.094+ |
| 20080929M | 0.093- |
| 19871026M | 0.092- |
| 20100506Th | 0.090- |
| 20081201M | 0.089+ |
| 19620529Tu | 0.089+ |
| 19871021W | 0.087+ |
| 20081016Th | 0.087+ |
| 20081006M | 0.085- |
| 20081022Th | 0.085- |
| 20020724Th | 0.081+ |
| 19980831M | 0.080- |

Note that of these twenty days, 7 were Mondays. We update this calculation to include data upto 2021, in which case we find that the following days entered the top twenty: 20200313F=0.088-. The US market was much less affected by the pandemic, with only one day from that period entering the top twenty.

Both markets were dominated by 2008 and 1987. The UK was also strongly affected by 2020. Perhaps overall, the US market is a little more volatile than the UK? This may be surprising since the S&P500 represents at least 10 times the value of the FTSE100 index. Some have argued that this may be explained by more innovation in the US? There is good volatility and bad volatility; perhaps not? Circuit breakers now limit the worst case, or perhaps spread it out over several days. For comparison, we look at the top ten most volatile days on the Yen/Dollar exchange rate. This seems mostly about 2008.

Yen/Dollar exchange rate:

| Date | Volatility |
|---|---|
| 20081208 | 0.17690151+ |
| 20081209 | 0.15504392- |
| 20081009 | 0.096103137- |
| 20081008 | 0.085058122+ |
| 19981007 | 0.066671738- |
| 20080409 | 0.058772426- |
| 20080408 | 0.056032779+ |
| 20081028 | 0.053715872+ |
| 20080509 | 0.050521790- |
| 19980617 | 0.044009698- |

We next show the realized range on JD.com and Alibaba two top Chinese companies.

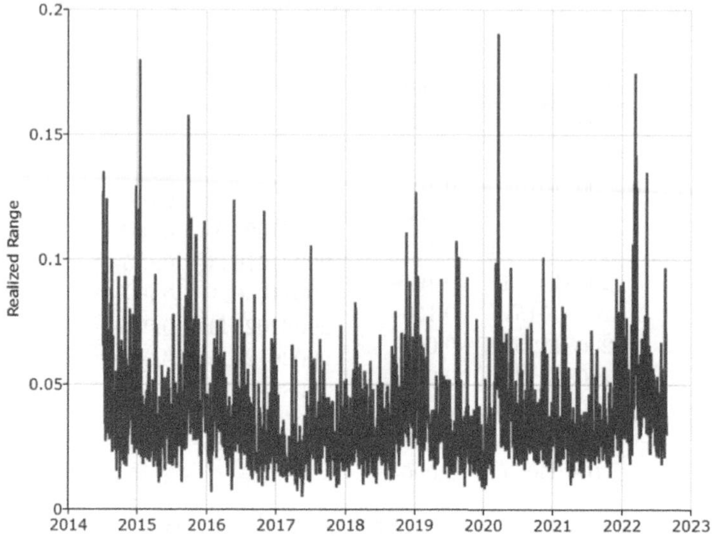


**FIGURE 12.10**
JD.com realized range

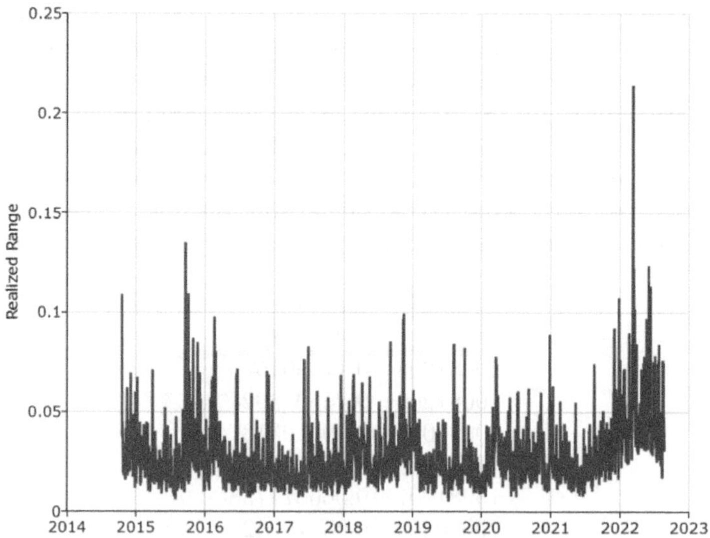


**FIGURE 12.11**
Ali Baba realized range

## 12.5 Implied Volatility from Option Prices

A (European) call option with exercise price $X$ and maturity $\tau$ on a stock with current price $P$ gives the owner (of the option) the right but not the obligation to buy the stock at maturity for the price $X$. If the price at maturity is above $X$, then the owner can buy at $X$ and sell at the prevailing price and make a profit. If the price at maturity is below $X$,, then the owner will not exercise the option. The gross profit to the option owner is $\max\{0, P(\tau) - X\}$, where $P(\tau)$ is the price of the stock at maturity (which is unknown at the time the option is purchased). This allows the option holder to profit if the stock price rises but limits his losses if the stock price falls, i.e., it provides insurance. Clearly, the option contract has a positive value, let's say $C$. Options are traded on exchanges such as the CME where the prices or values are determined by the interaction of traders. For example, on 20220929, a call option on the S&P500 with maturity one month and strike price $X = 3595$ (where the underlying was $P = 3641$) traded at $C = \$143.90$.

What is the value of this contract, i.e., what is the correct value for $C$ and on what does it depend? Black and Scholes (1973) showed that the option price $C$ should satisfy the following equation

$$\| C = P\Phi(d_1) - Xe^{-r_f \tau}\Phi(d_2) \|,$$

where $r_f$ is the risk-free rate, and:

$$d_1 = \frac{\log(P/X) + (r_f + \sigma^2/2)\tau}{\sigma\sqrt{\tau}} \quad ; \quad d_2 = \frac{\log(P/X) + (r_f - \sigma^2/2)\tau}{\sigma\sqrt{\tau}},$$

where $\Phi$ is the standard normal c.d.f. Here, $\sigma^2$ is the variance per unit time of the underlying stock. The value of the option increases in volatility, as can be shown by differentiation of $C$ with respect to $\sigma^2$.

Every day $t$ we observe the stock price $P_t$ and the risk free rate $r_{ft}$. We also observe many options contracts with different exercise prices $X$ and maturities $\tau$, and we observe their prices $C_t$. We can invert the Black-Scholes formula to obtain $\sigma^2$. In fact you can buy calculators that have this function built in. One can do this at every time period where we have these observations, thereby generating a time series of volatility $\sigma_t^2$. This is called **implied volatility**.

VIX is the ticker symbol for the Chicago Board Options Exchange Market Volatility Index, a popular measure of the implied volatility of S&P 500 index options. Often referred to as the **fear index** or the fear gauge, it represents one measure of the market's expectation of stock market volatility over the next 30 day period. The VIX is quoted in percentage points and translates, roughly, to the expected movement in the S&P 500 index over the next 30-day period, which is then annualized. The VIX is calculated and disseminated in real-time by the Chicago Board Options Exchange. This series is widely followed by traders, journalists, and academics.

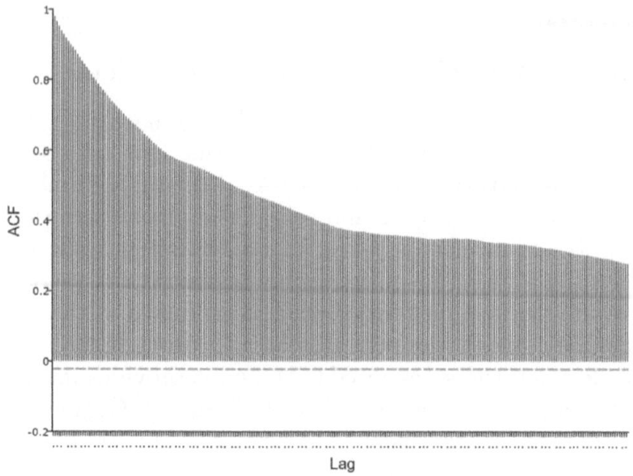


**FIGURE 12.12**
Autocorrelation on the daily VIX out to 255 lags

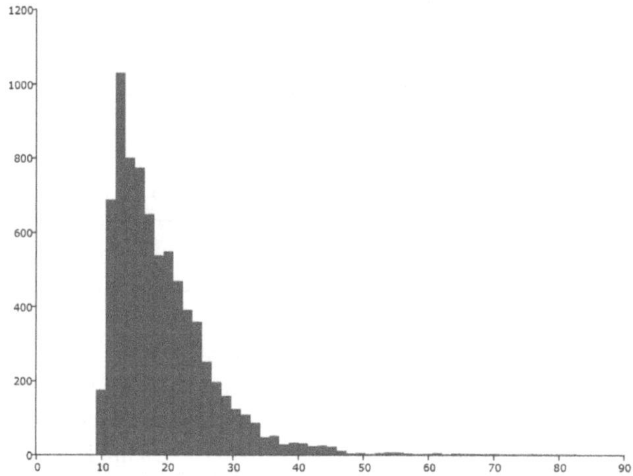

**FIGURE 12.13**
Histogram of daily VIX

What are the statistical properties of the VIX? It is a very persistent time series having strong positive autocorrelation at many lags.

We next show the marginal distribution of the VIX, which shows it is a very skewed distribution where most of the time it takes modest values, and occasionally takes a very large value relative to its mean.

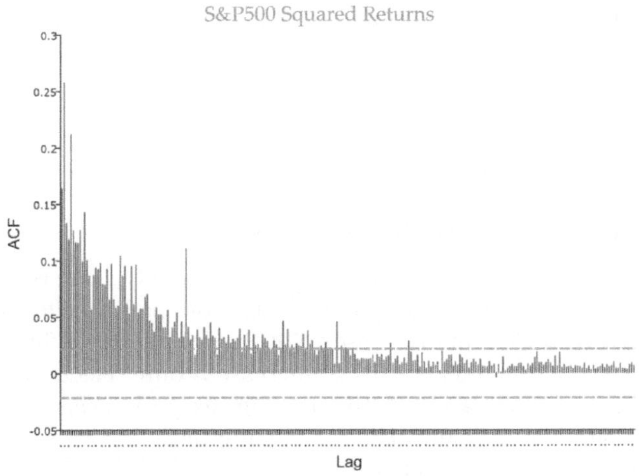


**FIGURE 12.14**
Autocorrelation of squared S&P500 daily returns out to 255 lags

## 12.6 Time Series GARCH Models

We next show the ACF of squared returns, which shows strong positive autocorrelation.

We are interested in ex-ante measures of volatility, i.e., what will volatility be tomorrow, not what volatility was last month. Investors want to trade off risk against return based on current knowledge. For S&P500 daily squared returns, we fit the multivariate regression of squared returns against past squared returns (estimates with standard errors below):

$$R_t^2 = \underset{(0.000007)}{0.000062} + \underset{(0.011)}{0.1617}R_{t-1}^2 + \underset{(0.011)}{0.0204}R_{t-2}^2 + \underset{(0.011)}{0.0278}R_{t-3}^2 + \underset{(0.011)}{0.2101}R_{t-4}^2 + \underset{(0.011)}{0.1004}R_{t-5}^2 + e_t.$$

The fitted value from the regression depends only on past values of the squared returns and is an ex ante volatility measure. Engle (1982), Bollerslev (1986) introduced the **Generalized AutoRegressive Conditional Heteroskedasticity** (GARCH) model, which is a general time series model that allows for the prediction of volatility, extending this regression idea.

**Definition 20** *The GARCH(1,1) model for returns is*

$$R_t = \mu + \sigma_t \varepsilon_t, \quad \sigma_t^2 = \omega + \beta\sigma_{t-1}^2 + \gamma\left(R_{t-1} - \mu\right)^2,$$

*where* $\varepsilon_t \sim N(0,1)$.

The quantity $\sigma_t^2$ is the conditional variance of returns given all past returns. The model parameters are $\omega, \beta, \gamma$ can be estimated by many software packages.

## 12.7 Applications in Event Studies

Volatility can be included in event studies as a target. That is, we may want to consider whether an event has had a positive or negative effect on volatility. For example, do stock splits increase volatility for the stock in question? For example, does stock market volatility increase around elections and referendums? We can do this easiest with the daily ex-post measures of volatility, such as the high-low measure. For a company daily volatility measure $V_t^{HL}$ we may consider the equivalent to the market model

$$\log(V_t^{HL}) = \alpha + \beta \log(V_{mt}^{HL}) + \varepsilon_t, \tag{12.4}$$

where $V_{mt}^{HL}$ is the high-low measure of market volatility. The error term here is mean zero and represents **idiosyncratic volatility**. The logarithm is used because it seems to provide a better model fit. The coefficient $\beta$ is expected to be positive and measures how company volatility moves with market volatility, in fact, it is the elasticity of company volatility with respect to market volatility. We show the result for Microsoft over the period 1986-2024 in Figure 12.15. We obtained the following regression estimates (with standard errors below)

$$\log(V_t^{HL}) = \underset{0.084}{-3.741} + \underset{0.0082}{0.485} \log(V_{mt}^{HL}) + erro, \quad R^2 = 0.286.$$

One potential adjustment to this model is include a lagged dependent variable in the regression, because the error terms in (12.4) are highly serially correlated. In this case we find

$$\log(V_t^{HL}) = \underset{0.084}{-1.388} + \underset{0.0077}{0.320} \log(V_{mt}^{HL}) + \underset{0.0084}{0.465} \log(V_{t-1}^{HL}) + error, \quad R^2 = 0.469,$$

which results in a significant improvement in the model fit. One may then proceed to calculate Abnormal Volatility and Cumulative Abnormal Volatility (as we did for returns) in an event window, and test whether there was a significant change in volatility. For economy-wide events, we instead propose the models

$$\log(V_{mt}^{HL}) = \alpha + \varepsilon_t, \quad \log(V_{mt}^{HL}) = \alpha + \gamma \log(V_{m,t-1}^{HL}) + \varepsilon_t$$

**Example 78** *Volatility around elections and major events. For example, the 2016 election was on November 8th. The average value of the S&P500 for the four years prior was 0.0096 with a standard deviation of 0.00564. The*

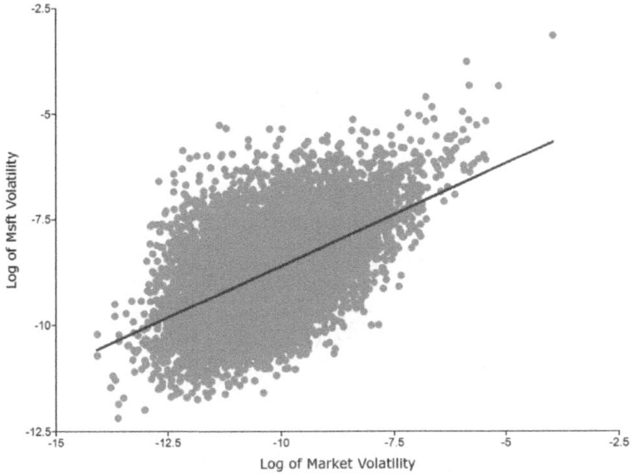


**FIGURE 12.15**
Regression of Msft volatility against market volatility

*value on 20161108. was 0.0110, the value on 20161109 was 0.021 (around 2 standard deviations above average), the value on 20161110 was 0.0145, the value on 20161111 was 0.0062, and the value on 20161114 was 0.00709. The regression model for log volatility is*

$$\log(V_{mt}^{HL}) = \underset{(0.137)}{-2.387} + \underset{(0.028)}{0.502} \log(V_{m,t-1}^{HL}) + \varepsilon_t, \quad \widehat{\sigma} = 0.454$$

*The residual on 20161109 was 0.788, which is slightly less than two standard deviations above normal.*

Inside the GARCH paradigm, one can include dummy variables inside the variance equation as follows

$$R_t = \sigma_t \varepsilon_t, \quad \sigma_t^2 = \omega + \beta \sigma_{t-1}^2 + \gamma R_{t-1}^2 + \sum_{j=1}^{E} \delta_j D_{jt},$$

where $D_{1t}$ is one if observation $t$ is equal to the first member of the event window etc. Suppose that

$$r_t = \alpha + \phi r_{t-1} + \sigma_t \varepsilon_t,$$

$$\sigma_t^2 = \omega + \beta \sigma_{t-1}^2 + \gamma u_{t-1}^2,$$

where $\varepsilon_t$ is i.i.d. with mean zero and variance one.

**Algorithm 23** *1. First estimate the model using the Estimation window data*

$\{r_1, \ldots, r_T\}$, *let* $\widehat{\alpha}, \widehat{\phi}, \widehat{\omega}, \widehat{\beta}, \widehat{\gamma}$ *be the parameter estimates,*
*2. Calculate*

$$\widehat{\varepsilon}_t^* = \frac{r_t - \widehat{\alpha} - \widehat{\phi} r_{t-1}}{\widehat{\sigma}_t}$$

$$\widehat{\sigma}_t^2 = \widehat{\omega} + \widehat{\beta}\widehat{\sigma}_{t-1}^2 + \widehat{\gamma}\left(r_{t-1} - \widehat{\alpha} - \widehat{\phi} r_{t-2}\right)^2,$$

*for all time periods in the Event window* $t = 1, \ldots, E$.
*3. Compute*

$$AR_t = \widehat{\varepsilon}_t^*, \quad AR2_t = (\widehat{\varepsilon}_t^*)^2 - 1, \quad CAR(\tau) = \sum_{t=1}^{\tau} AR_t, \quad CAR2(\tau) = \sum_{t=1}^{\tau} AR2_t.$$

*4. Compare with confidence intervals:*

$$\pm 1.96, \quad \pm 1.96 \times \sqrt{2}, \quad \pm 1.96\sqrt{\tau}, \quad \pm 1.96 \times \sqrt{2\tau},$$

*which are valid when* $\varepsilon_t \sim N(0,1)$ *because then* $\mathrm{var}(\varepsilon_t^2 - 1) = 2$.
*5. If* $\varepsilon_t$ *is not normal, then we can replace* 2 *by an estimate using the estimation window data*

$$\frac{1}{T}\sum_{t=1}^{T}\left(\widehat{\varepsilon}_t^2 - 1\right)^2.$$

## 12.8 Risk Management

The measurement and modeling of market risk became a big issue because of the concern of regulators and investors about the effects of large crashes, e.g., Black Monday, 1987, when there was a roughly 23% (and $23\sigma$) drop in the stock market value, which equated to roughly \$1trillion lost in one day. The long-term capital crisis of (1998) led to market-wide losses of around \$2 billion. The Asian crisis of 1997 and the Russian crisis of 1998 were other big events. The first Basel Capital Accord was signed in (1988), which introduced regulatory oversight of banks. This focused on the measure of risk called **Value-at-Risk** (VaR), which is the amount lost on a portfolio (investment) with a given small probability over a fixed time period. The regulations required the following. Banks must report their global Value-at-Risk for the following 10 days to supervisory authorities every day. The VaR is to be calculated for the 99% one-sided significance level. They should use at least one year of historical data and at least quarterly updates. The implied capital requirement is the higher of the previous day's VaR or the average over the last 60 trading days, times a multiplicative factor of 3 plus an add-on. Banks can use their own model to calculate the VaR, but regulators can audit. There are penalties for bad models. A second and third accord have since been signed with some updates on methodology and practice. See Basel Committee on Banking Supervision (2012).

The **Value at Risk** (at level $\alpha$) of an asset with random payoff $R$ is defined as $VaR_\alpha$, where

$$\Pr(R \le VaR_\alpha) = \alpha. \tag{12.5}$$

If $R \sim N(\mu, \sigma^2)$, then

$$VaR_\alpha = \mu + \sigma z_\alpha,$$

where $z_\alpha$ satisfies $\Pr(Z \le z_\alpha) = \alpha$ for a standard normal random variable $Z$. We may allow $\mu, \sigma$ to be time varying by the rolling window paradigm. Within the GARCH paradigm

$$VaR_\alpha = \mu + z_\alpha \sigma_t.$$

**Algorithm 24** *To estimate the $VaR_\alpha$ from sample data we let for example*

$$\widehat{VaR}_\alpha = \widehat{\mu} + z_\alpha \sigma_t(\widehat{\theta}).$$

## 12.9 Other Risk Measures

Some have argued that variance and its generalization are poor measures of risk. We may care about the probability of large losses on our portfolio, e.g., $\Pr(R_{\mathcal{P}} < -0.1)$ (10% losses on an annualized basis). Note that if $R_{\mathcal{P}} \sim N(\mu_{\mathcal{P}}, \sigma^2_{\mathcal{P}})$, then

$$\Pr(R_{\mathcal{P}} < -0.1) = \Pr\left(Z < \frac{-0.1 - \mu_{\mathcal{P}}}{\sigma_{\mathcal{P}}}\right) = \Phi\left(\frac{-0.1 - \mu_{\mathcal{P}}}{\sigma_{\mathcal{P}}}\right),$$

which can be calculated. This relies on the normal distribution (not a good approximation) and it is not allowing for change in risk and return over time.

We next show the density of daily S&P500 returns (red) and normal density with the same mean and variance (blue). The distributions are quite different in their behavior in the tails and at the mean.

If stock returns are normally distributed, what should be the largest/ smallest daily returns we should see? The probability of observing a 5 sigma event in daily returns at least once in a given year (according to the normal distribution and assuming independence) is

$$\begin{aligned} 1 - (1 - \Pr(X < \mu - 5\sigma))^{255} &= 7.3093490 \times 10^{-5} \\ &\simeq 255 \times \Pr(X < \mu - 5\sigma) \\ &= 7.3096151 \times 10^{-5}. \end{aligned}$$

In fact it happens almost every year (55 occurrences out of 93 years).

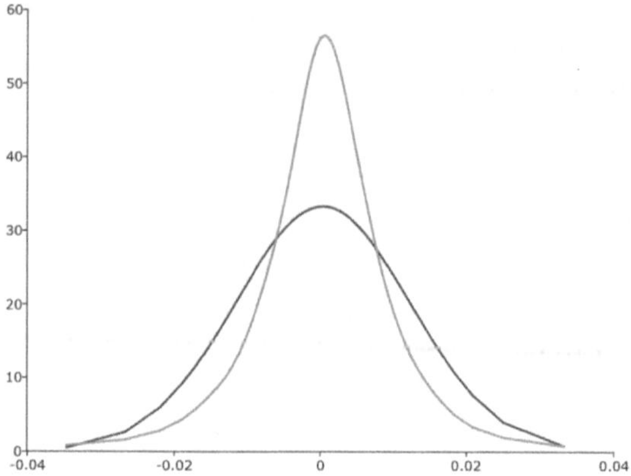


**FIGURE 12.16**
Density of daily stock returns in comparison with normal distribution

### 12.9.1 Semivariance

We have

$$\begin{aligned}\operatorname{var}(X) &= E\left[(X-E(X))^2\right] \\ &= \overbrace{E\left[(X-E(X))^2 1(X<E(X))\right]}^{\text{downside semivariance}} \\ &\quad + \overbrace{E\left[(X-E(X))^2 1(X>E(X))\right]}^{\text{upside semivariance}} \\ &\equiv \operatorname{var}_d(X)+\operatorname{var}_u(X)\end{aligned}$$

The downside semivariance and its square root $\operatorname{var}_d(X), \operatorname{stdev}_d(X)$ measures the part of the variance due to negative movements.

Some trading strategies work well under volatility, and some do not. Volatility or risk does not appear to be trending down. Rather, it has both up and down movements. This is unlike, say, the risk of dying in an airplane accident, which has consistently gone down over time. Some argue that there is good volatility (price going up) and bad volatility (price going down). Innovation leads to volatility by creative destruction, prices of successful companies go up, prices of unsuccessful companies go down, overall market goes up when there is innovation, good for society.

## 12.10 Key Points

1. Volatility is the name given to the econometric measurement of risk. Its measurement is a key component of risk management. There

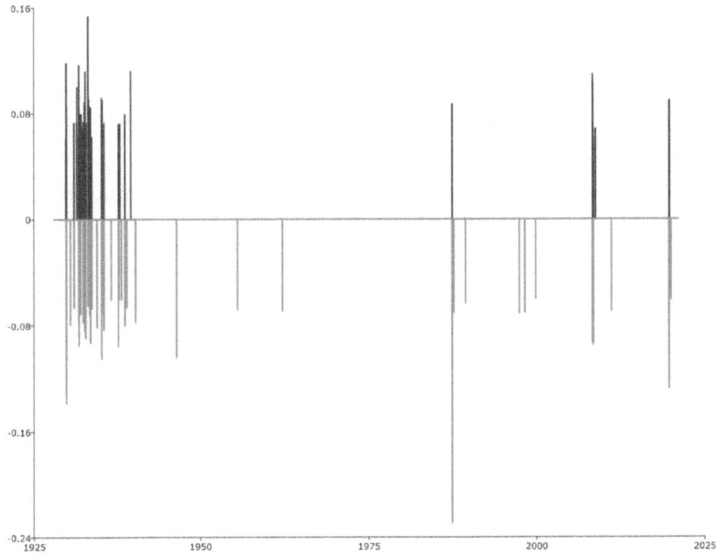


**FIGURE 12.17**
Five sigma returns on S&P500

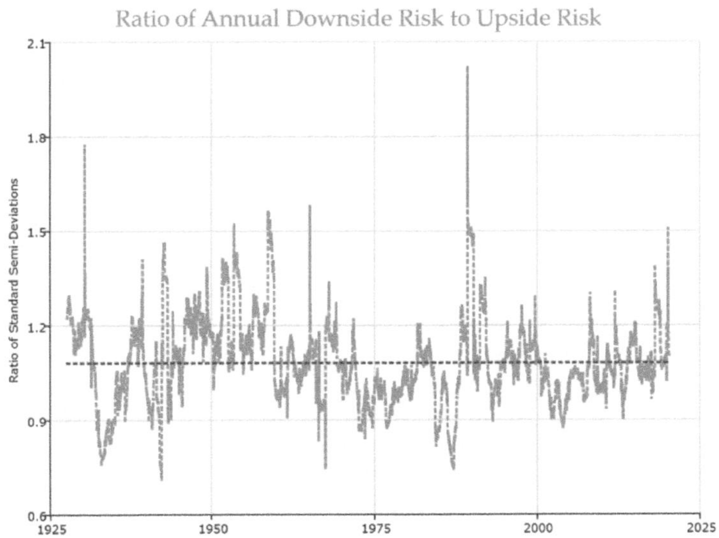


**FIGURE 12.18**
Ratio of downside to upside semivariance

are many different ways of measuring or estimating volatility at the daily horizon.

2. Measured volatility varies over time in a systematic way, i.e., it clusters with periods of high volatility persisting for some time, and periods of low volatility persisting also.
3. Volatility varies over assets (with Bitcoin, for example, having high volatility), and over time.

# 13

# Complements

## 13.1 What is Research?

- You want to find an answer to a question.
- You want to understand how some part of the world works or why things happen the way they do.
- You want to improve on some existing way of doing things.
- You want to generalize from some specific setting more widely.

**Data**

- Data can typically be downloaded in .csv or .xlsx or .txt format.
- First step should be to look at the data in the spreadsheet and check
  - whether there are missing observations
  - what is the format of each field, text or numeric, and if numeric, how many digits
  - do the numbers roughly make sense
- Save the data in a simple-to-use file name (change typically from the source name) inside a well-named directory inside your project directory.
- Document where you got the data from, and be prepared to update the file at a later date.
- Example download from Yahoo Finance.

**Software**

- Different software have their own advantages and disadvantages. Excel, R (R-studio) and Python are free, whereas MATLAB® typically requires a subscription. Differ according to
  - how easy it is to code

DOI: 10.1201/9781003543121-13

  - how powerful in terms of ability to webscrape and how fast to compute
  - how easy it is to access others code to use in applications

- Usually, you will find your favorite programming language and stick with it, but occasionally you may have to use other languages if your coauthor favors them.

- Spend time learning the basics, like how to import data. Follow examples.

- Software for writing an article, LaTeX, Word, or other.

# Bibliography


Andersen, T. G., T. Bollerslev, F. X. Diebold, and P. Labys (2003). "Modeling and forecasting realized volatility." *Econometrica* 71, 579–626.

Anderson, N., Breedon, F., Deacon, M., Derry, A. and Murphy, G. (1996). *Estimating and interpreting the yield curve.* John Wiley Series in Financial Economics and Quantitative Analysis. Chichester.

Arrow, K. (1965). *Aspects of the Theory of Risk Bearing.* Yrjö Jahnsson lectures, Helsinki.

Bachelier, L. (1900). *Theorie de la speculation.* Paris: Gauthier-Villars.

Barber, B. M. and J. D. Lyon. (1997) "Detecting long-run abnormal stock returns: The empirical power and specification of test statistics". *Journal of Financial Economics*, 43, 341–372.

Bartram, Söhnke M. and Brown, Gregory W. and Stulz, René M., (2012). "Why are U.S. Stocks More Volatile?" *Journal of Finance*, Vol. 67, No. 4, 1329–1370.

Black, F. and M. Scholes (1973). "The Pricing of Options and Corporate Liabilities". *Journal of Political Economy.* 81 (3), 637–654. doi:10.1086/260062.

Blanchard, O. J. and M. W. Watson (1982). "Bubbles, Rational Expectations and Financial Markets" *Crises in the Economic and Financial Structure*, Paul Wachtel, editor, pp. 295–316. Lexington, MA: D.C. Heathand Company.

Bliss, R., (1997), "Testing Term Structure Estimation Methods," *Advances in Futures and Options Research*, 9, 197–231.

Bollerslev, T. (1986) "Generalized autoregressive conditional heteroskedasticity". *Journal of Econometrics*, 31(3), 307–327.

Bollerslev, T., R.F. Engle, and D. Nelson (1994). "ARCH Models" in *The Handbook of Econometrics, vol. IV*, eds. D.F. McFadden and R.F. Engle. North Holland.

Boudoukh, J., Richardson, M. P. and Whitelaw, R. E. (1994). "A tale of three schools: Insights on autocorrelations of short-horizon stock returns". *Review of Financial Studies*, 7(3), 539–573.

Boudoukh, J., Richardson, M. P. and Whitelaw, R. E. (2008). "The Myth of Long-Horizon Predictability". *Review of Financial Studies* 21, 1577–1605.

Brown, S.J. and J.B. Warner (1980). "Using daily stock returns: The case of event studies". *Journal of Financial Economics* 14 (1), 3–31.

Brunnermeier, Markus K. (2008). "Bubbles". in *New Palgrave Dictionary.* Ed. Lawrence Blume & Steven Durlauf.

Castura, J., R. Litzenberger, and R. Gorelick (2010) "Market Efficiency and Microstructure Evolution in US Equity Markets: A High Frequency Perspective", October 2010, and March 2012 Available at `https://www.sec.gov/comments/s7-02-10/s70210-364.pdf`

CBOE (2010) "CBOE Volatility Index". Available at `http://www.cboe.com/micro/vix/vixwhite.pdf`

Chou, R.Y., H.C. Chou, and N. Liu (2009). "Range Volatility Models and Their Applications in Finance". In *The Handbook of Quantitative Finance and Risk Management, Springer, Part V*, pp. 1273–1281.

Cochrane, J.H. (1999). "New Facts in Finance". NBER Working Paper No. 7169.

Cochrane, J.H. (2001). *Asset Pricing.* Princeton University Press.

Cram, D. (1997). http://web.mit.edu/doncram/www/eventstudy.html

Cutler, D.M., J.M. Poterba, and L.H. Summers (1989). "What Moves Stock Prices?" NBER Working Paper No. 2538 (Also Reprint No. r1232) *The Journal of Portfolio Management*, 15(3), 4–12.

De Bondt, W.F.M. and R. Thaler (1985), "Does the stock market overreact?" *Journal of Finance* 40, 793–805.

De Bondt, W. and R. Thaler (1987), "Further evidence of investor overreaction and stock market seasonality," *Journal of Finance* 42, 557–581.

Dimson, E., Marsh, P. and Staunton, M. (2008). "The worldwide equity premium: A smaller puzzle". in R. Mehra, ed., *Handbook of the Equity Risk Premium.* Amsterdam: Elsevier.

Dolley, J.C. (1933) "Characteristics and Procedure of Common Stock Split-Ups", *Harvard Business Review*, 11, 316–326.

Dubow, B. and N. Monteiro (2006). "Measuring market cleanliness". Financial Services Authority Occasional paper no 23.

Engle, R.F. (1982): "Autoregressive Conditional Heteroscedasticity with Estimates of the Variance of United Kingdom Inflation". *Econometrica* 50, 987–1007.

Faber, M., (2010). "Relative Strength Strategies for Investing". Available at `https://ssrn.com/abstract=1585517` or `http://dx.doi.org/10.2139/ssrn.1585517`

Faber, M. (2013). "Quantitative Approach to Tactical Asset Allocation", Available at `https://ssrn.com/abstract=962461`

Fair, R.C., (2002) "Events that Shook the Market". *Journal of Business*, 75(4), October 2002. Available at `https://ssrn.com/abstract=334004`

Fama, E (1963). "Mandelbrot and the stable Paretian hypothesis". *Journal of Business* 36, 420–429.

Fama, E. (1965). "The behaviour of stock market prices". *Journal of Business* 38, 34–105.

Fama, E (1970). "Efficient Capital Markets: A review of Theory and Empirical work". *Journal of Finance* 25(2), 383–417.

Fama, E., Fisher, L., Jensen, M., and R. Roll (1969). "The Adjustment of Stock Prices to New Information". *International Economic Review*, 10(1), 1–21. doi:10.2307/2525569

Fernandez, P., (2015). "CAPM: An Absurd Model". Available at `https://ssrn.com/abstract=2505597orhttp://dx.doi.org/10.2139/ssrn.2505597`

Fernandez, P. and O. Pizarro Alberto and I. Fernández Acín (2015) "Discount Rate (Risk-Free Rate and Market Risk Premium) Used for 41 Countries in 2015: A Survey". Available at `https://ssrn.com/abstract=2598104` or `http://dx.doi.org/10.2139/ssrn.2598104`

Foresight (2012) "The future of computer trading in financial markets". UK Government office for science final project report. Available at `https://www.gov.uk/government/publications/future-of-computer-trading-in-financial-markets-an-international-perspective`

Foster, D.P. and D.B. Nelson (1996). "Continuous Record Asymptotics For Rolling Sample Variance Estimators," *Econometrica*, 64(1), 139–174.

French, K. R. and Roll, R. (1986). "Stock return variances: The arrival of information and the reaction of traders". *Journal of Financial Economics*, 17(1), 5–26.

Friedman, M. and L.J. Savage (1948). "Utility Analysis of Choices Involving Risk". *Journal of Political Economy* 56(4), 279–304. doi:10.1086/256692

Gabaix, X. (2008), "Power Laws", *New Palgrave Dictionary of Economics*, 2nd Edition.

Garber, P.M. Famous First Bubbles (1990). *The Journal of Economic Perspectives*, 4(2), 35–54.

Garman, M.B., and M.J. Klass (1980). "On the estimation of security price volatilities from historical data". *Journal of Business* 53(1), 67–78.

Goyal, A., and I. Welch, (2003). "Predicting the equity premium with dividend ratios". *Management Science*, 49(5), 639–654.

Goyal, A. and I. Welch (2008), "A Comprehensive Look at the Empirical Performance of Equity Premium Prediction, *Review of Financial Studies* 21(4), 1455–1508.

Graham, B. and D. Dodd (1928,2008) *Security Analysis.* Sixth Edition, McGraw Hill.

Grinold, R.C. and R.N. Kahn (1999) *Active Portfolio Management : A quantative approach for producing superior returns and selecting superior money managers*, Wiley.

Grossman, S.J., and J.E. Stiglitz. (1980). "On the Impossibility of Informationally Efficient Markets." *The American Economic Review*, 70(3), 393–408.

Hertzberg, D. (2010). "The Great Stock Myth: Why the market's rate of return—and your nest egg—may never recover". *The Atlantic.* Available at http://www.theatlantic.com/magazine/archive/2010/09/the-great-stock-myth/308178/

IBES. `http://thomsonreuters.com/products\_services/financial/financial\_products/a-z/ibes/`

Ikenberry, D. L., G. Rankine and E. K. Stice (1996). "What Do Stock Splits Really Signal?" *The Journal of Financial and Quantitative Analysis*, 31(3), 357–375.

Ioannidis, John P. A. (2005)"Why Most Published Research Findings Are False", `https://doi.org/10.1371/journal.pmed.0020124`

ITG http://www.itg.com/news_events/papers/CitiSplit2.pdf

Jegadeesh, N., and S. Titman (1993) "Returns to Buying Winners and Selling Losers: Implications for Stock Market Efficiency." *Journal of Finance*, 48(1), 65–91. JSTOR, JSTOR, www.jstor.org/stable/2328882

Kahneman, D., and A. Tversky (1979). "Prospect Theory: An Analysis of Decision under Risk." *Econometrica*, 47(2), 263–291.

Keim, D. (1983), "Size related anomalies and stock return seasonality: further empirical evidence," *Journal of Financial Economics* 12, 13–32.

Khandani, A. and Lo, A.W. (2011) "What happened to the quants in August 2007? Evidence from factors and transactions data", *Journal of Financial Markets*, 14(1), 1–46.

Kirilenko, A., M. Samadi, A. S. Kyle, and T. Tuzun (2017). "The flash crash: The impact of high frequency trading on an electronic market". *Journal of Finance* 72(3), 967–998.

Linton, O. (2016). *Probability, Statistics and Econometrics.* Academic Press, October 2016. 400pp. ISBN 9780128104958

Lo, A.W. (2004). "The adaptive markets hypothesis". *Journal of Portfolio Management*, 30(5), 15–29.

Lo, A.W. (2005). "Reconciling efficient markets with behavioral finance: the adaptive markets hypothesis". *Journal of Investment Consulting*, 7(2), 21–44.

Lo, A.W., and J. Hasanhodzic (2010). *The Evolution of Technical Analysis: Financial Prediction from Babylonian Tablets to Bloomberg Terminals.* Wiley.

Lo, A.W. and MacKinlay, A. C. (1999). *A Non-Random Walk Down Wall Street.* New Jersey: Princeton University Press.

Malthus, T. (1798). *An Essay on the Principle of Population, as it Affects the Future Improvement of Society with Remarks on the Speculations of Mr. Godwin, M. Condorcet, and Other Writers.* London. Printed for J. Johnson, in St. Paul's Church-Yard.

Malkiel, B.G. (2015). *A Random Walk down Wall Street: The Time-tested Strategy for Successful Investing.* W.W. Norton.

Mandelbrot, B. (1963). "The variation of certain speculative prices". *Journal of Business* 36, 394–419.

Markowitz, H.M. (1952a). "The Utility of Wealth" *Journal of Political Economy.* 60(2), 151–158. doi:10.1086/257177

Markowitz, H. M. (1952b), "Portfolio Selection", *Journal of Finance* 7(1), 77–91.

Markowitz, H. M. (1959), *Portfolio Selection: Efficient Diversification of Investments*, John Wiely & Sons, New York, USA. Available at: http://cowles.econ.yale.edu/P/cm/m16/index.htm

Marsh, T.A. and R.C. Merton (1986) "Dividend Variability and Variance Bounds Tests for the Rationality of Stock Market Prices," *The American Economic Review*, 76, 483–498.

Mehra, R. and E.C. Prescott (1985), "The Equity Premium: A Puzzle." *Journal of Monetary Economics* 15, 145–161.

Newey, W.K, and K.D. West (1987). "A Simple, Positive Semi-definite, Heteroskedasticity and Autocorrelation Consistent Covariance Matrix". *Econometrica* 55(3), 703–708. doi:10.2307/1913610. JSTOR 1913610

Ng, R. (2014). "An Empirical Study of Risk and Return in Chinese A- and H-share Markets". Cambridge, mimeo.

Ohlson, J. and S.H. Penman (1985). "Volatility increases subsequent to stock splits: An empirical aberration" *Journal of Financial Economics*, 14(2), 251-

Parkinson, M., (1980). "The extreme value method for estimating the variance of the rate of return". *Journal of Business* 53(1), 61–65.

Parzen, E. (1957). "On consistency of the spectrum of a stationary time series". *Annals of Mathematical Statistics* 28(2), 329–334.

Pástor, L. and P. Veronesi (2006) "Was There a Nasdaq Bubble in the Late 1990s?" *Journal of Financial Economics* 81, 61–100.

Patton, A. (2009). "Are "Market Neutral" Hedge Funds Really Market Neutral?" *Review of Financial Studies*, 22, 2495–2530.

Poterba, J. M. and L.H. Summers (1988). "Mean reversion in stock prices: Evidence and Implications". *Journal of Financial Economics*, 22(1), 27–59.

Pratt, J.W. (1964). "Risk Aversion in the Small and in the Large," *Econometrica* 32, 122–136.

Press, S.J. (1967). "A Compound Events Model for Security Prices". *Journal of Business*, 40, 317.

Rashes, M.S. (2001). "Massively Confused Investors Making Conspicuously Ignorant Choices (MCI-MCIC)." The *Journal of Finance*, 56(5), 1911–1927.

Rogers, L.C.G., and S.E. Satchell (1991). "Estimating variances from high, low, and closing prices". *Annals of Applied Probability* 1(4), 504–512.

Rogers commission. (1986). `https://spaceflight.nasa.gov/outreach/SignificantIncidents/assets/rogers\_commission\_report.pdf`

Roll, R. (1984a). "A simple implicit measure of the effective bid-ask spread in an efficient market". *Journal of Finance*, 39(4), 1127–1139.

Roll, R. (1984b). "Orange Juice and Weather." *American Economic Review* 74(5), 861–880.

Ross, S.A. (2005). *Neoclassical Finance.* Princeton University Press.

Scheinkman, J.A. (2014). *Speculation, Trading, and Bubbles.* Columbia University Press.

Schwert, G.W. (1989) "Why does stock market volatility change over time". *Journal of Finance* 44, 1115–1153.

Schwert, G.W. (2011). "Stock Volatility during the Recent Financial Crisis", *European Financial Management,* 17, 789–805.

Shiller, R.J. (1981). "Do stock prices move too much to be justified by subsequent changes in dividends?" *The American Economic Review* 71(3), 421–436.

Shiller, R.J. (2000). *Irrational Exuberance.* Princeton University Press. ISBN 1400824362.

Stambaugh, R.F. (1999). "Predictive regressions". *Journal of Financial Economics* 54(3), 375–421.

Taleb, N.N. (2010) *The Black Swan,* Second Edition, Penguin.

Thaler, R.H. (2016). "Behavioral Economics: Past, Present, and Future." *The American Economic Review,* 106(7), 1577–1600. DOI: 10.1257/aer.106.7.1577

Tylervigen (2015?) `https://www.tylervigen.com/spurious-correlations`

Weld, W.C., R. Michaely, R.H. Thaler, and S. Benartzi (2009). "The Nominal Share Price Puzzle." *Journal of Economic Perspectives,* 23(2), 121–142.

White, H. (2000). "A Reality Check for Data Snooping". *Econometrica* 68, 1097–1126.

http://math.ucsd.edu/~crypto/cgi-bin/MontyKnows/monty2?2+7883

See `https://thehustle.co/professor-who-beat-roulette/`

`https://news.stanford.edu/pr/2004/diaconis-69.html`

`https://www.betfair.com/exchange/plus/politics/market/1.128151441`

See `https://stockstotrade.com/head-and-shoulders-pattern` and `https://investinganswers.com/dictionary/d/double-bottom`

# Index